Moroccan Islam

Tradition and Society in a Pilgrimage Center

Modern Middle East Series, No. 1

Sponsored by the Center for Middle Eastern Studies
The University of Texas at Austin

Moroccan Islam

Tradition and Society in a Pilgrimage Center

by Dale F. Eickelman

University of Texas Press
Austin and London

Library of Congress Cataloging in Publication Data

Eickelman, Dale F   1942–
        Moroccan Islam.

        (Modern Middle East series; no. 1)
        Bibliography: p.
        Includes index.
        1. Muslim saints—Morocco—Boujad. 2. Islam—Morocco. 3.
Boujad, Morocco—Social life and customs. 4. Morocco—Social life
and customs. I. Title. II. Series: Modern Middle East series (Austin,
Tex.); no. 1.
BP64.M62B653   297'.0964   75–45136
ISBN 0–292–75025–0

To Christine

For this book to be worthwhile, it is not necessary in my view that it should be assumed to embody the truth for years to come and with regard to the tiniest details. I shall be satisfied if it is credited with the modest achievement of having left a difficult problem in a rather less unsatisfactory state than it was before.

Claude Lévi-Strauss
The Raw and the Cooked
trans. John and Doreen Weightman

Contents

Tables

Figures

Note on Transliteration

Most Arabic words, even those which occur in written, classical Arabic, are transliterated as they are pronounced in the spoken Arabic of the region in which I worked. The text would have been unnecessarily complicated had I followed separate conventions for the spoken and written variants. For example, Boujad, the town in which I worked, is spoken as *Bja'd*, written as *Abū l-Ja'd*. The word for "marabout" is *mrabet* in western Morocco, *murābit* in classical Arabic. In any case, specialists will easily be able to reconstitute the classical forms. There are exceptions to strict transliteration, primarily of words and place names that have fairly conventional European forms. Also, I have represented most words only in the singular, with plurals indicated by *-s*. The exceptions to this convention, like the others, are meant to make my text read as smoothly as possible. Plurals that commonly occur in Islamic literature in western languages (e.g., *'ulama*) have been kept intact. Similarly, descendants of the marabout Sidi Mhammed Sherqi, who figure largely in my discussion, are called Sherqawi in the masculine singular, Sherqawa in the plural. I have also found it easier to call a resident of Boujad a Boujadi, as he is called in Arabic, than to resort to awkward circumlocutions.

I have preferred Richard S. Harrell's system for transliterating Moroccan Arabic vowels (Harrell, ed. 1966:xiii–xix) for two reasons. First, it is more accurate than the system of the International Congress of Orientalists (ICO), designed primarily for classical Arabic. Second, Harrell's system contains the publishing advantage of eliminating the macron for long vowels. There are six vowels: *e*, very short but like the *e* in English *masses*; *o*, very short but like the *u* of *put*; *a*, usually like the *a* of *mad*; *ă*, a shorter version of *a*; *i*, exactly as in French *vite*; *u*, like the *ou* in French *fou*. The ICO system has, however, been retained for consonants, since it is more widely known.

Fifteen out of thirty-one Moroccan Arabic consonants are almost identical with those which occur in English. The others are listed below:

> ': a glottal stop, like the *tt* in Brooklynese *bottle*
> *ḅ, ḍ, ḷ, ṃ, ṛ, ṣ, ṭ, ẓ*: emphatic consonants
> *q*: similar to *k* but pronounced farther back in the mouth
> *kh*: the same as the *ch* of German *Bach*
> *gh*: described by Harrell as "similar to a light gargle accompanied by a musical buzz from the adam's apple" (Harrell, ed. 1966:xvii)
> *ḥ*: "similar to an English 'h' pronounced in a loud stage whisper" (ibid.)
> ': the Arabic *'ayn*, technically a pharyngeal fricative, with no equivalent in a European language
> *l*: like the *l* in French *louche*
> *r*: like the *r* in Spanish *para*

Preface

The fieldwork on which this study is based was conducted in Boujad, Morocco, and its environs between October 1968 and June 1970. Boujad's significance lies in its continuing domination by the Sherqawi religious lodge (*zawya*) located there, which makes it perhaps the most important pilgrimage center on Morocco's western plains. I consider neither the Sherqawi religious lodge nor Boujad as a microcosm of any larger entity. They are merely the loci of an intensive social anthropological study of popular Islam which I conducted there. The data collected there merely form the evidential base for a series of hypotheses about what Clifford Geertz has called "the curve of social discourse" (1973).

In one sense this study is an ethnography and follows the canons of such a study. I do not intend it as just another narrowly circumscribed, brick-laid-on-brick ethnography. Meaningful work in any social science must be based upon the concrete and the specific, but I doubt whether most readers of this book will be motivated primarily by a desire to learn more about Boujad, the Sherqawa, or perhaps even North Africa. The intensive microsociological study I present here is meant to serve as a base for discussion of key traditional Moroccan conceptions of the social order and of the problems of providing an adequate description of religion in a complex Islamic society. In the course of the work, I implicitly present my own vision of the nature of social anthropology and its relation with history, which I consider to be its sister discipline. It is these issues that initially motivated and have continued to sustain this study.

Retrospectively, it appears that the study of a pilgrimage center has probably placed the outline of religious belief and ritual in bolder relief than would have been possible elsewhere. The relatively heterogeneous population of this center and the availability of rich manuscript and oral historical data provided a more solid substance to the "curve" of religious discourse over the last century than I could have expected from most other vantage points. I say that these advantages appeared retrospectively because during a large part of my early fieldwork the difficulties of studying a place with such religious significance were much more vividly apparent to me. Boujad is an important pilgrimage center in an implicit popular pattern of Islam that is in many respects incongruent with the formal tenets of Islam. Both Boujadi-s and tribesmen were quite aware of this and often were quite reserved with the inquisitive "Roman" (*rumi*) writer who evinced such an avid interest in the town and its religious practices. A Boujad merchant who in his youth had studied the traditional religious sciences (and who later became a leading local nationalist) told me that he had once written a newspaper article characterizing Boujad as *namsi*, a subtle Arabic term which indicates someone or something evasive, secretive, elusive, and, if need be, wily. *Namsi* was to him and to most Boujadi-s a positive quality, a fact which I discovered only gradually, as my perceptions of the social world about me assumed a meaningful pattern. I appreciate the combination of sincere hospitality and discretion with which Boujadi-s initially welcomed me all the more for the trust and confidence which I was eventually accorded.

Many individuals in Morocco and elsewhere have contributed to this study. Many Boujadi-s and Sherqawa have preferred to remain anonymous, but this in no way lessens my gratitude to them. The *qaḍi* of Boujad during much of my stay was Ḥajj 'Abd er-Raḥman l-Manṣuri, a rare exemplar of the distinguished tradition of the religious sciences in Islam. After almost a year of my fieldwork he tacitly decided that, however curious my research techniques and goals might be, they constituted a "science" in their own right. Consequently he offered me sustained intellectual and practical support, particularly in bringing his legal and scholarly training to bear on criticizing and furthering my interpretation of manuscript historical sources. I alone am responsible for the result, but my work would have been greatly handicapped without his interest in it.

Claude Ecorcheville, a *contrôleur civil* of Boujad during the 1930's, allowed me to consult his collection of transcribed royal proclamations relating to Boujad and an account of Boujad's history which he prepared in 1938. These have been of great value to me in the present work. Mohammed Cherkaoui (Sherqawi) has also been kind enough to speak with me at length on the history of the Sherqawa.

The Moroccan Department of Urbanism and Housing, part of the Ministry of the Interior during my initial fieldwork and now a separate ministry, actively facilitated my work at every stage. To its officials and to others at the provincial and local levels of government I owe my sincere thanks.

One of the intellectual pleasures of working in North Africa and the Middle East is the interdisciplinary, international collegiality that characterizes most area specialists. I found this the case from my student days at the Institute of Islamic Studies at McGill University through those at the University of Chicago. I was particularly fortunate to be at Chicago during a period of sustained faculty and student interest in Islam and the Middle East in the Department of Anthropology. Clifford Geertz, Lloyd A. Fallers, Robert McC. Adams, and Nur Yalman were then all on the faculty. Through both formal and informal seminars, Cliff quietly but vigorously insisted that each of us develop individually a style of thought and analysis. Especially since several of us were working in the same region and freely exchanging ideas, it would have been easy to lapse into a "school." Cliff delicately managed to convey his own rigorous standard of scholarship without "guiding" me. This has been the case from our first discussions to his reading the penultimate version of this book. I am deeply grateful. Hildred Geertz and Lawrence Rosen were active participants in the Moroccan discussion group that Cliff initiated in 1968, and both have commented on the manuscript of this book. To a certain extent all of us have been concerned with similar issues, particularly the ideas concerning social structure that I develop in Chapters 4 and 5. Our concern has been not so much with "owning" ideas as with testing them on each other. Rosen particularly has discussed his ideas with me at length; I am pleased to work with such open colleagues.

This manuscript was essentially completed in June 1974, a month before the tragic death of Lloyd A. Fallers. I regret that he never got to read it, because many of the interpretations of my material were developed through extended dialogues that began in 1970 and continued until a few weeks before his death. In 1973–1974 he invited me to return to Chicago as a Fellow of the Committee for the Comparative Study of New Nations and of the Center for Middle Eastern Studies. I hope that in some small way this book merits his confidence in me. Robert McC. Adams has also served for years as a skeptical devil's advocate. His ruthlessly constructive criticisms have been invaluable.

T. O. Beidelman, my colleague at New York University, patiently read several versions of this manuscript with the same critical intensity that he applies to his own work. Our many hours of discussion over the entire field of anthropology have been a major formative influence on me. Nicholas Hopkins of New York University, Ross Dunn of the California State University, San Diego, Robert and Elizabeth Fernea of the University of Texas at Austin, and Jacques Berque of the Collège de France have also provided generous and incisive comments. For helpful discussions I wish to thank Kenneth Brown, Edmund Burke III, Jacques Cagne, Ernest Gellner, Mohammed Guessous, David Hart, Abdelkebir Khatibi, Ira Lapidus, Rémy Leveau, John Middleton, and Abdulhamid el-Zein. John Kirchner prepared the base for all the maps except Figure 3. Bouzekri Draioui of the University Muḥammed V checked the accuracy of the transliteration. The book is dedicated to my wife, who has lived with it and shaped it since its inception.

My initial fieldwork was supported by the Foreign Area Fellowship Program and the National Institute of Mental Health. Additional work in Morocco, although not primarily in Boujad, was made possible in the summer of 1972 by the Smithsonian Foreign Currency Program and the following summer by the Social Science Research Council. An earlier version of the first half of Chapter 4 originally appeared in the *International Journal of Middle East Studies* 5 (1974).

Moroccan Islam

Tradition and Society in a Pilgrimage Center

Introduction

This is a study of Islam as it is locally received and understood in a regional pilgrimage center of western Morocco. I am particularly interested in describing and analyzing the processes by which religious symbols and institutions are reinterpreted and modified to accommodate new and evolving social and historical realities. I am also concerned with describing how religious ideologies, implicit or explicit, themselves shape the social order.

I have attempted to portray certain aspects of a particular culture and society through time. Patterns of belief and ritual, like all systems of meaning, are maintained by persons in the course of social action. As Max Weber was concerned to demonstrate by his empirical studies of the major world religious traditions (e.g., Weber 1952), beliefs and ritual action are often invested with new meanings or change direction as they are introduced in novel situations and social frameworks different from those in which they were initially developed. For this reason, ideas and systems of ideas, especially those which fundamentally shape men's attitudes toward the world and their conduct in it, cannot be analytically construed as ahistorical Platonic entities, unaffected by the ravages of time. They are in a constant tension with social reality, shaping it and in turn being shaped. My intention, however, is not to write social history, although I think this study serves to document Marshall Hodgson's claim that the so-called "folk" culture of Islam shares substantially the same dynamic force that he found more visible in Islam's "high" culture (1975:I,80). My primary goal is to make sociological sense of the changing forms in which certain key, contradictory elements of a major religious tradition have been understood in a specific locale over the last century.

Some anthropologists might consider the above objective primarily ethnographic, informed by theory but not devoted to it. I think that would be a mistake. My presentation implicitly explores the utility of what might be called a "Weberian" paradigm for the study of social and cultural change and as such constitutes a marked departure from many anthropological treatments of these topics. As Stephen Toulmin writes, anthropology and sociology, among other fields, have recently experienced a sudden transition of their dominant paradigms. For over half a century, both fields had been dominated by a theoretical preoccupation with static, ahistorical patterns and procedures (1971: 53–54, 56). Problems of historical change were relegated to second place or even considered outside the scope of "science." For example, Talcott Parsons has argued that a synchronic, or functional, under-standing of social systems has to precede a diachronic understanding (1964:480). His reason for this is that a comprehensive sociological theory must seek logical "closure," attainable only if society is treated abstractly and as if it were in an equilibrium. To Parsons, Weber's lack of concern for such closure in his own writings constituted his "failure" (introduction to Weber 1964:20–25).[1] Other social scientists have gone so far as to insist that sociological abstractions can be made only from ahistorical studies. They argue that, since processes of historical change are particularistic and nonrecurrent, they fall outside the domain of sociological abstraction (e.g., Devons and Gluckman 1964:159–160, 201). A less extreme variation on this argument has been to deal with historical change in synchronic form by juxtaposing several earlier and later descriptions of a single culture or society. The limitation of this strategy is that it serves more to contrast the end points of certain processes than to focus on the nature of the changes taking place. This encourages a conception of historical change in terms of discrete, episodic units, rather than as a continuous process.

There is an increasing awareness of the limitation of ahistorical paradigms for the study of diachronic processes, but it would be a mistake to look, as a consequence, for exclusively diachronic ones. There is no reason to assume a radical dichotomy between stringent historical nominalism and the use of sociological ideal types. Both historians and social scientists continuously interweave the two approaches in the narratives and explanations which they present. This study will try to document empirically the lack of an inherent contradiction between attempts to explain specific events and attempts to seek to confirm recurrent regularities.

Perhaps the clearest illustration of the sociological explanation of specific historical situations remains the paradigm implicit in Max Weber's *The Protestant Ethic and the Spirit of Capitalism*. Leaving aside the empirical accuracy of Weber's argument, his basic problem focuses on a historically unique phenomenon, the emergence of what he calls "rational" capitalism in the West. He seeks to explain this in general, systemic terms by relating developments in the economic order to a particular religious ethos (Weber 1958:25, 166). Weber carefully specifies that the core of his argument concerns the dialectical interrelation of these two elements; but he does not postulate a sequence of unidirectional causation between them (1958:182–183). Weber was simply interested in showing that the two variables, as logically delimited, were in significant tension with each other. He did not seek to validate his thesis by presenting these two elements in a logically closed system. This lack of logical "functional" closure makes Weber's style of sociology amenable to the analysis of specific historical situations. It also has the advantage of lending itself more easily to a conceptualization of sociological variables over time than the style of argument in which the historical dimension is presented only in superimposed synchronic layers.

The usefulness of such a paradigm for the study of society must be tested not by its pretensions to logical "closure" but by its capacity to provide the best available explanation—consistent, plausible, and in accord with all the evidence—for the problem at hand. This goal is both realistic and attainable if one assumes, as I do, that events in the social world always contain unpredictable and accidental elements and that any paradigm for the study of society must somehow take account of these elements in order to offer an adequate comprehension of social action. The compelling advantage of the Weberian paradigm over other approaches (such as those assuming historical "laws") is its capacity to achieve a more comprehensive understanding of the sociological features of particular historical developments. The purpose of comparative studies within such an approach is not the gossamer pursuit of general "laws" of history or society but the sharper understanding of particular historical situations and the social forces at work in them. I shall return to these issues throughout my discussion.

I realize that the questions that I raise regarding the nature of religious change in a complex society are difficult and capable of no easy answer. At times my discussion becomes necessarily tentative, and, in fairness to the reader, I will point out such instances as they occur. I have preferred this course to that of sacrificing what I feel are significant issues for less crucial ones that lend themselves to at least a surface elegance or a "neat" representation within more conventional explanatory paradigms used by anthropologists. Similarly, my argument is occasionally more detailed ethnographically and historically than may appear immediately necessary for my implicit theoretical argument. This is deliberate. The main features of North African Islam have often been taken for granted or otherwise misrepresented in much of the literature on the region. A fuller presentation, such as I have attempted here, at least permits the reader to check some of my more abstract conclusions and to discern other possible analytical implications than those which I have chosen to emphasize.

The fieldwork on which this book is based was conducted in Boujad, a town of eighteen thousand people (est. 1970), and its tribal and religious hinterland (see Fig. 1). The town's significance lies in its continuing dominance by the Sherqawi religious lodge (*zawya*) located there, which was founded in the late sixteenth century by the marabout Sidi Mḥammed Sherqi (d. 1601). Roughly one-third of the town's population claims descent from him. Collectively, his descendants are called the Sherqawa. The powers attributed to them and certain of their enshrined ancestors form the magnet that attracts pilgrims from throughout western Morocco.

The most striking feature of North African Islam is the presence of marabouts, such as Sidi Mḥammed Sherqi. They are persons, living or dead,[2] to whom is attributed a special relation toward God which makes them particularly well placed to serve as intermediaries with the supernatural and to communicate God's grace (*baraka*) to their clients. On the basis of this conception, marabouts in the past have played key religious, political, and economic roles in North African society, particularly in Morocco. Until the end of the nineteenth century, maraboutism was virtually without contest the prevailing form of rural and urban Islam throughout North Africa (Merad 1967:58). The complex of beliefs surrounding marabouts was—and for many North Africans continues to be (although in significantly modified forms, as will become clear)—a central and integral element in a coherent vision both of the realities of the social world and of man's relations to the supernatural.[3] A concrete indication of this is the proliferation of maraboutic shrines throughout the Maghreb, particularly in Morocco. In Morocco's rural areas, one rarely loses sight of the squat, whitewashed, and—in the case of the more popular ones—domed maraboutic shrines. In towns, more lavish shrines with green-tiled roofs are often found, with vast courtyards and adjoining mosques and hostels for pilgrims. The shrine of Sidi Mhammed Sherqi takes this form, as do those of several of his descendants that are also situated in Boujad.

Tens of thousands of pilgrims, singly and in groups, visit these shrines throughout the year. The greatest influx is during the annual festival (*musem*) of Sidi Mhammed Sherqi, held in late September or early October. For a two-week interval, the town doubles in size, as client groups, each of which stays an average of three days, renew their covenants with the Sherqawa. At other times of the year, the descendants of marabouts go out to their clients and say invocations on their behalf in exchange for customary offerings. In all, the activities associated with marabouts are impressive. Few others so thoroughly involve the active participation of the majority of the region's rural population and activate social ties that transcend ordinary economic, social, and administrative boundaries. This fact is not lost upon government officials, despite their formal assertion that maraboutism constitutes an atavistic ideological residue of the least "evolved" segment of the population. Seventy percent of the country's population was rural as of 1970 (as opposed to an estimated 93 percent in 1900) (Noin 1970:II, 100) and, as I shall indicate below, it is reasonable to assume that the majority of the rural population supports maraboutic activities in some form. In the past much of the urban population also supported such activities.

In this study I am not trying to generalize directly from Boujad to any larger entity. I consider neither the Sherqawi religious lodge nor Boujad as a microcosm of a larger whole. The study of such a pilgrimage center as Boujad undoubtedly places the outline of

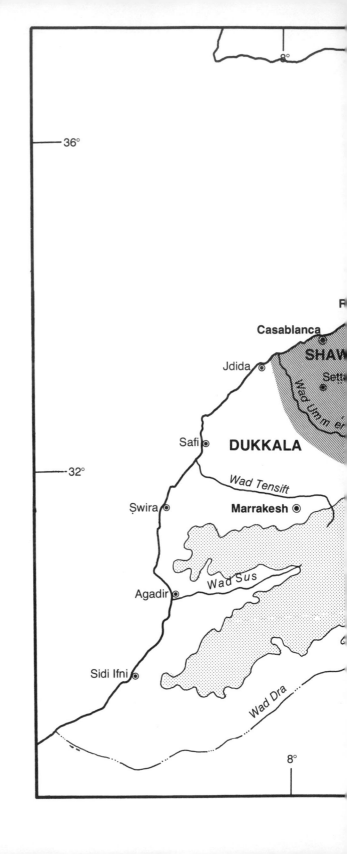

Figure 1.
Morocco.

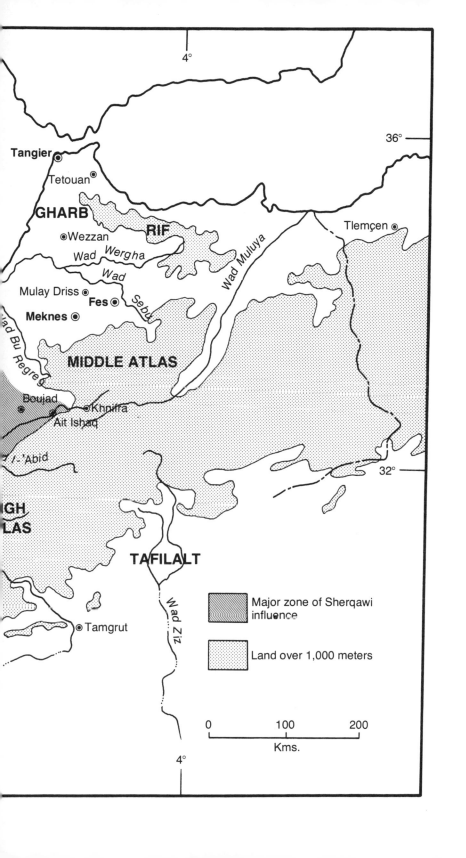

4°

36°

Tangier ◉

Tetouan ◉

GHARB

◉ Wezzan

RIF

Tlemçen ◉

Wad *Wergha*

Wad *Muluya*

Wad

Mulay Driss ◉

Fes ◉

Sebu

Meknes ◉

Wad Bu Regreg

MIDDLE ATLAS

Boujad
◉

◉ Khnifra

Ait Ishaq

? / 'Abid

32°

IGH

LAS

TAFILALT

Wad Ziz

Major zone of Sherqawi influence

Land over 1,000 meters

◉ Tamgrut

0   100   200

Kms.

4°

religious belief and ritual in bolder relief than would have been possible elsewhere. Moreover, manuscript and oral historical sources, both French and Moroccan, were available for Boujad. These were invaluable for tracing the curve of religious understandings and transformations of religious institutions over the last century, especially through the turbulent years that immediately preceded the French protectorate in 1912. Boujad's role as a "company town" for the descendants of Sidi Mhammed Sherqi notwithstanding, the activities of its population are heterogeneous, as would be expected in a regional market center, which the town also is. There are no more full-time religious specialists in Boujad than in other towns of commensurate size. What is important is that roughly the same range of coexisting understandings of Islam is found in Boujad as elsewhere in Morocco, although there is considerable variation in the pattern of religiously oriented activities or institutions.

Understanding the character of Islam in Boujad, particularly the role of marabouts and its temporal transformations, goes in one key sense beyond its ethnographic importance for a particular region of Morocco or even North Africa. Figures similar to marabouts, ambiguously and often misleadingly labeled as saints, Sufi-s (mystics), or holy men, exist throughout the Islamic world. This is not to say that they all play similar social or cultural roles. They decidedly do not. But everywhere they popularly represent an implicitly hierarchical conception of the relations between man and God.

Their supporters see marabouts and similar "holy men" as a hierarchy of intermediaries through whom the supernatural pervades, sustains, and affects the universe. Analytically, an observer may hold such a conception of access to the divine to be, in Weber's sense of the term, a "magical" accretion to Islam; but from the viewpoint of tribesmen, peasants, and others who hold such beliefs and act upon them, intermediaries with God are part of Islam as they understand it. Supporters of this conception do not in general systematically articulate their beliefs, but they certainly would reject the notion that they are an amalgam of Islamic and non-Islamic elements. They regard themselves as Muslims, pure and simple. In what sense, then, can such beliefs be considered to form a part of Islam?

Ernst Troeltsch (1960) posed a similar question of the Christian tradition. He argued that, sociologically, Christianity could be seen as constantly in tension with social reality. Consequently, its sociological history is one of shifts at various levels between compromise and noncompromise with the world. A similar pattern can be seen in Islam. Maraboutic assumptions about the relations between man and God (and similar assumptions elsewhere in the Muslim world) are diametrically opposed to what most contemporary educated Muslims consider to be the "scripturalist" core of Islamic belief and ritual, but at the same time bear closer relation to the existing framework of social relations. Let me briefly, perhaps too abstractly, outline these opposed assumptions. Scripturalists and Islamic modernists assume that all men, including the Prophet Muhammed, are considered equals before God, even if they are not so in the eyes of each other. They also assume that there is no human or nonhuman hierarchy that has privileged access to God. There are supernatural beings besides God—angels, *jinn*-s, Satan, and saints (*wali*-s), but none of these serve as intermediaries. These assumptions are explicit in the Qur'an and in the teachings of numerous reformist movements which have been an integral part of the Islamic tradition since the time of the Prophet (Merad 1967:29; Rahman 1968:245). These "formal" doctrinal tenets have been aggressively propagated by an articulate, reformist elite in recent decades (and periodically in the past— the first "reform" movements began not long after the death of Muhammed) and have had a decided impact upon popular belief, especially with the spread of "modern," city-oriented life-styles. Characterizing these beliefs as "formal" Islam is not entirely satisfactory, but it reflects their emphasis upon the equality of men before God and the fact that most educated, articulate Muslims now adhere to these interpretations of Islam rather than to any others.

Those who remain in client relations with marabouts and their descendants are aware of the disfavor with which their beliefs are viewed by educated Muslims. For this reason, maraboutic beliefs and rituals are often denied before outsiders or dissimulated in favor of the formal tenets of Islam. Still, maraboutic beliefs are tenaciously seen by the clients of marabouts to be the way things really are in the relations between man and God.

Unfortunately, the hierarchical assumptions implicit in much of popular Islam are largely unrecorded and poorly understood. Relatively few studies of Islam have ventured beyond the presentation and analysis of written texts and the explicit ideologies of an articulate religious intelligentsia. In contrast to various reformist movements that have explicit ideologies and representatives willing to discuss them, little attention has been given to the description and analysis of popular, "traditional" beliefs and their social context (Merad 1967). The works of Jacques Berque and, more recently, Clifford Geertz constitute singular exceptions to this neglect. Most reformist Muslims and scholars of Islam typically attribute the continuing strength of traditional, maraboutic beliefs to an ignorance of "true" Islam on the part of many Muslims both now and in the past. Such "ignorant" persons are thus, according to reformists, at the mercy of charlatans, parasites, opportunists, and other varieties of "spiritual delinquents" (Rahman 1968:185).

At least for North Africa, such accounts of the persistence of marabouts are exceedingly unconvincing. As I discovered early in my fieldwork, the supporters of marabouts are fully aware, at least in outline, of the interpretations of Islam offered by the scripturalists; yet they continue to regard maraboutic Islam as a meaningful religious representation of reality.

What then, are the implications of the coexistence of these antithetical notions of Islam? I think it is useful to anticipate part of my argument. In the Islamic tradition as it has emerged in various parts of the world, the conceptions of man's relations to God as comprising or lacking intermediaries are correlative rather than mutually exclusive and are in a dialectical tension with each other and with social reality. Both now and in the past, these conceptions have been known at least in bold outline to all believers. Taken together in various syntheses according to temporal and social contexts, these two conceptions have enabled Islam to encompass many varieties of social experience and to be regarded at any given time as a meaningful religious representation of reality. I believe that the proper study of any world religious tradition involves understanding its variants over time and place and their interrelation. The career of maraboutism and of marabouts in Boujad provides a concrete instance of how a world religion has remained living and meaningful to those who sustain it.

The order of presentation of this study is somewhat unorthodox for an anthropological monograph. In order to make my discussion of the relation of religious ideologies to society as clear as possible, I have found it convenient not to follow a strictly historical progression. In any case, Boujadi-s themselves have multiple conceptions of the past which they often invoke with varying degrees of consciousness to facilitate their comprehension of social action. My own shifting between past and present has much the same intention. Only the first two chapters are ordered in strict chronology. Chapter 1 outlines in a very general way the implantation and early development of Islam in Morocco. In large part it is meant to orient readers unfamiliar with North Africa. I am particularly concerned with the fourteenth through the sixteenth centuries, the so-called Maraboutic Crisis, during which maraboutic Islam gained hegemony. In a sense, the "filling out" of maraboutic Islam that occurred during this period is the inverse process to the chief concern of this book, the loosening hold of that same pattern over the last century. Although both Moroccan and foreign historians have been attracted to the analysis of this period, the social bases of maraboutism are generally assumed rather than described. Since traditional chronicles present only those aspects of maraboutism congruent with the formal tenets of Islam, this is not surprising. I try to correct some of these lacunae in my ensuing discussion of the preprotectorate history and sociological characteristics of the Sherqawi religious lodge in Chapter 2. Because precolonial sources for the political activities of marabouts are almost nonexistent, I discuss my sources in detail in an appendix.

The next major section of the book, Chapters 3–5, presents the economic activities and social institutions of Boujad and its rural hinterland, their social structure, and some of the basic common-sense assumptions that Boujadi-s and tribesmen make about the social order. These are not just "contextual" chapters prefacing the intensive discussion of maraboutism and the changing local consciousness of Islam, the subject of the final three chapters. Of course, maraboutism as an implicit, unarticulated pattern of belief and ritual action has derived much of its strength from a congruence with the values that guide everyday conduct. Such congruences have hardly gone unreported in the classic monographs of social anthropology. But these congruences are neither total nor permanent. For this reason, of perhaps greater interest are those situations, both now and in the preprotectorate past, in which such congruences have been denied or questioned, and which have led to shifts in patterns of belief and ritual and, equally, to altered conceptions of the social order.

I

Morocco, Islam, and the Maraboutic Crisis

The Geographical Background

Of all the countries of North Africa, Morocco shows the most marked ecological diversity. In the Middle East as a whole, perhaps only Iraq shows a similar range of variation, although Morocco does not share the latter country's sharp ethnic and religious cleavages. Geographers divide Morocco into twenty-three distinct ecological zones. although these can be grouped into three major regions: the Rif and Atlas mountain chains, the coastal and interior plains situated roughly between Marrakesh and Fes, and the semiarid pre-Sahara of the south (Noin 1970:I,88–89). The first two of these regions show little marked discontinuity with the southern half of Spain, a resemblance complemented by others in traditional rural *genres de vie* and in the spatial organization of traditional towns.

Except for Marrakesh, Morocco's most important towns and cities are located on the plains to the northwest, especially the Sais, Gharb, and Shawya. This region also has the heaviest rainfall and the richest agricultural land. Consequently, with the exception of certain densely populated pockets of the Rif Mountains, it carries the highest population concentration of the country, roughly sixty persons per square kilometer. This density affords a dramatic contrast to the average of five persons per square kilometer in the arid southeast (Martin et al. 1967:57).

As one proceeds southward from these plains, Morocco becomes progressively more arid. This is especially the case south of the Umm er-Rbi' River. Nevertheless, large parts of these plains have been provided with modern irrigation since the 1930's and thus now form a part of what the French (and by imitation the Spanish, who administered a small northern zone) used to call *le Maroc utile* ("useful Morocco"), the agriculturally rich and economically exploitable regions that once attracted the major part of colonial settlement and investment. Prior to the protectorate the tribes of these coastal and interior plains were also "useful" to the Makhzen, or central government, in that taxes and other levies could be more regularly exacted from them than from the tribes of other regions. For this reason "useful Morocco" was also known as the "land of the Makhzen" (*blad l-Makhzen*). The term *Makhzen* literally means "a place to store treasure." Its popular connotations are obvious. The core of *le Maroc inutile* from the point of view of colonial economics was the two major mountain chains and the pre-Sahara. These regions also broadly coincided with what colonial ethnographers and Makhzen officials called the "lands of dissidence" (*blad es-siba*), zones only sporadically under the control of the Makhzen.

Perhaps the most important ecological features which have affected Morocco's political fortunes are its two mountain chains. In the north, the Rif Mountains impede easy access from the Mediterranean to the interior of the country. To the west and the south, the Middle and High Atlas mountain chains have been characterized as a "natural barrier" to the rest of the continent. Traditionally, these mountainous regions have offered natural zones of refuge from the Makhzen for the predominantly Berber-speaking tribes that populate them. Some of these tribes are sedentarized; others, even to the present, largely transhumant. Except during intermittent periods when charismatic religious and political leaders emerged to unite them, these tribes have remained relatively fragmented and autonomous. Even France, with the resources of a modern colonial power, took twenty-one years, from 1912 to 1933, to "pacify" all of its possession.

Nonetheless, the importance of these mountains and the lack of natural harbors in isolating Morocco has often been exaggerated. The use of such geographical factors as natural barriers to explain the course of Moroccan history has primarily a metaphorical utility. During most of the Middle Ages of Europe, the fortunes of Morocco were closely linked with those of the Iberian Peninsula; for certain extended periods, the Iberian Peninsula was even ruled from Morocco. From at least the seventeenth through the nineteenth centuries it was less any natural barriers than the policies of its successive rulers which isolated Morocco both from Europe and, to a lesser extent, from the Middle East as well. General Franco, in launching his campaign against Republican Spain from Morocco in 1936 with significant numbers of Riffian tribesmen in his ranks, was only the last of a large number of conquerors to show the permeability of the boundary between North Africa and southern Europe.

Similarly, the Atlas Mountains to the south may have impeded, but in no way cut, communications. From the middle of the ninth through the fourteenth century, most of the gold trade from Black Africa to the Middle East flowed through Morocco. At the end of the nineteenth century there was a significant, if no longer flourishing, trans-Saharan caravan traffic linking sub-Saharan Africa with Marrakesh, Fes, and other major Moroccan cities (Dunn 1971). The remote Tafilalt oasis in Morocco's southeast, far from being politically peripheral, was strategically situated along one of the major north-south caravan routes and was the birthplace of the 'Alawi dynasty, which has controlled the Moroccan empire (a kingdom since 1956) from 1666 to the present. The earlier Sa'adi dynasty (1555–1659) came from the Dra Valley. Both dynasties have based their legitimacy upon patrilineal descent from the Prophet Muhammed.

Islam in Morocco: The Early Stages

Islam first came to Morocco in 681, with the raid of the Muslim general 'Uqba ben Nafi. This lightning expedition, which occurred less than fifty years after the death of the Prophet Muhammed, did not immediately lead to a permanent Arab and Muslim presence. Not much is known of the process of Islamization or the consolidation of Arab hegemony for this period, but they seem to have varied considerably according to tribal and other political divisions of any given region. More certain is that by the middle of the eighth century at least a nominal Islam had been firmly established throughout Morocco, but the systematic Islamization of the Berber-speaking tribes was a slow process which stretched out over the next few centuries and occasionally encountered determined opposition. The fact that some of the resistance was led by prophets claiming revelations in Berber dialects rather than Arabic reflects the formidable linguistic and, to a certain extent, cultural barriers which had to be overcome in the spread of Islam (Brignon et al. 1968:49–57; Bel 1938:166–188; Julien 1972:127–128, 370).

Throughout the early period of Islamization, there was a constant, although often antagonistic, contact between the autochthonous Berber tribesmen and the Arab conquerors. At first, the cutting edge for the diffusion of Islam was the towns and fortresses (*rbat*-s) where Arab contingents were stationed. Arabic gradually became the language of the towns and of contact with the garrisons (Bel 1938: 363–365; Brignon et al. 1968:53–62). One of the first Arab dynasties of Morocco, the Idrissi (788–1016), dates from this period. It was founded by Idris I (d. 791), who escaped the massacre of his family in the Muslim Orient and fled to Morocco. As a claimed descendant of the Prophet Muḥammed, he was enthusiastically received and supported by certain Berber tribes. The reign (803–828/829) of his successor, Idris II, a son by a Berber concubine, marked the beginning of an effective government, although essentially confined to the plains between the Rif and Middle Atlas mountains, and of a more profound and systematic Islamization of the Berber tribes.

Although from the ninth century onward the interaction of townsmen and tribesmen in Morocco was continuous and intense, it would be an error to reduce this to a simple manifestation of Arab-Berber conflict, or of mutually impermeable urban and tribal life-styles. As Clifford Geertz has pointed out, Morocco is at the frontier of the grain-growing world and developed no stable buffer of peasants between the cities and tribes as occurred elsewhere (1968:5–7). Colonial historiographers often portrayed Morocco's towns and cities as foreign bodies in a vast sea of tribesmen. But from the advent of the Muslim conquest they progressively became and remained very much interdependent economically with their rural hinterlands and involved in the same range of political activities. Only since the onset of the protectorate has the gap between the two again widened.

The fluid interpenetration of towns with tribal areas is particularly salient in the period 1050–1450, characterized as the Great Age of Berber Islam and the formative period of Morocco as a nation. In contrast with the superficial Islamization accomplished by the first wave of Muslim conquerors, in this period it was Berber tribesmen who enhanced Islam as a symbol of Moroccan identity. Both the Almoravid (1061–1147) and Almohad (1130–1269) dynasties were founded and consolidated by charismatic Berber leaders who, to use Geertz's striking phrase, combined "strong-man politics with holy-man piety" (1968:8). They managed to fuse Berber tribes into effective political forces and incorporate towns and, for significant periods, even much of the Iberian Peninsula into their empires. For religious reasons both dynasties provided an impetus for Arabization. Moreover, a second influx of Arab tribal migrations in the eleventh century, the so-called Hilali Invasion of colonial historians, led to a further erosion of distinctions between Berber and Arabic-speaking tribes. This further strengthened the political base of these dynasties and contributed to the formation of a distinct Moroccan identity.

By the fifteenth century, however, the unifying ideology which sustained these two dynasties was exhausted and the political order which they forged had collapsed. It was in the period of intense ideological and political dislocation which followed, the Maraboutic Crisis, that Morocco developed a distinct style of polity and of religious expression which was to persist largely intact until the early part of this century.

The Maraboutic Crisis and Its Assessment

The Maraboutic Crisis lasted roughly from the fifteenth to the end of the seventeenth century. Its beginning was not sharply marked by any one event but rather by the constellation of several historical developments. As the Almoravid and Almohad dynasties declined, they were followed by that of the Merinids (1146–1546). This dynasty, in turn, eased into a period of prolonged decline. A major economic factor contributing to this political weakness was Morocco's diminished control of the lucrative trans-Saharan gold trade with the development of alternate routes. Further, Spanish and Portuguese "crusaders" had established enclaves along Morocco's coasts. The Merinids had constantly to compromise with them and with the Christian powers of southern Europe. Many of the dynasty's subjects criticized it for yielding unnecessarily to Christian demands. The Ottomans in Algeria, who were not under direct pressure from Christian powers, played on this sentiment and exacerbated the difficulties of the Moroccan dynasty by supporting opposition to it.

In this same general period, Berber tribesmen from the extreme south of Morocco began a vast movement into the central regions and plains which was to continue over the next few centuries. The overall effect was to create a period of prolonged civil and dynastic strife (Burke 1969:70–75; Bel 1938:376–400; Lacoste 1974). Religious and political authority was open to competition at every level of articulation of society, hard to maintain, and subject to reversal (C. Geertz 1968). Under these conditions the sultanate, rather than being the center of authority and legitimacy, was just one of a number of competing centers of power.

I think it is useful here to specify exactly how a discussion of this period fits into this study. In one sense, that pursued by Geertz in *Islam Observed* (1968), it is important as the formative period that shaped much of Morocco's prevailing religious and political style for ensuing centuries. This is of interest because, as I have mentioned, it is the inverse of that same style that concerns me here. But the lack of sources that reveal the sociological nature of this period limits its possibilities for a comparative study. Instead, I want to concentrate here upon some of the ways in which this period has been construed historiographically and by contemporary educated Moroccans. This concern brings into sharp focus some of the obstacles to the study of Islam as popularly understood.

One component of understanding any historical action, at least for contemporary social historians, is an effort to see events as they were originally comprehended by participants in them. In reconstructing this aspect of the past, historians are professionally aware of the necessarily arbitrary process of selection and abstraction involved in their work. In other words, the comprehension of historical action involves the observer's consciousness about what is essential in past action interacting with what is known of past events. Consequently, it is possible to have multiple conceptions of the past. Far from being a sterile relativism or the despair of hard-bitten positivists, an attention to these problems of perception enhances the social historian's (and the social anthropologist's) sensitivity toward temporal shifts in cultural understandings prevailing at any given time. This applies to the investigation of the present as much as the past, since the shape of the past and attitudes toward it serve as major elements in defining contemporary social realities.

This has been the case for the Maraboutic Crisis. Despite the general thinness of sources for the period, it has been used by colonial historians and many educated Moroccans in recent decades as a sort of Rorschach protocol for elaborating their conceptions of Moroccan (or, alternatively for some, Muslim) society. Although differing in other respects, both colonial historians and Muslim scripturalists assume that Moroccan culture and society became "frozen" during this period and did not alter in essential form until the protectorate era. For the moment, I want to leave aside the question of the dubious accuracy of this assumption and concentrate upon what the historiography of the Maraboutic Crisis reveals about attitudes toward the popular understanding of Islam.

With the exception of the recent work of Abdallah Laroui (1970), the most elaborate assessment of the Maraboutic Crisis remains that developed by French colonial historians, basing themselves upon historical and ethnographic research conducted in the first part of this century. Such studies were primarily undertaken by individuals directly or indirectly concerned with establishing or maintaining the machinery of the protectorate. Like India for the English, Morocco tended to attract a higher caliber of French personnel than other colonies, so that the work of these scholars remains the starting point for reappraisals of Morocco's past. Or, to be more exact, the "colonial vulgate" is now an inherent part of that past.

Key elements of what the French saw as "traditional," here as in other colonies, were frozen into place to serve as the symbols of legitimacy for the "protecting" power. The French felt that, with their early ethnographic inquiries, often carried out by military intelligence officers, they had ascertained the essential features of *le Maroc disparu* ("the Morocco that was"), the colonial phrase used to describe Morocco as it presumably was for an indeterminate period prior to the protectorate. The French then formally maintained that their task as "protector" was to preserve and to enhance what they considered to be the positive features of preprotectorate Morocco. As French rule became established, the early ethnographic formulations of the nature of indigenous society tended increasingly to be invoked rather than reassessed in the light of changing conditions. At least in the early part of the protectorate, the French were able to make their view of Moroccan society a significant component of social reality.

French administrators and scholars occasionally described North African society as totally static from the exit of the Romans to the establishment of French control.[1] This state of affairs sometimes was attributed to the impact of Islam (e.g., van Gennep 1914: esp. 157–194) or, alternatively, to the fixed religious conceptions of the indigenous Berber population (e.g., Bel 1938). Lucien Lévy-Bruhl's concept of the "primitive mentality" was avidly picked up by colonial specialists on Morocco as a way of theoretically justifying their assumption that Islam had such a grip on society that the minds of Moroccans were collectively stocked with a fixed set of images impermeable to modification or change (Brunot 1923; 1934; Hardy 1926).[2] As late as 1951 a leading French administrator and ethnographer wrote that in Islam "evolution is boundlessly slow. For Islam, *even more than for other religions,* one has to count not in years but in centuries" (Montagne, foreword to Drague 1951:5; italics added).[3]

Relatively few scholars engaged in the hyperbole of seeing the forms of North African society as fixed from the time of the Romans. But, as I have indicated, most were willing to see the Maraboutic Crisis as the decisive period in which Islamic beliefs and institutions were refashioned so as to be in accord with what were assumed, rather than demonstrated, to be certain "fundamental" notions of the indigenous population of North Africa.

The "Fundamental" Beliefs of Barbary

One of the most influential colonial accounts of the religious synthesis which occurred during the Maraboutic Crisis was that of Alfred Bel. Bel was a French orientalist who for many years taught in Algeria and Morocco and who, among other tasks early in the Moroccan protectorate, was responsible for reorganizing the traditional religious teaching at the Qarawiyin Mosque in Fes, which once was one of the great centers of Islamic learning in North Africa. In the 1930's his lectures on Islam, on which his *La Religion musulmane en Berbérie* (1938) is based, were a standard part of the curriculum for training the protectorate's native-affairs officers. Jacques Berque has pointed out to me that Bel's work was out of date by the time it was published. This is undoubtedly the case. But the fact remains that Bel had a prolonged influence on educated colonial officials and others and that better general accounts written for a wider public, such as Henri Terrasse's *Histoire du Maroc* (1949–1950), became available only much later.

Bel's account is particularly interesting because it tries to demonstrate thoroughly the complex interrelation between Moroccan religious beliefs and the political developments of the period which he discusses. His assessment of this interrelation contains obvious distortions, especially in his acceptance of a stratigraphy of religious beliefs and of an image of "true" religion as somehow independent from other aspects of society. Bel nevertheless carefully considers all available documentation.

Bel's argument is an idealist one. He sees a long-term historical evolution which occasioned a gradual erosion of essential Islamic tenets. This purported trend is the result of his assuming an earlier period when Islamic beliefs were understood and practiced virtually in idealized, pure forms almost exclusively by the Islamicized urban elite of North African society. Almost no explicit sociological context is provided for this period. By adding sociological detail and depicting the understanding of Islamic beliefs in popular milieus for later periods, Bel manages to suggest the decline and compromise of Islam, which he indistinguishably conceives as a "religious faith" and as a civilization.

In many ways the structure of Bel's study resembles that of Fustel de Coulanges's *The Ancient City*. Like earlier commentators on Morocco (e.g., Doutté 1903), Bel presumes a stratigraphic model of the historical development of religion and society. His book begins with an account of what he assumes to be the first known religious practices of North Africa; later chapters deal successively with various periods up to the sixteenth century. A single concluding chapter presents religious beliefs as they presumably have remained over the last four centuries.[4] In this chapter alone, Bel frequently introduces ethnographic materials, but he apologizes for presenting "popular religious fictions" and "pious legends," since these he considers only a "muddle" of actual historical events in contrast with written accounts (1938: 390–400).

In detail, Bel argues that after Islam was first introduced in "Barbary"—the standard colonial term for North Africa prior to and after the Islamic conquest—both its formal rituals and Islamic mysticism (*tasawwuf*, Sufism) were understood and practiced primarily by an urban elite. Tribesmen who came to towns to pursue the study of Islam were invariably assimilated into the towns and did not try to carry their knowledge to the countryside (Bel 1938: 364–365).

Beginning with the thirteenth century, rural religious lodges (*zawya*-s) began to complement those already in the towns. The

teachings of these lodges tended to emphasize Sufism over other aspects of Islam. The principles and ritual necessary to progress in the
stages of the mystic way (*tariqa*) were a primary concern.[5] Each
religious lodge was directed by a Sufi master, called a *shaykh*. It is
indicative of his idealistic assumptions toward his material and an
implicit comparison with institutionalized European mysticism that
Bel glosses the term *shaykh* as *directeur de conscience* ("spiritual
director"). Each *shaykh* had an entourage of disciples; collectively,
shaykh-s and their disciples were known as *foqra* (sg., *fqir*), a term
defined in Sufi texts as "those who have abandoned everything in
quest of God." The *foqra* of each religious lodge were materially
sustained by gifts and contributions made by the inhabitants of the
surrounding region (Bel 1938:352–353).

The spread of *zawya*-s from the towns to the countryside provoked
a fundamental change in the nature of Sufism. Bel writes that the
strict rules, the severe rituals, the monotheistic conception of God,
and the more subtle aspects of mystic doctrines were incompre-
hensible to "unpolished, minimally educated" tribal disciples. These
were incapable of accurately comprehending the fundamental tenets
of Islam. Islam in the countryside thus had to be "reduced" to the
understanding of the "vulgar populace" (*l'homme du peuple*). The
abstract components of Islamic doctrine could not survive in the
emerging synthesis of Islamic populism (Bel 1938:355, 369; also see
Michaux-Bellaire 1927:4). Religious lodges in tribal areas humbly
began as centers to propagate a "correct" understanding of Islamic
doctrine and practice, writes Bel, but became increasingly enmeshed
in local society and tribal politics. In the political disorders of the
fifteenth century and later, the rural population turned increasingly
to the religious leaders of these lodges to relieve them of oppressive
government, repurchase captives held for ransom by Christian in-
vaders, and alleviate other forms of need or misfortune (Bel 1938:
353).

According to Bel, the main reason that these rural *zawya*-s were
incapable of "raising" the level of understanding of religion was the
impermeability of what he calls the "fundamental religion" of the
Berbers. Bel admits that the evidence for the nature of these beliefs
is negligible or uncertain but says that, as far back as can be traced,
Berbers seem to have believed in a mix of good and bad "forces" and
in magical techniques of protection against vague, malevolent spirits.

For Bel, one proof of the existence and pervasiveness of this religious substratum was the relatively short period of time during which the Almoravid and Almohad ideologies managed to hold sway over the Berber populations. Another indication of these fundamental beliefs for Bel was the rapid and widespread success of vulgarized Sufism, in which Sufi *shaykh*-s in rural regions were quickly assimilated into the pre-existing religious framework and had attributed to them the ability to convey supernatural blessings, *baraka*. Bel explains the popularity of this conception as follows: "Does not the idea of the tutelary God of Islam—more powerful than demonic spirits—lead to that by which God can transmit to certain men, his friends [*sic*], a part of his power, his *baraka*? To become one of these men by Sufi exercises, to gather from these human fetishes (*hommes fétiches*) a parcel of their beneficent influence, which chases and destroys the forces of evil, was a perspective well in accord with everyone's aspirations" (1938:342).

A key element in Bel's presentation of the fusion of various concepts into an Islam compatible with pre-existing "fundamental beliefs" during the Maraboutic Crisis was the increasing significance attached to descendants of the Prophet Muhammed, collectively called *shorfa* (sg., *shrif*).

Prior to the fifteenth century the concept of descent from the Prophet and that of maraboutism were largely separate. Gradually, some of the more successful marabouts, such as the Berber mystic al-Jazuli (d. 1465/1466), who was reputed to have had twelve thousand disciples at the time of his death, claimed descent from the Prophet. Increasingly the concepts of maraboutism and descent from Muhammed fused. From the fifteenth century onward, writes Bel, there was an "epidemic" of claims by marabouts of descent from the Prophet. Even the names of many tribes changed during this period to indicate such descent.

Similarly, before the fifteenth century a marabout was "one who is tied to God" and thus was equivalent to a Sufi *shaykh*. The term also signified the early propagators of Islam, who lived in fortified enclosures (*rbat*-s—a word derived from the same triliteral root as *mrabet*, "marabout"). By the fifteenth century, however, the meaning of *marabout* had significantly shifted. By that time marabouts were regarded as saints (*wali*-s and *saleh*-s). It was popularly believed that for temporal success men had to attach themselves to marabouts, who were capable of communicating God's grace (*baraka*) to them. In part, this capacity was considered hereditary. A reputation for being a marabout could be based upon varying combinations of descent from the Prophet Muḥammed (or from 'Umar ben l-Khaṭṭab, his second successor, or caliph [*khalifa*], in all but prophetic powers), religious scholarship (*'ilm*), mystic insight, and the possession of un- canny powers. These attributes were permeable, in that possession of one frequently constituted evidence for the others. Thus, feats of religious scholarship gave one the reputation of being a marabout (e.g., Bel 1938:371). A reputation as a marabout conversely legit- imated claims to descent from the Prophet (e.g., Lévi-Provençal 1922:201).

Throughout these developments, Bel writes that the carriers of Islamic learning (*'ilm*) continued their teaching in the cities, al- though their scholarship, insulated from contemporary realities and popular acceptance, became increasingly pedantic and fossilized. Marabouts were left to purvey to the masses a "vulgar" mysticism and fatalistic resignation to the world, stripped of the more rigorous aspects of the Islamic tradition. Thus their synthesis of Islamic populism was devoid of a critical spirit. The hegemony of mara- boutism was, nevertheless, to last almost unchallenged until the early twentieth century. It signaled for Bel the general collapse (*fléchisse- ment*) of Muslim civilization in North Africa (1938:369–372, 388).

The political consequences of maraboutism were far-reaching. The Sa'adi and 'Alawi dynasties of Morocco both claimed legitimacy on the basis of descent from the Prophet Muḥammed. Marabouts helped both of these dynasties to power but at the same time struggled to establish and maintain their own local and regional political autonomy. By the late sixteenth century maraboutism was firmly established as the idiom of political action. Both the Ottomans, in possession of Tlemçen from 1555 and Tunis from 1574, and the Moroccan dynasties increasingly pursued a maraboutic style of politics and associated marabouts with their own political ends in order to maintain popular support of the "Berber" tribal majority. Religious lodges and marabouts claiming ties with the mystic *shaykh* al-Jazuli predominated in regions allied with the Moroccan dynasties. Those claiming ties with *shaykh* 'Abd l-Qader l-Jilani (d. 1166) were primarily allied with the Ottomans. As mentioned, Moroccan dynas- ties were compelled to temporize with the Christian powers, while both the Ottomans and marabouts (whether or not they were allied with the Ottomans) were able to call uncompromisingly for holy war (*jihad*) against the infidels.

Bel writes that, under these circumstances, Morocco found itself "prey" to marabouts who consciously exploited their reputation for sanctity as a conscious device for temporal aggrandizement. Citing approvingly an earlier source, Bel writes that, from the sixteenth century onward, marabouts "under the cover of religion" founded feudal "fiefs" (1938:376–388).[6] Such statements sharply reveal Bel's implicit assumption of what is "properly" religious. But Bel does seem correct in emphasizing that from at least the sixteenth century to the protectorate there was considerable tension between marabouts and the sultanate. Both marabouts and the sultan shared some of the same bases of popular legitimacy. By formal accounts the sultan (since 1956 the king) is the temporal center of the Moroccan empire. At the same time, by virtue of descent from the Prophet Muhammed, the sultan is also popularly considered to be the caliph, God's deputy on earth (*khalifet Allah fel-l-ard*).[7] As such, he is also Morocco's spiritual leader. Since French policy from shortly prior to the protectorate was to support the institution of the sultanate as the basis on which the French presence was legitimized, this doctrine was further elaborated in the early colonial era. But the sultan has a second popular basis of legitimacy that is ambiguously shared with marabouts. This is the possession of divine grace (*baraka*) and the ability to transmit it. This basis of legitimacy even figured in a proposed Moroccan constitution of 1908.[8]

The tension inherent in this ambiguity is apparent in a royal decree (*daher*) dated 12 July 1820 / 10 Shawwal 1235,[9] in which Sultan Mulay Sliman invested an eleven-year-old marabout as lord (*sid* or *mqaddem*) of the Sherqawi religious lodge. In the decree the boy is told that he inherits the "secret of your ancestors" (*sirr aslafikum*), that is, the powers of a marabout, and that he is responsible to God alone. There is no explicit mention of the duty of submission to the sultan, presumably because of the marabout's "special" relationship with God. But by investing the boy (and passing over an elder, more mature brother who had spent a considerable period of time in the sultan's entourage), the sultan in effect demonstrated a pragmatic, if not formal, dependency on his will.

Because of this shared basis of legitimacy, the sultanate was limited in its capacity to attack the ideological basis of maraboutism, although individual marabouts were on occasion killed, imprisoned, or exiled when their influence became a threat (e.g., Morsy 1972). Hence, according to Bel, the static nature of Islam and the Moroccan polity over a period of four centuries.

Clearly, some of Bel's assumptions about the nature of religion—Islam in particular—and its relation to other aspects of society have strongly influenced the form of his argument. A key assumption is that "true" religion expresses itself only in institutions independent of other aspects of society. Bel is not concerned with demonstrating that such a conception is held by Muslims themselves. Hence he asserts that the popular religious leaders who emerged during the Maraboutic Crisis merely used religion as a "cover," since they acquired military, political, and economic advantages. Presumably only when religious leaders lack such advantages does he consider them genuinely religious. Significantly, Bel's distaste for the leaders of popular Sufism is shared by many Muslim modernists. I have already cited one such scholar, Fazlur Rahman, who speaks of the popular development of Sufism throughout the Muslim world as in the hands of "spiritual delinquents" from the fourteenth century onward (1968: 185.) Rahman is much more precise than Bel on periodization and nuances of doctrine, and broader in scope, since he is concerned with the entire Muslim world. But his overall argument on the detrimental effect of popular Sufism as a doctrine upon the Muslim masses through at least the eighteenth century—and, in such areas as North Africa, well beyond—is largely in accord with that formulated by Bel (Rahman 1968:153–202, 237–260).

Given the emphasis of such colonial historians as Bel and of such Muslim modernists as Rahman upon the widespread appeal of popular Sufism, it is surprising how little detail is presented on the exact nature of such beliefs or, for that matter, of what prompts their popular acceptance. The issue of whether certain marabouts were "sincere" or charlatans is a red herring. Unless the Muslim masses at various historical periods are viewed as inert consumers of their religious tradition and passively open to all forms of deception (or, as Bel also argues, saddled with a religious understanding of the world fixed for all time), it seems reasonable to attempt to formulate as explicitly as possible just what these popular beliefs are. Admittedly, there is a significant French colonial literature which traces the spiritual genealogies of marabouts and the assumed links between religious orders. Such studies thus follow the form of traditional legitimation used by marabouts (which I will later discuss in detail) and give little indication of why they are popular. These studies particularly flourished in the late nineteenth and early twentieth centuries. The French were uneasy about the formation of a "pan-Islamic" movement which, spread through the transnational routes of the pilgrimage and the transcolonial links of religious orders, constituted a potential threat to European rule (e.g., Rinn 1884). With few exceptions, even later colonial literature (e.g., Drague 1951) reads more like police dossiers on the potential influence of various orders, together with certain formal, written elements of their doctrines, than an attempt to understand their popular character and appeal.

What, then, is the driving force of popular conceptions of Islam which have sustained rituals and beliefs associated with maraboutism over a period of centuries? Why do men maintain ties with marabouts? Claiming that many marabouts are "charlatans" or "spiritual delinquents" hardly constitutes a response to this basic question. Even if, as Bel says, there is a religious substratum so powerful in North Africa that it severely limited the form which Islam could take in that region, perhaps it will be rewarding to look unapologetically in detail at what he terms "popular religious fictions" and "pious legends." The following chapters are intended to construct a base for understanding such conceptions.

2
Marabouts and Local Histories: The Sherqawa

The Importance of Local History

The Maraboutic Crisis, like much of Moroccan history until the nineteenth century, consists of a plurality of local histories. One of their dominant themes is the struggle of various sultans to overcome and manipulate various regional and local loyalties and alliances. Marabouts played major roles in these struggles.

Still, little attention has been paid to marabouts and maraboutism. The contemporary Moroccan historian Abdallah Laroui suggests that the Maraboutic Crisis and maraboutism are regarded by Moroccans as issues that belong to a period of disunity and even "decadence." As a consequence, he continues, Moroccan historians have hardly begun to investigate the resources available for their study (Laroui 1970:212–213, 256).[1] Admittedly, such inquiries present difficulties, particularly for historians confined to the study of written sources. Most discussion of marabouts and maraboutism in traditional chronicles has been accurately characterized as little more than stereotyped responses to questionnaires fixed by tradition (Lévi-Provençal 1922:49, 56). These sources tacitly omit any aspect of maraboutism incongruous with the formal tenets of Islam. Marabouts are generally referred to only as pious religious scholars and as saints (*wali*-s) devoted to the praise of God, with highly circuitous references, or none at all, to their political and other mundane activities. One reason for this was that marabouts constituted real or potential threats to the power and authority of the Makhzen. Since most traditional chroniclers were attached to the sultan's entourage or dependent upon his good favor for their well-being, it was circumspect to ignore the whole issue (Lévi-Provençal 1922:43). Nevertheless, at least some events concerning marabouts are signaled, if not described, in these texts. The structure of traditional chronicles indicates that they were intended for a discerning Moroccan audience intimately acquainted with the social fabric in which the actions they report took place, as well as with the key personalities whose actions are described. Such accounts are not intended to be complete in themselves. For their original audience, an oblique reference to an incident was sufficient to induce the reader to seek out, if necessary, alternative, nonwritten sources of information. Of course, the major transformations in the social fabric over the last century have led to the contraction and disappearance of such alternative sources and of interest in them. The result is that, for many Moroccans, even the events of the nineteenth century, let alone those of earlier periods, are no longer fully intelligible.

This chapter presents elements of a social history of the Sherqawi religious lodge. The period from the origins of the Sherqawa in the late sixteenth century to the beginning of the nineteenth century is presented primarily on the basis of traditional chronicles. These sources are complemented for the nineteenth century by the accounts of European travelers and, more importantly, by correspondence between the Sherqawa and various sultans, Makhzen officials, merchants, religious scholars, tribal councils (*jma'a*-s), overseers of agricultural estates, and, for the beginning of the twentieth century, the French. This material is invaluable for understanding the social and political context in which marabouts operated during the nineteenth century. It also clarifies earlier periods, for, as Laroui implies, there is no reason to assume any radical discontinuity in the Moroccan social order between the sixteenth century and the opening of the twentieth (1970:213). An appendix presents in more detail some of the complex political intrigues of the late nineteenth century. The relegation of this material to an appendix does not mean that I regard it as of secondary importance. To my knowledge, no other detailed account of precolonial maraboutic factionalism exists. Although such evidence is closely tied to my main argument, its presentation requires a more microscopic attention to detail than the other elements of this chapter.

The Rise of the Sherqawi Zawya

From its foundation in the late sixteenth century until the beginning of the French protectorate in 1912, Boujad was the only settlement of significance on the Tadla Plain and was considered one of the most important religious centers in the Moroccan interior (A. Nasiri 1906–1907: I, 346–347; Foucauld 1939: 121; Lévi-Provençal 1922: 297–298), with a population composed of the maraboutic Sherqawa and their slaves and clients. The latter included a significant Jewish community.

Boujad's location makes sense primarily in terms of the configuration of the maraboutic geopolitics of preprotectorate Morocco. To paraphrase Marc Bloch (1964: 83–84), it is necessary to lay aside the spectacles of men of this century to understand the implications of maraboutism. Moroccans of the sixteenth century and later never lacked a vigorous realism. Part of this realism was attaching as much importance to marabouts, visits to their shrines, and pilgrimages to Mecca as to battles, trade, and contests over the sultanate. As a local pilgrimage center, Boujad served as a mediating point between local patterns of Islamic ritual and belief and those forms shared with the rest of the Muslim world. Largely as a consequence of this original role, complex lines of communication grew up around the town. Boujad emerged as a mediating point for trade and political negotiation with the Berber highlands to its immediate east and as a local market center. Nevertheless, the most important ties between the Sherqawa and their tribal clientele for at least the last 150 years have been with the Arabic-speaking tribes of the western plains, Shawya, Tadla, and Dukkala. These ties continue to the present.

The town is located near, but significantly not at, points of former strategic importance. In the frequent campaigns of reconquest characteristic of the more ambitious sultans in precolonial Morocco, the main route of penetration of the western plains and the Middle Atlas Mountains was along the Umm er-Rbi' River. A religious lodge located along this route would have been more vulnerable to the vicissitudes of Makhzen politics. Similarly, settlement closer to the Middle Atlas

Mountains would have left the town more open to attacks from the Berber highlands. Such threats remained significant several years after the French established a military post in Boujad in 1913. The town of Bni Mellal to the south, located directly at the base of the mountains, was still subject to the incursions of "dissident" tribesmen in the early 1930's.

Although founded in the late 1500's, the Sherqawi *zawya* did not become a significant factor in Morocco until a century later. Its ascendancy is closely linked with the decline of another religious lodge, that of ed-Dila, which played a critical role in the last stages of the Maraboutic Crisis.[2] A brief discussion of the vicissitudes of this *zawya* places the rise of the Sherqawa in perspective. The ruins of ed-Dila are located approximately fifty kilometers to the southeast of Boujad, near the present Middle Atlas settlement of Ait Ishaq. A fast-moving series of alliances and conquests culminated in 1650 with ed-Dila's conquest of Fes, which was held for about a decade. At its apogee the marabouts of the *zawya* held a good part of the plains of northeastern Morocco, as well as the Middle Atlas Mountains, where they commanded the loyalty of the region's Berber-speaking tribesmen. For a few years Meknes, Salé, the Gharb Plain, and the region from the south of the Middle Atlas Mountains to the outskirts of Tafilalt was in their domain. At the center of this "maraboutic fiefdom," ed-Dila, the Qur'an was reportedly recited nonstop night and day.

Ed-Dila's power against the sultanate is demonstrated by the fact that it served as a sanctuary for the 'Alawi Mulay Rashid when he revolted against his reigning brother in 1659. Later, in 1668, during his reign as sultan (1664–1672), Mulay Rashid saw ed-Dila as a threat, destroyed it, dispersed its client tribes, and sent its principal marabout and his entourage in exile to Ottoman-controlled Tlemçen, in what is now Algeria.

A grandson of the exiled marabout tried a comeback with Ottoman support in 1677, during the reign (1672–1727) of the strong-man consolidator of the 'Alawi dynasty, Sultan Mulay Isma'il. Ed-Dila was rebuilt and again supported by most of the tribes of both the Middle Atlas Mountains and the Tadla Plain. Mulay Isma'il managed to destroy the lodge, but only after several unsuccessful, heavily resisted expeditions. Tribal resistance was only gradually broken. To keep it that way, by the late seventeenth century Mulay Isma'il had established a chain of fortresses and garrisons along his principal lines of communication. One such fortress was Qaṣba Tadla (built in 1687), thirty kilometers to the southeast of Boujad (Chapelle 1931: 26–27; A. Naṣiri 1906–1907:I, 65, 70, 92, 107).

The role of the Sherqawa in this vital conflict is uncertain, except that they were closely linked with both sides and at the critical moment managed to cast their lot with the 'Alawi dynasty.[3] The historian al-Ifrani (d. 1670), who wrote at least part of his account of the earlier Sa'adi dynasty while at Boujad,[4] portrayed the second principal marabout of ed-Dila, Sidi Muḥammed ben Abu Bakr (1560–1637), as the disciple of a number of leading saints in the Maghreb until finally he declared that Sidi Mḥammed Sherqi was his "spiritual guide" above all others. Thus Sidi Mḥammed Sherqi acquired "an authority and consideration superior to that of his contemporaries" (Ifrani 1888:276–280). Sidi Muḥammed ben Abu Bakr's successor during ed-Dila's apogee, Sidi Muḥammed l-Ḥajj (1589–1671), is also said to have exchanged "correspondence and reproaches" with a grandson of Sidi Mḥammed Sherqi, Sidi Muḥammed Mfaddel ben Ḥmed l-Mursli (d. 1664) (A. Naṣiri 1906–1907:I, 141–142). Neither al-Ifrani nor other writers further elaborate the nature of ed-Dila's ties with Sidi Mḥammed Sherqi or any of his successors as marabout (see Fig. 2).

Such relations were clearly of paramount significance. since in the 1680's Boujad became the most prominent of the "loyalist" *zawya*-s supporting the sultan: "Sultan Mulay Isma'il, when he was certain that the Sherqawa had no desire for temporal power, showered them with consideration and honors; the tomb of the ancestor of the Sherqawa became one of the most visited sanctuaries of the Empire. By the end of the seventeenth century this *zawya* acquired an importance which had only previously been obtained in the Tadla region by the house of Dila" (Lévi-Provençal 1922:297–298).

The Sherqawa through Traditional Sources

Traditional accounts, such as that of al-Qadiri (d. 1712), based on earlier manuscript sources, provide only stylized information concerning Sidi Mḥammed Sherqi and his successors.[5] Al-Qadiri devotes a large part of his biographical notice to the proper orthography of the founding marabout's name, his patrilineal antecedents (including doubts as to whether he really is a descendant of the caliph 'Umar), a listing of his Sufi masters, the fact that he had moments of "mystic

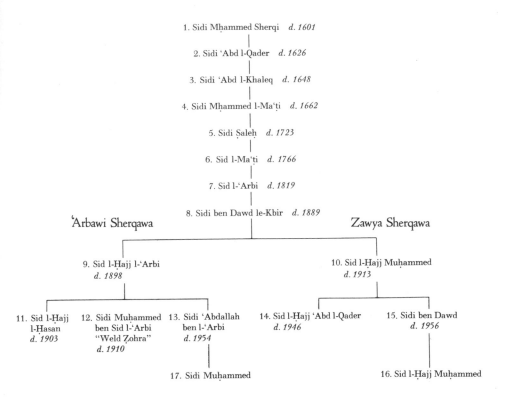

1. Sidi Mhammed Sherqi   *d. 1601*

2. Sidi 'Abd l-Qader   *d. 1626*

3. Sidi 'Abd l-Khaleq   *d. 1648*

4. Sidi Mhammed l-Ma'ti   *d. 1662*

5. Sidi Saleh   *d. 1723*

6. Sid l-Ma'ti   *d. 1766*

7. Sid l-'Arbi   *d. 1819*

8. Sidi ben Dawd le-Kbir   *d. 1889*

'Arbawi Sherqawa   Zawya Sherqawa

9. Sid l-Hajj l-'Arbi
d. 1898

10. Sid l-Hajj Muhammed
d. 1913

11. Sid l-Hajj
l-Hasan
d. 1903

12. Sidi Muhammed
ben Sid l-'Arbi
"Weld Zohra"
d. 1910

13. Sidi 'Abdallah
ben l-'Arbi
d. 1954

14. Sid l-Hajj 'Abd l-Qader
d. 1946

15. Sidi ben Dawd
d. 1956

17. Sidi Muhammed

16. Sid l-Hajj Muhammed

Figure 2.
Lords of the Sherqawi zawya.

exaltation," and a brief anecdote suggesting his theological position on God's attributes versus that of Sidi Hmed bel Gasem, a neighboring marabout in Bni Mellal (Qadiri 1913:127–129).

For anthropological purposes, most of the traditional accounts appear at first to have a thin yield. There is no material that suggests the nature of maraboutic succession, the internal organization of *zawya*-s, or their economic activities, and exceedingly little on popular attitudes toward marabouts. For instance, al-Qadiri makes no attempt to elaborate the implications of 'Umari descent as claimed by the Sherqawa and certain other maraboutic groups. In the political context of the seventeenth century such a claim could be considered as a means of placing marabouts and their descendants outside of direct contention for the sultanate, which required descent from the Prophet. At the same time, 'Umari descent maintained all other distinctions from "commoner" descent, including the right to marry female descendants of the Prophet. Similarly, the marabout's origin is said to be the Werdigha tribe, which presently is one of the client groups to the Sherqawa. But no other mention is made of his relations with local tribes or the fact, at least in terms of the oral history of contemporary Sherqawa, that the marabout first established a *zawya* at Taghzirt, a village to the south of Qasba Tadla, but left there following friction with neighboring marabouts.

Al-Qadiri writes tautologically that Sidi Mhammed Sherqi was one of the great Sufi *shaykh*-s because of his widespread reputation and numerous disciples. "Through him God showered rewards on a multitude of faithful, of whom many distinguished themselves by their outstanding virtues and their *baraka*" (1913:127–129). No context is given which allows a more precise understanding of *baraka*, its recognition or transmission, the importance attached to claims of genealogical descent, or other issues which would clarify the significance of marabouts in Moroccan society. All such concerns are either taken for granted (a fact that in itself is critically important) or considered beneath mention.

Only a faint echo of maraboutic geopolitics enters the quasi-official, Makhzen-centered traditional historiography. Sidi Mhammed Sherqi received religious and mystic instruction from his father, Sidi bel Gasem (not the same person as Sidi Hmed bel Gasem of Bni Mellal), and from two other *shaykh*-s, who themselves had been instructed by Shaykh 'Abd l-'Aziz et-Tebba (d. 1508), al-Jazuli (d. 1465/1466), and (through other intermediaries) esh-Shadili (d.

1258). This particular chain (*silsila*) of instruction places the
Sherqawi marabout in the pro-Moroccan mystic tradition mentioned
in the last chapter. Al-Qadiri's anecdote regarding the relations of
Sidi Mhammed Sherqi with Sidi Hmed bel Gasem of Bni Mellal states
that the two were "like the grindstones of a mill, crushing anyone
who came between them," despite their theological differences on the
nature of God's attributes. A more politicized account of the relations
of the two marabouts is provided by al-Ifrani. He writes that in the
late sixteenth century the governor of Tadla, en-Naser l-Ghaleb
Billah, revolted against his paternal uncle, the Sa'adi sultan Hmed
ben Mansur (1578–1603). Sidi Hmed bel Gasem supported en-Naser,
who was soon captured, paraded throughout the Tadla Plain, and
finally beheaded. Sidi Mhammed Sherqi, who by inference was more
successful in his alliances, is reported to have said of his unfortunate
maraboutic colleague "Poor Baba Hmed! He saw en-Naser's head
enter Tadla and thought it was en-Naser!" (Ifrani 1888:101).[6] Such
political activities become clear only for the later period of the nineteenth century, when information beyond that of the traditional
chronicles becomes available.

   The traditional accounts are valuable at least in revealing aspects
of the Sherqawi *zawya* that existed only in truncated form at later
times. During the seventeenth and eighteenth centuries, the Sherqawi
lodge had a substantial reputation as a center of religious learning,
so that in this respect it is accurately represented by the traditional
paradigm of hagiographic historiography. Thus, during the lordship
of Sidi Saleh (d. 1723) (2-5),[7] the historian al-Ifrani was resident in
Boujad. At such close range to the Sherqawa, the historian must have
been familiar with the full scope of their activities but generally
recorded only those which fell within the available historiographical
paradigm. The conclusion of his history of the Sa'adi dynasty (1888:
310) is a panegyric to Sidi Saleh, at one point calling him "the seal
[i.e., the most perfect] of the saints" (*khatem el-'awliya*), a phrase
echoing that reserved for Muhammed, "the seal of the prophets."
Al-Ifrani and the marabout carried on a frequent correspondence,
through which the former often sought subsidies for his writings
(Lévi-Provençal 1922:119–120). Sidi Saleh himself appears to have
been highly educated and in touch with, if not an internal part of,
the network of urban-oriented religious scholars (*'ulama*; sg., *'alem*).
As a youth he studied in Fes at the Medrasa Mesbahiya, the school
of the Qarawiyin Mosque-University which seems to have particular-

ly attracted students from the Tadla. Among his teachers was Sidi Ḥmed ben Naṣer, later to become one of the principal marabouts of the important Naṣiriya religious order situated in Tamgrut, in Morocco's pre-Saharan south (Ecorcheville 1938).

Sid l-Maʿti (d. 1766) (2-6), Sidi Ṣaleḥ's son and maraboutic successor, studied the religious sciences under his father, a paternal uncle, and three non-Sherqawi religious scholars who were attached to the *zawya*. A fourth taught him medicine. From childhood he is said to have possessed mystic inspiration (*ḥal*) and to have often gone into trances (*ghaḍb*). At least one account uncharacteristically refers to "magical" acts performed by him, although these are not described in any detail (Lakhdar 1971:227). Sid l-Maʿti was best known for a sixty-volume collection of prayers which he compiled with the aid of three of his disciples and secretaries. Both Sid l-Maʿti and his father had their biographies written by secretaries who came from Wlad 'Abdun (Shawya) and Bni Khiran (Lévi-Provençal 1922:297–298; Niegel 1913:290), tribal groups over which the Sherqawa have exercised considerable influence since at least the nineteenth century and probably much earlier. Names of other secretaries and students (*tolba*; sg., *taleb*) indicate provenance from most of the principal regions of Morocco; occasional references prior to the nineteenth century also suggest that Sherqawa established themselves in major cities elsewhere (e.g., A. Nasiri 1906–1907:I, 155).

The overall picture that emerges from these small details is that the Sherqawi *zawya* and its marabouts played an important role in Morocco's intellectual life. The sharp dichotomy between rural religious leaders and religious scholars which tended to characterize Morocco (with the possible exception of the Sus region in the south) during the colonial era and independent Morocco of the nineteenth century is thus no accurate indication of the earlier realities.

The Sherqawa were linked with many of the other major maraboutic centers in the country, although, barring new sources, it is impossible to trace these with any precision. Thus Sidi Mhammed l-Maʿti (d. 1662) (2-4) was initiated into the Naṣiriya religious order by the marabout Mhammed ben Naṣer (d. 1674) (Drague 1951:205),[8] as was his son Sidi Ṣaleḥ. Similarly, Sidi 'Ali ben Ḥamdush (d. ca. 1720), founder of the ecstatic Ḥmadsha order of Meknes, was a disciple of Sid l-Ḥafyan ben Sid l-Mursli esh-Sherqawi,[9] whose shrine in Boujad is regularly visited by Ḥmadsha pilgrims.

The last Sherqawi lord discussed in traditional sources is Sid l-'Arbi (d. 1819) (2-7). These sources are particularly interesting because they are complemented both by oral tradition of the Sherqawi elite and by the testimony of a foreign observer. The late-nineteenth century Moroccan historian, al-Naṣiri, describes the Sherqawi *zawya* as "one of the most renowned of the Maghreb," which "for centuries . . . has been directed by eminent men who have transmitted from one to the other the heritage of saintliness and preeminence" and who have been treated with "care and respect" by the 'Alawi dynasty. These remarks preface his report that Sultan Muhammed ben 'Abdallah (1757–1790), himself "glorious and noble," destroyed most of Boujad during a military expedition in 1784/1785. Al-Naṣiri provides no explanation for the friction which existed between the two except to say that chiefs must act severely towards those they command and that no man is perfect except those whom God has so created (1906–1907:I,346–347).

Oral tradition, substantiated in part by written documentation, places the destruction of Boujad in 1784/1785 in a more meaningful context. Until the late eighteenth century, the Sherqawi *zawya* served as a collective granary for nearby client tribes and as a sanctuary powerful enough to provide security for refugee tribesmen and Makhzen officials negotiating amnesties (*aman*-s) from the Makhzen. Sid l-'Arbi (2-7) had extensive land holdings (see Fig. 4) and reputedly possessed a vast fortune, considered by some to rival the sultan's (Ecorcheville 1938). Under these circumstances, the sultan appears to have seen the Sherqawi lodge as a threat. The tactics he used in destroying the *zawya* may have struck al-Naṣiri as less than "glorious and noble," for he fails to report them. According to members of the Sherqawi elite in the 1930's, Sultan Muhammed ben 'Abdallah sent a message to Sid l-'Arbi to join the royal expedition as it approached Boujad. The first Makhzen troops began arriving just as the *sid* left Boujad. Sensing deceit, he quickly returned. Later, after destruction of the town and the granaries had begun, the sultan told Sid l-'Arbi that he was not taking action against the Sherqawa, only against certain non-Sherqawa who had sought refuge in Boujad. For two days the troops sacked the town, took tribesmen as prisoners, and left intact only the shrines of Sidi Mhammed Sherqi and Sid l-Ma'ti and the houses which stood between them. When the pillaging ended, the sultan provided Sid l-'Arbi a convoy of sixty mules and brought him to Marrakesh (Ecorcheville 1938:49–51). The marabout remained in a sort of "forced residence" in Marrakesh and its region for eight years, at least two of which were spent in the nearby village of Bzu (see Eickelman 1972–1973:44).

Sid l-'Arbi's exile seems to have diminished neither his prestige nor his personal wealth. During it at least twenty-nine large estates in the Bzu-Demnat region were given him by tribes anxious to secure his intercession. These are still collectively owned by his descendants and yield substantial revenues. The sultan also recognized the marabout's continuing influence. At least twice, Sid l-'Arbi served as emissary (together with Mulay 'Ali, principal marabout of the *zawya* of Wezzan) to the sultan's son Mulay Yezid, who, with the support of Berber marabouts and tribesmen in the Rif and Middle Atlas mountains, had revolted against his father.

When Sultan Muhammed ben 'Abdallah died in 1790, Sid l-'Arbi was caught in an untenable position in the ensuing struggle over his succession. One of the sultan's sons, Mulay Hisham, was recognized as sultan in Marrakesh, where the marabout was residing. Mulay Yezid was recognized elsewhere. Sid l-'Arbi was compelled to give his oath of allegiance (*bay'a*) to Mulay Hisham and was allowed to return to Boujad. After a bitter struggle which lasted two years, a third son, Mulay Sliman (1792–1822), was recognized as sultan throughout Morocco. Sid l-'Arbi went to Fes to appease him but was treated contemptuously and not allowed to return to Boujad until twenty months later (Drague 1951:86, 232; Ecorcheville 1938: 51–52; cf. A. Nasiri 1906–1907:I,347).

The continuing strength of the Sherqawa through this period is clear from the account of Ali Bey (Domingo Badia y Leblich). Ali Bey was in Morocco from June 1803 to October 1805 and saw a nephew of Sid l-'Arbi in Marrakesh. On the basis of what he learned, Ali Bey depicted Sid l-'Arbi and the lord of the *zawya* of Wezzan as the "two greatest saints of all the empire of Morocco . . . These two saints decide almost on the fate of the whole empire, as it is supposed that they attract the blessings of heaven on the country." The region surrounding the Sherqawi lodge was described as having no representative of the sultan and paying no taxes to the Makhzen. The marabout's household was obviously substantial, as he is described as keeping, besides his wives and common concubines, eighteen young Negro girls. When Sid l-'Arbi visited other regions, he gave "orders and advice" to the governors of the sultan, received substantial presents and alms, and was avidly consulted by women and followed by crowds of poor people who sang his praises. He traveled surrounded by an armed retinue "ready to defend the divine cause with their weapons." The marabout himself was "easy on horseback, and a clever shot." Politically, Sid l-'Arbi preached "submission to the Sultan, domestic peace, and the practice of virtue" (Ali Bey 1816: 176–177).

Sid l-'Arbi's relations with Mulay Sliman appear to have been generally satisfactory. As a youth, Mulay Sliman spent several years in Boujad, and later, as sultan, he maintained a large house there.[10] In 1805 he built what remains Boujad's principal mosque. These actions suggest close ties with the Sherqawa. Nonetheless, Ali Bey wrote that the sultan and the Sherqawi marabout had a falling-out, after which Sid l-'Arbi converted the mosque into a stable. To end the quarrel, the sultan sent the marabout a thousand ducats, which the marabout reciprocated with a thousand sheep, to indicate that the matter was settled. Ali Bey speculates that the quarrel rested on nothing but "some little want of attention" (1816:178).

North African maraboutism did not operate in a sealed vacuum throughout this period. Toward the latter part of his reign, Mulay Sliman was strongly influenced by Wahhabi emissaries from Arabia. These persuaded him to write a treatise condemning maraboutism as against the fundamental tenets of Islam and to issue a proclamation forbidding maraboutic festivals (*musem*-s) and visits to maraboutic shrines (Abun-Nasr 1963:94–95). Such an attempt was markedly unrealistic in the context of North Africa. Sid l-'Arbi remained a loyalist when the sultan faced a series of revolts led by Berber marabouts. He also advised the sultan not to take a personal part in a punitive expedition to the Middle Atlas in 1818. The sultan ignored this advice, suffered a major defeat, and was taken prisoner (but, because of his *baraka*, was personally unharmed) after having been betrayed by a *qaid* from Shawya. After the sultan was released, the rebel *qaid* sought sanctuary (*horma*) in Boujad, where he was later assassinated (Mission Scientifique du Maroc 1915:I,164). The inviolability of the right of sanctuary appears to have been weighed against the question of Sherqawi relations with the Makhzen.

The Makhzen paid equal attention to the nuances of Sherqawi affairs and presumably to those of other major maraboutic lodges. When Sid l-'Arbi died of the plague in 1819 (A. Nasiri 1906–1907: II,50), Sultan Mulay Sliman delayed a year in confirming a successor. This probably was in order to assess the suitability of the various contenders to the Sherqawi lordship in the light of Makhzen interests as well as the strength of various contending factions. The elder son of Sid l-'Arbi had been in the sultan's entourage as a student (perhaps also as a guarantee of the marabout's loyalty?), but the sultan had earlier suggested to Sid l-'Arbi that his son should discontinue his studies "since it is impossible for a married man with one wife, let alone two, to pursue studies" (E, 6 July 1810 / 5 Rejeb 1225). He was passed over in favor of a younger brother, Sidi ben Dawd (2-8), then eleven years old. In a decree addressed to the elder brother, Sidi ben Dawd was invested with "possession of that which is due him by paternal, maternal, and fraternal succession," as well as with the "secret" of his ancestors (E, S, 12 July 1820 / 10 Shawwal 1235). Presumably the choice of the younger brother was to favor a faction within the Sherqawa that would be dependent upon the Makhzen for its well-being. In any case, there are numerous subsequent requests from Mulay Sliman and succeeding sultans throughout the nineteenth century ordering Sidi ben Dawd to furnish the Makhzen with specified numbers of horsemen from tribes in a client relationship with the Sherqawa (e.g., E, 6 March 1821 / 26 Jumada I 1236) and to perform other services on their behalf.

Such incidents as the above indicate that a key determining factor in the roles played by the Sherqawa was their relative strength and capability in relation to that of the sultan and his entourage. Sherqawi power and influence were no more given, fixed elements in "traditional" Morocco than any other component of society. There is evidence that the scope of Sherqawi political interest was remarkably wide. The Sherqawa followed not only the intricacies of Makhzen politics but also those of the Ottomans and those of the French in Algeria (e.g., E, Mulay 'Abd er-Rahman to Sidi ben Dawd, 7 October 1844 / 24 Ramadan 1260). Undated notes in Boujad also indicate that travelers were regularly questioned on the news of important personages in their own locality.

The Zawya in the Late Nineteenth Century

A fuller picture of the social role of the Sherqawi lodge can only be given beginning with the 1880's. A particularly valuable, although not always accurate, source is the French explorer-priest Charles de Foucauld, who traveled through Morocco disguised as an Algerian Jew and stayed at Boujad from 6 to 17 September 1883. By that time,

Boujad no longer served as a collective granary for tribes of the region—this function had presumably ended in the previous century. Boujad still served, however, as a major market center. Some Sherqawa participated in the market as merchants (as did many non-Sherqawa) and as guarantors of the market's peace. The weapons of tribesmen were deposited with the lord of the *zawya* or one of his kinsmen for its duration. Sherqawa also served as escorts (*zettat*-s) for caravans of merchants and other persons seeking safe passage through their region of influence. A Sherqawi riding on a mule with a red saddle, followed, if he had sufficient prestige, by a slave holding a parasol, was a familiar sight alongside such caravans. Escorts were chosen and fees assessed according to the value of the caravan. A two- or three-hundred-camel caravan, for instance, was escorted by a close relative of the leading marabout (Foucauld 1939:130). The average fee during the reign (1873–1894) of Mulay Ḥasan I was one-half *ryal* per camel, according to an elderly Sherqawi notary. From manuscript letters between Sherqawa and leading merchants elsewhere in Morocco, it is clear that the main commercial route to Boujad was through Casablanca, a journey of approximately four days in good weather. Goods from Fes, Rabat, and overseas also came to Boujad through Casablanca, although a certain amount of trade was carried on directly with Marrakesh, an eight-day voyage. But this route was considered in general to be much more precarious, since many tribes of the Marrakesh region had no regular relations with the Sherqawa. Subsidiary caravan routes linked Boujad with Bni Mellal and Khnifra. Only exceptionally was there direct contact with Fes via the Middle Atlas Mountains, as when Fes, the Middle Atlas tribes, and a faction of the Sherqawa supported the insurgent Mulay Ḥafeḍ against his brother Mulay 'Abd l-'Aziz in the struggle for the sultanate that erupted in 1907 (Martin 1923:473).

Principal goods included tea, rice, sugar, spices, cloth, perfume, jewelry, household utensils, and luxury clothing (Foucauld 1939: 127). These were exchanged for animal hides, wax, wool, horses, camels, sheep, goats, and grain from tribesmen. Most of the same range of animal products were offered the Sherqawa as donations from their clients. Much of this extralocal commerce was typically in the hands of dyadic trading partners who could claim complex, diffuse bonds of kinship or common origin. For instance, Sherqawa and other Boujadi-s lived in their own quarter in Khnifra, where they worked as muleteers and representatives for merchants in Boujad (F. Berger 1929:44–45). Similar arrangements existed in Bni Mellal, Casablanca, and other centers linked economically with Boujad.[11] The extent to which the Sherqawa actively engaged in this commerce is not clear from the sources. Regular correspondence and gifts were exchanged between prominent Sherqawa and leading merchants of Rabat and Casablanca, as well as with the sultan and other Makhzen officials. Those ties were not strictly limited to commerce. A letter from a major Fassi merchant, Hajj Tayyeb Gsus (Guessous), ensured Foucauld a good reception upon his arrival in Boujad (Foucauld 1939:128). Itinerant artisanal specialists, such as those from Marrakesh who carved the intricate woodwork characteristic of the houses of leading Sherqawa and shaped the domes of shrines, were also engaged through such contacts.

Foucauld estimated Boujad's population at 1,700, including the Sherqawa, their slaves, and their clients. The latter included around two hundred Jews. In Boujad, as in Demnat to the south (Flamand 1952) and other Moroccan towns, Jews were not confined to a special quarter (*mellah*). Only the quarter containing the synagogue (3-10) was called the *mellah* by Boujadi-s, although Foucauld used the term to refer generically to any residential cluster of Jews, including two (3-11, 3-12) without synagogues. In the preprotectorate period, Jews clustered about the houses of the wealthiest and most prominent Jewish merchants. Foucauld makes no specific mention of the economic activities of the Jewish community. Both Muslims and Jews engaged in grain trading; largely Jewish specialties included work as bellowsmakers (*rwabzi*-s), itinerant jewelers, and cloth merchants. Many Jewish merchants and craftsmen made the rounds of the small rural markets. Others, such as butchers, dealt exclusively with the Jewish community itself. In general, each Jewish household had ties with particular Sherqawa and relied upon these for protection in time of crisis.

The religious and political influence of the Sherqawa extended considerably beyond the range of tribes which used Boujad as a weekly market. Foucauld wrote that almost all tribes within two days' journey of Boujad in any direction were in a client relation to the Sherqawa. These included the Bni Zemmur, Sma'la, Bni Khiran, Werdigha, Bni Meskin, Ait Rba', Bni 'Amir, and Bni Musa tribes. Regular gifts—Foucauld calls those of tribal collectivities "tribute"—

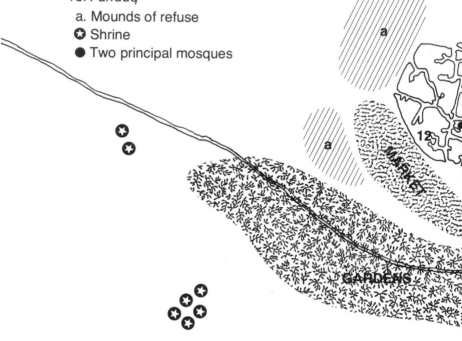

1. Mosque of Mulay Sliman
2. Mosque of Sidi Mḥammed Sherqi
3. Three Sherqawi shrines
4. Shrine of Sidi Mḥammed Sherqi
5. House of Sidi ben Dawd (2-8)
6. House of Sidi 'Umar
7. House of Sidi Muḥammed ben Driss
8. House of Sid l-Ḥajj Driss
9. House of Musa 'Allun
10. *Mellaḥ* (includes synagogue)
11. Jewish houses
12. Jewish houses
13. *Funduq*
a. Mounds of refuse
✪ Shrine
● Two principal mosques

Figure 3.
Boujad, 1883. (Based on Foucauld 1888:55.)

BOUJAD
1883

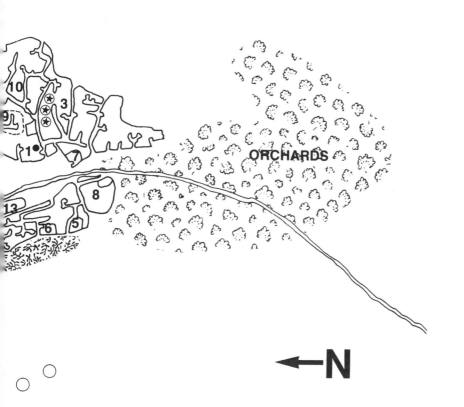

ORCHARDS

←N

also came from most of the tribes of the Shawya, as well as Middle
Atlas tribes including Ait Seri and Ishqern (Foucauld 1939:117–118,
122).

Foucauld estimated the gifts in wheat alone which arrived at the
zawya as four hundred camel loads the week before his arrival and
two hundred during his twelve-day stay (1939:122, 125). This figure
must be adjusted seasonally, however, as September is the only time
at which collective, tribal pilgrimages are made. These collective offerings were made primarily to the lord (*sid*) of the *zawya*, although
many also were made to other Sherqawi marabouts having special
relationships with particular groups. Some of this wealth was re-
distributed among the Sherqawa. The most prominent (and wealthy)
saw to the well-being, or at least the maintenance, of their less fortunate kinsmen. A limited amount of Sherqawi wealth found its way
back to the tribes in the form of seeds for fall planting and, in at least
one case (Foucauld 1939:121), the construction of a fortified enclo-
sure for the Bni Zemmur. Offerings and sacrifices made at other times
of the year were primarily made by individual pilgrims or their proxies—tribesmen, influential merchants, the sultan, and members of his
entourage. These were directed to any Sherqawi regarded as capable
of obtaining God's blessings (*baraka*) for the supplicant. Neither
Foucauld nor other commentators on maraboutic activities during the
nineteenth century make any distinction between regular offerings
and sacrifices made by tribal collectivities and occasional ones made
by both tribal and nontribal individuals.

Foucauld wrote that the Sherqawa lived exclusively from offerings,
but this claim is misleading. They also had revenues from commercial activities, the vast holdings of land in the hands of individual
Sherqawa or their legal heirs (such as those of Sid l-Ḥajj l-'Arbi
[2-9]), pious endowments (*aḥbas*; sg., *ḥabus*), agricultural estates
(*'azib*-s), and a substantial traffic in influence with the Makhzen.

The *'azib*-s are particularly important for what they reveal of the
nature of Sherqawi relations with other centers of power in Moroccan society. But the exact meaning of *'azib* is also difficult to elicit
from nineteenth-century sources. In a general sense, *'azib* refers to
any agricultural estate with an absentee owner (Aubin 1906:15).
In reference to the Sherqawa and other marabouts, the term is more
complex. According to context, *'azib* can refer alternatively to an
agricultural estate with special privileges recognized by the sultan or
to workers or tribesmen attached to such an estate. Agricultural

holdings beyond the pale of effective influence of the sultan, such as the holdings acquired by Sid l-'Arbi (2-7), are never referred to by this term, although rights to them were firmly established in Islamic law and safe from tribal incursions. Much of the Sherqawi agricultural land in the Boujad region was held by individual Sherqawa or their descendants by Islamic law. Most of these holdings were irrigated orchards that were cultivated by slaves or other clients of the Sherqawa and constituted the only permanent rural settlements in Boujad's region. Evidently only the supernatural sanctions available to the Sherqawa were capable of insulating these enclaves from the region's general insecurity. Figure 4 represents both these individual holdings and those of *'azib*-s as they were roughly from the end of the reign (1873–1894) of Mulay Hasan I to the eve of the protectorate. Not shown are urban properties—houses, baths, subsidiary *zawya*-s—in Casablanca, Meknes, Fes, and Salé, as well as scattered holdings in the High Atlas mountains.[12] The status of *'azib*-s was more indefinite than that of the individual holdings. Some of these estates were occupied by Sherqawi clients; others were occupied by Sherqawa who had left Boujad and settled in tribal regions, often at the invitation of the host group. The documentation for these estates, consisting primarily of royal decrees (*daher*-s) and correspondence with Makhzen officials (E, S), indicates that both the estates and their inhabitants were exempt from direct Makhzen authority. Their inhabitants were not subject to *corvée* labor or to requests for troops, as was the case with other subjects of the Makhzen (e.g., E, decree of Sultan Muhammed IV, 3 September 1864 / 1 Rbi'a II 1281). Royal decrees also specified that the taxes (*zakat* and *'ashur*) imposed on the inhabitants of Sherqawi *'azib*-s were to be paid directly to the lord (*mqaddem*) of the Sherqawi *zawya* in Boujad and used for his benefit. As the map indicates, most estates were concentrated in the Shawya region of western Morocco and were in the midst of tribes submitted to the direct Makhzen control. This location is in itself significant. Edouard Michaux-Bellaire, a prominent French ethnographer in the early days of the protectorate who was also concerned with various political affairs, arbitrarily saw *'azib*-s as a means of extending Makhzen sovereignty to peripheral regions by vesting it in maraboutic proxies. This may have been true in some instances but was decidedly not the case for Sherqawi holdings (Michaux-Bellaire 1913:229; cf. Eickelman 1972–1973:42–46).

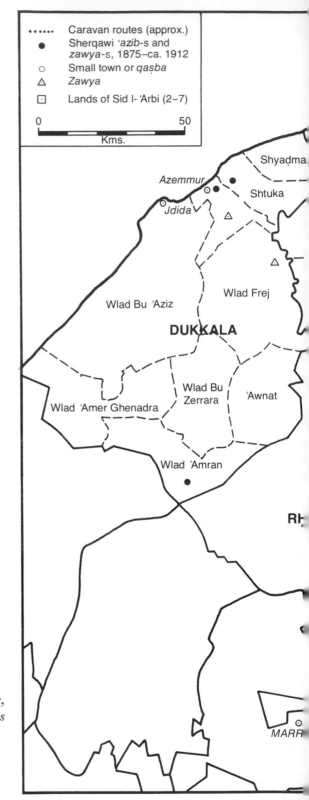

Figure 4.
*Western Morocco and the
Sherqawa in the late
nineteenth century.*

*Names of tribes and tribal
sections are in roman type,
names of small settlements
or towns in italic.*

Significantly, the status of these estates appears to have been constantly tested by the Sherqawa of Boujad, subsidiary groups of Sherqawa located outside of Boujad, tribes, local officials of the Makhzen, and the Makhzen itself. It is not always clear whether a royal decree was granted voluntarily by the sultan or whether it was simply the de facto recognition of a pre-existing situation.[13] The renewals of royal decrees show the range of these variations. Predictably, all decrees were renewed either singly or collectively at the accession of a new sultan. Many were also intermittently reaffirmed, indicating the constantly contested nature of these privileges (e.g., E: Mulay Ḥasan I, 29 November 1875 / 9 Qaʿada 1292; Mulay ʿAbd l-ʿAziz to Sid l-Ḥajj l-Ḥasan, 3 June 1901 / 15 Ṣafar 1319; Mulay ʿAbd l-ʿAziz to Sid l-Ḥajj l-ʿArbi, 4 May 1896 / 21 Qaʿada 1313; Mulay ʿAbd l-ʿAziz to Sid l-Ḥajj l-Ḥasan, 29 January 1901 / 8 Shawwal 1318). Sherqawi lords frequently complained to the sultan that local *qaid*-s and neighboring tribes did not respect or recognize presumed Sherqawi privileges. The Makhzen itself sometimes questioned the status of claimed estates (e.g., E: two decrees of Mulay Ḥasan I dated 22 September 1884 / 1 Dhu Ḥijja 1301; Mulay ʿAbd l-ʿAziz to Sid l-Ḥasan, 28 May 1899 / 17 Muḥarrem 1317; Driss ben ʿUmar to Muḥammed ben Dawd, February 1894 / Shaʿban 1311). *Qaid*-s also complained that Sherqawi estates, over which they had no direct authority, were used as bases to raid neighboring tribes (e.g., E, Sultan Mulay ʿAbd er-Raḥman to Sidi ben Dawd, 24 September 1853 / 20 Dhu Ḥijja 1269).

Certain estates were attached to subsidiary *zawya*-s founded by Sherqawa who had left Boujad, often at the invitation of client tribes. Sometimes these *zawya*-s were permanent settlements; in other cases they were local communities (*dǎwwar*-s) living in tents, which were transhumant like the tribal section to which they were attached. Most subsidiary *zawya*-s were situated on the Tadla and Shawya plains, although a few were located in the High Atlas and one in the Sahara at Tata, visited by Foucauld (Eickelman 1972–1973; Foucald 1939:136). Fields surrounding such a *zawya* often were cultivated for the profit of its maraboutic inhabitants, who then sent annual contributions to the lord of the Sherqawa at Boujad. In exchange for these donations, the Sherqawi lord in Boujad secured *ʿazib* status from the Makhzen for the subsidiary lodge. When the support of the Sherqawa in Boujad was no longer considered necessary, such offerings were cut to token amounts or were discontinued.

When this happened, a "subsidiary" *zawya* became autonomous.

The uncertain status of these Sherqawi estates directly reflects the fluctuating and complex nature of Sherqawi relations with the Makhzen and tribal groups, as well as internal tensions among the Sherqawa. Foucauld's statement that the Tadla Plain in the 1880's was a sort of "theocracy" subject only to the "authority" of the lord of the Sherqawi *zawya* (1939:121) is misleading.[14] This claim is based on what the Sherqawa told him. The Sherqawa most concerned with Foucauld's visit believed that the direct intervention of France in Morocco's affairs was imminent and thus were anxious to emphasize their prominence (Foucauld 1939:135–136). They also were aware of his French identity. Admittedly, there is no indication that taxes were regularly collected by the Makhzen from the tribes of the upper Tadla Plain. Nevertheless, Boujad had a *qadi* (judge of Islamic law) appointed by the sultan.[15] There was also at least a nominal *qaid* over the neighboring tribes during part of the reign of Mulay Hasan I, and an overseer (*nadir*) of pious endowments from at least the eighteenth century (E, decree of Mulay 'Abd er-Rahman, 17 May 1827 / 20 Shawwal 1242). More significantly, the Makhzen often asserted a decisive role, as previously indicated, in the selection of Sherqawi lords. Reciprocally, the Sherqawa exercised considerable influence over the Makhzen policy toward the tribes of western Morocco. Correspondence indicates that, at least from the 1840's, the Sherqawi lords were asked by the sultan to suggest *qaid*-s for the tribes of the immediate region: Werdigha, Sma'la, and Bni Zemmur (E, Mulay 'Abd er-Rahman to Sidi ben Dawd, 11 August 1845 / 7 Sha'ban 1261). These may have been only nominal appointments or only intermittently effective. In the 1845 letter, the sultan also asked the Sherqawi lord to report on the popular acceptance of the nominees. Any candidate unacceptable to the tribal councils (*jma'a*-s) of the groups involved was not to be confirmed. Clearly such *qaid*-s owed their position to the Sherqawa. Moreover, at least some of them built houses in Boujad, suggesting long-term associations with the Sherqawa. By the reign of Mulay Hasan I, the Sherqawa also had a strong voice in nominating *qaid*-s for the Shawya. Later accounts indicate that Sherqawi nominations were commonly purchased.

In return for the power of nominating *qaid*-s, the Sherqawi lord was held responsible by the Makhzen for their performance. Among other obligations, the Sherqawa were asked to secure the oath of

allegiance from tribal councils at the inauguration of a new sultan
(e.g., E, 31 August 1875 / 29 Rejeb 1292), provide troops from their
client tribes upon request, arrange for the settlement of local disputes
inimical to the interests of the Makhzen, and conduct other sensitive
negotiations on its behalf. At the request of either the Makhzen or
the tribes involved, the *sid* was often called upon to arrange amnesties
(*aman*-s), not only for rebellious tribes of the Tadla, but also for
those in Sraghna and, at least on one occasion, the Bni Mṭir of the
Meknes region, whose council (*jma'a*) had come to Boujad to seek
an amnesty (E, Mulay Ḥasan I to Sidi ben Dawd, 26 January
1883 / 17 Rbi'a I 1300). The settlement of intertribal disputes took
the form of the "great *'ar*" (*'ar kbir*), or contingent supernatural
curse (see Westermarck 1926:518–569). After preliminary negotiations, a Sherqawi marabout interceded between the conflicting groups,
often carrying the cloth cover (*ghoṭa*) of the sepulcher of one of his
ancestors, and asked in the name of his maraboutic ancestor that
hostilities cease. By popular belief, those who refused to cease fighting
would sooner or later be struck with major misfortune. This form of
compulsion is known primarily from sources for later periods; hence,
I will discuss it at more length in a subsequent chapter.

More mundane tasks ordered by the sultan included taking an
inventory of goods of a deceased *qaid* and the purchase of "young,
prolific goats" for his herds (E, Sultan Mulay Ḥasan I to Sidi ben
Dawd, 7 March 1886 / 3 Jumada II 1303). The lord of the *zawya*
or his counselors also arranged, for a price, the release of prisoners
held by the Makhzen, the return of runaway slaves to their owners,[16]
and the issuance of royal decrees certifying tribal groups as descendants of the Prophet (*shorfa*). Presumably such descent carried with
it certain privileges, such as exemption from military service occasionally demanded by the Makhzen.

Throughout the nineteenth century, there is no question of the
favor of the Sherqawa in the eyes of the Makhzen. Local *qaid*-s and
members of the sultan's entourage sought intermarriage with the
Sherqawa and exchanged as presents concubines, animals, and other
objects of value, especially on the occasion of major festivals. Likewise, the Makhzen saw to the repair of Sherqawi shrines.

To monitor events in the Makhzen entourage, close relatives of
the Sherqawi lord generally accompanied it (or, as I earlier indicated,
may have been obligated to remain with it). One was the elder son

of Sid l-'Arbi (2-7), already mentioned. Until he became the lord of the *zawya* himself, a later Sid l-'Arbi (2-9) attended court, as did Driss ben 'Umar, the grandson of Sidi ben Dawd (2-8), who acted as escort to Charles de Foucauld in 1883 and from 1904 on worked as a translator-informant for the French and Sherqawi factotum in Casablanca. In addition, the Sherqawi lord always accompanied the sultan whenever he passed through the region of Sherqawi influence.

For the late nineteenth century, there is documentation of the internal division of leadership among the Sherqawa. Typically, the leading marabout allowed a close kinsman to undertake the more mundane, often lucrative, political tasks in order to leave unsullied his reputation of aloofness from such concern. In the latter part of the lordship of Sidi ben Dawd and for a considerable period after his death, this role was filled by his son Sidi 'Umar, a consummate politician. Foucauld and present-day elderly Sherqawa represent him as the *zawya*'s "grey eminence." It was he who negotiated the release of prisoners with the appropriate Makhzen officials. During Foucauld's visit, 'Umar detailed his son Driss (d. 1915), then twenty-five years old, to remain in close contact with the explorer in order to discern the real intention of his visit. Prior to Foucauld's visit Driss, like many other prominent Sherqawa, had made the pilgrimage (*hajj*) to Mecca. On his return Driss had visited Tunis and many of the principal cities of Algeria (Foucauld 1939:125, 130). Foucauld writes that he possessed a fair understanding of France's activities in Algeria and the potential consequences to the Sherqawa of direct French intervention in Morocco.[17] Foucauld makes clear, however, that Driss and his father kept Foucauld's true identity from Sidi ben Dawd, asserting that the latter was old and did not "understand" how to deal with the French. Such concealment also kept major political decisions in 'Umar's control.

Foucauld was evidently unaware of a major political maneuver undertaken by 'Umar immediately prior to his visit. In the spring of 1881 'Umar had arranged a meeting in Boujad between Sultan Mulay Hasan I and the Berber chieftain Mha u Hammu ez-Zayyani, after which Mha was made a *qaid* (Arnaud 1952:61).[18] This was part of the sultan's strategy of extending his effective authority over the Berber-speaking tribes of the Middle Atlas Mountains. Mha received arms and ammunition from the sultan, the deliveries of which were escorted by the Sherqawa through regions where they had influence.

So preponderant was 'Umar's political role in Sherqawi affairs that one anonymous correspondent complained to Sidi ben Dawd that "some say it is his *zawya*, not yours."[19]

Relations between the Sherqawi marabouts and outside groups were clearly not fixed during the nineteenth century or, presumably, for earlier periods. The status of the lord of the *zawya* and at least some of his prerogatives were legitimated by proclamations of the sultan. But the extent to which he actually was regarded as a marabout depended only in part upon the sultan. The rest depended upon the marabout's own capabilities in dominating other rival Sherqawa and maintaining a sizable tribal clientele. Competition among the Sherqawa themselves; political manipulation by tribes, the sultan, and his entourage; and an uncertain flow of events caused allegiances to marabouts to be constantly realigned. Accounts of this competition are almost totally absent from the traditional sources and, for that matter, most ethnographic presentations. Yet they are crucial to understanding the social role of marabouts.

In Boujad itself, competition for prestige in the nineteenth century and at earlier periods was largely in terms of acquiring a reputation for *baraka*, even if this was manifested (as in the case of Sidi 'Umar) by sagacious political negotiations on behalf of the *zawya*. Sherqawa unsuccessful in acquiring prestige on the basis of this attribute had the options of becoming dependent upon their more successful relatives, of leaving Boujad to form their own "subsidiary" *zawya*-s, or, to a much lesser extent, of leaving Boujad for the possibilities afforded by life in an urban center.

Fortunately, there is a fairly substantial documentation on the development of factions among the Sherqawa from the early 1890's through the beginning of the protectorate in 1912. This period is of particular interest because it is the last in which marabouts were considered capable of playing significant social and political roles based upon their "special" relationship with God. As mentioned, there are virtually no other accounts of internal factionalism in North African religious lodges outside of the circumstances of colonial hegemony. Hence I present this account in detail in the appendix, concentrating upon the problems of succession. In any case, this data will be more comprehensible after my ensuing account of contemporary Boujad and the Sherqawa. This is because many of the implicit understandings involved in these factional alignments and in the popular legitimations of claims to maraboutic qualities become clear only in the light of later events known in a fuller social context.

There are two significant features of the conflicts over maraboutic succession that developed in the 1890's: their articulation with extra-local events and their persistence over time. Tribal disputes, Makhzen manipulations of local rivalries, internal splits within the Makhzen, and the perception of opportunities by individual Sherqawa—all were closely related to maraboutic succession. After 1907 (when the French occupied Casablanca and the Shawya), colonial manipulation of local and national disputes constituted an additional factor, although French intervention was soon to alter radically the nature of these rivalries and the assumptions held by Moroccans about the powers of marabouts. No person engaged in the contest for dominance or prestige knew with certainty what style of conduct would be successful in any given situation. Loyalty to a given sultan, which in some circumstances might carry with it significant rewards, could also be a handicap should the authority of that sultan be challenged or cease to be effective. Excessive zeal in support of the Makhzen was as dangerous for powerful individuals as a reserve toward it. Positions were constantly tested and adjusted in line with personal evaluations of "the way things were."

Such conflicts showed surprising continuity over time. Shortly after Sidi ben Dawd (2-8) died in 1889, Sultan Mulay Hasan I designated the eldest of his twenty-one sons, Sid l-Hajj l-'Arbi (2-9), to succeed him. The very number of these sons, added to the descendants of earlier marabouts, gives some idea of the possibilities for intrigue among close kinsmen. All male descendants were technically entitled to equal inheritance from their father (with lesser amounts for daughters, wives, and other relatives). As indicated in detail in the appendix, even when a marabout chose his successor, there were often bitter and prolonged conflicts. Until the death of the sultan in 1894, there was no effective opposition to the Sherqawi lord, Sid l-Hajj l-'Arbi. He enjoyed the unqualified support of Mulay Hasan I. After the sultan's death, a still minor son, Mulay 'Abd l-'Aziz (reigned 1894–1908) came to the throne. Some of his entourage were particularly hostile to the Sherqawa and sought ways to weaken their influence. The first step was to pay regular subsidies to another son of Sidi ben Dawd, Sid l-Hajj Muhammed (2-16). Both 'Umar and his son Driss (who lived in Casablanca and from there kept in touch with the Makhzen and, after 1904, the French) had close ties with Sid l-Hajj Muhammed. This rival faction was nurtured by the Makhzen until finally, in 1901, both Sid l-Hajj Muhammed and his paternal nephew, Sid l-Hajj l-Hasan (2-11) (who succeeded his father, Sid l-Hajj l-'Arbi, as lord of the Sherqawa on the latter's death in 1898), were called by the sultan to Marrakesh. There he announced that the *zawya* and its holdings were to be divided equally between them and that henceforth they were to be the co-lords of the Sherqawa (E, decree of 20 October 1901 / 7 Rejeb 1319). The timing of the announcement, just after the fall festival in which tribesmen massed in Boujad, avoided confrontation with the Makhzen. The sultan also detained Sid l-Hajj l-Hasan in Marrakesh for several months, enabling his rival, Sid l-Hajj Muhammed, to consolidate his position. Henceforth the two rival groups of descendants (and clients) of Sidi ben Dawd were known as the 'Arbawi Sherqawa and the Zawya Sherqawa. The first were so named because their core consisted of descendants of Sid l-Hajj l-'Arbi (2-9) and those who stressed close ties with them. The Zawya Sherqawa, led initially by Sid l-Hajj Muhammed, were so named because after 1901 they assumed control of the house (3-5) of Sidi ben Dawd, at which pilgrims were traditionally received. The whole quarter was, and is, known as the Zawya quarter. Although the minor personnel of these two factions could on occasion shift loyalties, their leaders were locked into positions that limited their room for sudden reversals.

The Makhzen's divisive move was successful. For years, the proponents of both factions were engaged in bitter struggles over property rights and worked to draw clients away from each other. The Zawya Sherqawa were the weaker faction in terms of popular legitimacy; hence, they were more dependent upon the Makhzen for support. In 1907, the contest became even more bitter when a brother of Sultan Mulay 'Abd l-'Aziz, Mulay Hafed, rebelled and was recognized as sultan in Marrakesh, Fes, and the Middle Atlas Mountains. This major national movement had significant local repercussions. The 'Arbawi faction swore allegiance to Mulay Hafed. After a short interval the 'Arbawi lord was rewarded with a royal decree from Mulay Hafed declaring him the exclusive lord of the Sherqawa.

In effect, each of the two Sherqawi factions now controlled regional appointments for the sultans they respectively recognized. It was not uncommon for two rival *qaid*-s to be appointed over the same tribe. Alliances and loyalties rapidly dissolved into short-term strategic maneuvers. The Zawya Sherqawa, anxious over the loss of support for 'Abd l-'Aziz, intensified their ties with the French. They became the main conduit of French intelligence for the upper Tadla Plain and for several years managed to convince the French that the members of the rival faction were merely "malcontents" with no real following. At first, the French saw this alliance as useful in providing intelligence and influencing events in western Morocco. Sid l-Ḥajj Muḥammed was even accorded a consular Patent of Protection in 1910, exempting him from direct Makhzen authority. The French tended to accept the Zawya Sherqawa accounts of the nature of their "traditional" influence but gradually found that the Zawya lord did not possess the sort of firm political control over his clients that the French were led to expect, or even absolute control over the Sherqawi lodge. But even in the light of direct evidence of the strength of the rival 'Arbawi faction, which accompanied a punitive military expedition in 1910, the French continued to regard the Zawya lord as the sole legitimate one.

As the French consolidated their hold over the Shawya, they increasingly regarded their reliance upon the Sherqawa and other marabouts as unnecessary. Gradually, the Sherqawa and other marabouts were denied certain prerogatives previously accorded them, including exemption from taxes and *corvée* labor for themselves and their clients. The French intended to separate what they considered "spiritual" from "temporal" power. The Sherqawa no longer were consulted on *qaid*-ships in the Shawya, although in the first months of the protectorate Sid l-Ḥajj Muḥammed was still consulted on appointments of *qaid*-s for the upper Tadla Plain. After 1912, in recognition of their services as "friends of France," the French gave the sinecure of *qadi*, or religious judge, to the 'Arbawi lord and that of *qaid* of Boujad to the Zawya lord. But in these offices they were treated the same as other local functionaries elsewhere in Morocco and no longer were called upon as marabouts to settle tribal disputes or other matters. The result, quickly perceived by their maraboutic clients, was a de facto secularization that later will be discussed at length.

Maraboutic Islam in the Nineteenth Century

Until now I have said relatively little about the popular religious beliefs that were at the base of Sherqawi prestige. It is clear that the Sherqawa and other prominent maraboutic groups enjoyed recognition and acceptance among all elements of Moroccan society, from

the tribesmen of the Middle Atlas Mountains or the upper Tadla
Plain to the sultan and his entourage (Doutté 1903:314–327). The
prestige of marabouts was not confined to tribesmen. By the nineteenth century, the intellectual and scholarly activities of the *zawya*
were on a much lower level than in earlier centuries. Foucauld reported that Sidi ben Dawd possessed an excellent but rarely consulted library. This is in accord with the report of the first Native Affairs
officer in Boujad that after the death of Sid l-'Arbi in 1819, no Sherqawi lord personally taught at the *zawya*, as had been the practice
since the days of Sidi Mḥammed Sherqi (Niegel 1913:291). Still,
there were eighty students at the school (*madrasa*) connected with
the *zawya* as late as 1908, supported by revenues from Sherqawi
estates. The political disorders which followed reduced their numbers
to fifteen, together with a single, non-Sherqawi teacher, by 1913
(Niegel 1913:292–293). Nonetheless, the prestige enjoyed by the
Sherqawa for being living exemplars of the "maraboutic synthesis"
of Islam—knowledge of the religious sciences, mysticism, the ability
to convey God's grace—remained intact. In correspondence, Sherqawi marabouts were addressed as *sidna*, "our lord." In contemporary
usage, this term is reserved exclusively for the king.

Throughout the nineteenth century and earlier, the difference between the "maraboutic synthesis" and the formal, "orthodox" teachings of Islam was recognized by religious scholars. As previously
mentioned, foreign observers of Morocco in the late eighteenth and
early nineteenth centuries reported interviews with marabouts and
religious scholars who sharply distinguished between maraboutism
and the formal tenets of Islam (Chenier 1788:179–191; Ali Bey
1816:48–49). Although these remarks were made to foreigners, there
was anything but evangelical fervor in the efforts of such learned
men toward popularizing a "proper" comprehension of Islam. This
passivity toward maraboutism among religious scholars lasted well
into the twentieth century and can be interpreted as reflecting the
strength of maraboutism (Doutté 1903:319; Merad 1967).

Significantly, such scruples about maraboutism were invoked only
in private and to foreigners. With the exception of Sultan Mulay Sliman, the idea of maraboutism encountered few significant popular or
public challengers. Maraboutism was nourished by a quasi-orthodox
interpretation and legitimation. As already indicated, the sultan invested marabouts. The proclamation which invested Sidi ben Dawd
in 1820 was much more explicit in attributing to him the "secret of

his ancestors" than were proclamations for marabouts of the late nineteenth and early twentieth centuries. The later decrees only tersely conveyed the fact of investiture, but they were still issued as late as 1930. Maraboutic politics remained significant. Similarly, members of the urban-based religious elite kept in touch with their Sherqawi counterparts. To provide one instance at length, both Sidi ben Dawd and his son 'Umar corresponded with 'Arbi ben Sayh, a religious scholar (*'alem*) in Salé. The undated correspondence between 'Arbi ben Sayh and 'Umar primarily concerns a theological discussion of how the hands should be positioned when making a request to God. Of more practical interest is a letter from Sayh to Sidi ben Dawd, requesting that an escort be provided for an associate of his (S, 20 November 1875 / 21 Shawwal 1292). The introductory section (*isti'ar*) praises Sidi ben Dawd in flawless Arabic prose as the eminence whose "light travels as far as the light of the sun, whose breath blows its *baraka* over land and sea." The marabout also is described as the point that mediates the formal religious sciences (*al-ma'aref*) with those known to the mystics (*al-asrar*) and that links his ancestors with his descendants in the transmission of these gifts. 'Arbi ben Sayh also announces his intention of visiting Boujad before the end of the year. In a word, the letter affirms the continuing vitality of the maraboutic synthesis among all elements of the population.

There are other contemporary justifications of maraboutism by religious scholars. The Fassi scholar Muhammed al-Kittani in *Salwat al-Anfas* (1895) tried to demonstrate that a devotion to saints accorded perfectly with the letter of Islam, even if nothing was known of the saint. He argued that, even if a pilgrim got no profit from a visit to a saint, it would do him no harm (cited in Lévi-Provençal 1922:381–382). The same writer also wrote of *baraka* on earth as causing "productivity and abundance of the means of the living" and being transmitted through saints. "Without [saints] the sky would not send rain, the earth would not cause its plants to grow, and calamity would pour upon the inhabitants of the earth" (cited by Abun-Nasr 1965:5–6).

The question remains as to what extent these implicit statements of religious ideology by a literate elite reflected more popular beliefs of, for instance, tribesmen who were clients to the Sherqawa. This is a difficult question, for, as I have shown, written sources are silent on many aspects of the popular concept of marabouts. The written sources that do exist, such as those cited above, suggest that there was no clear educated consensus in the nineteenth century of a "formal" Islam distinct from popular beliefs, such as was to begin to emerge by the 1920's, at least for the literate urban intelligentsia. Hence, there was no sharp distinction between popular religious beliefs and those expressed by the literate elite. Fortunately, there is valuable confirmation in the form of correspondence (or drafts of correspondence) from Sherqawa (including Driss ben 'Umar) with a faulty knowledge of written Arabic (S). Individuals trained in Arabic letters tend to substitute for concepts verbalized and understood by their contemporaries in colloquial Arabic those available from their repertoire of classical Arabic and its literature. This shift often alters meaning. Persons with imperfect knowledge of Arabic letters use colloquial Arabic more often and neglect to excise references to popular religious assumptions incompatible with the traditions of written, classical expression. Thus, one such letter from Driss bluntly stated to the tribal council (*jma'a*) of a specific group that their offering was insufficient and that their donation would have to be increased in order to have prayers said on their behalf. Another threatened a tribal council with a supernatural curse (*'ar*) unless it saw to the return of sheep stolen from the herd of a Sherqawi marabout.

A second source of evidence is Foucauld's brief description of Boujad. He states, accurately, that the Sherqawa are not a religious order (*tariqa*) but a maraboutic descent group claiming descent from 'Umar.[20] Foucauld writes that the principal marabout, Sidi ben Dawd, was the carrier of "special graces" which made his blessing "fertilize the earth and make herds prosper." He further writes that the marabout's blessing opened "the doors of Paradise for men and [assured] them of the intercession of 'Umar (the Prophet's Caliph) and all his saintly descendants on Judgement Day" (1939:122).

There are, of course, ethnographic accounts of maraboutism in the late nineteenth and early twentieth centuries. Taken by themselves these accounts, like the material of this chapter, serve more to suggest the importance of marabouts than to present and analyze the beliefs which sustained them in their influence over most elements of Moroccan society. Outstanding among these accounts is Edward Westermarck's massive *Ritual and Belief in Morocco* (1926), based upon fieldwork initiated several decades earlier and reflecting a careful reading of other ethnographers, especially Edmond Doutté. Unfortunately, Westermarck's chapters devoted to magic, supernatural compulsion (*'ar*), *baraka*, sacred groves, genies (*jinn*), the seasons, and other topics are ordered by an external scheme which by its itemistic association of data does not attempt to elicit the underlying framework of Moroccan beliefs or place them in a specific historical context. It is clear that Westermarck was an extremely talented ethnographer. One constantly regrets that he lacked a concept of culture as an interrelated set of symbols and meanings.

Westermarck conveyed an image of a world in which the supernatural was all-pervasive. Signs of supernatural intervention were everywhere and capable of interpretation by residents of any given locality. Rocks, trees, springs, the memory of uncanny events, maraboutic shrines, the gestures of daily life—all were part of a coherent, largely unquestioned way of looking at the world. Marabouts, at least in the form represented by the Sherqawa, provided concrete links between local, manifest representations of the supernatural and more universalistic patterns of Islamic belief. Even the pilgrimage to Mecca, symbolic of involvement with the wider Muslim world, seems to have been confined largely to the Sherqawa on the upper Tadla Plain. For some, the Sherqawa to this day are thought to provide a link with a more universalistic pattern of Islam, although this pattern of belief is rarely taken for granted as it was in the nineteenth century and at the time of Westermarck's research.

I am aware that the above brief description, which I have based as rigorously as possible upon documentation contemporary to the nineteenth and early twentieth centuries, leaves many lacunae. In one way, these sharpen the value of the extant evidence. To render intelligible the evidence for the nineteenth century, I have had to develop implicitly a set of working assumptions, or at least expectations, as to the shape of religious belief and ritual in particular social and temporal contexts. These assumptions do not spring out of a void. From an analysis of maraboutism in its contemporary context and an attempt to comprehend the fundamental assumptions which Moroccans now make about social reality, one develops a sense of expectation of what is crucial or often absent in evidence concerning earlier periods. This is not to assume blindly that the perceptions of reality of contemporary Moroccans have been identical over the period of a century or more. Rather, the careful examination of such perceptions serves as a sort of first approximation. Although my discussion of the nineteenth century comes before my discussion of the present, large parts of it were necessarily thought out only after considerable im-

mersion in the contemporary aspects of maraboutic Islam. But in ex-
amining the contemporary role of marabouts, it became clear that
something was missing, that what I saw were fragments of a pattern
of beliefs, once solid, that was beginning to crumble. This idea was
reinforced as I worked with informants capable of detailed recollec-
tions of past events and with manuscript correspondence. Soon I
found it convenient to think of both past and present simultaneously,
as it were, to make sense of various patterns of activity.

This approach to understanding the past—and the present—is not
entirely an artificial strategem, although as a social anthropologist I
have been concerned with making these assumptions much more explicit than a Moroccan (or anyone else, for that matter) would ordinarily find a need to do. It is the same means by which Moroccans,
with varying degrees of interest and accuracy, also construe the past,
whether the past in question is their personal, lived experience or a
more distant past, such as that discussed in this chapter. Educated
Moroccans have a sharp sense of historical transformations and present elaborate accounts of what marabouts were and how they became what they are today. Even tribesmen who maintain a firm belief in marabouts are aware that marabouts and their descendants
play a different role today than they did in the past.

In the ensuing chapters, my discussion deals mostly with the present. My first concern is to describe how Moroccans conceive the social world. This description and the analysis of maraboutic Islam are
largely complementary; hence the following three chapters are meant
to do more than merely provide the social and cultural context for
the explicitly religious issues of Chapters 6–8. Moroccan understandings of the nature of the social world are not a static backdrop but are
themselves profoundly affected by changing patterns of religious
belief.

3
Boujad:
The Town and Its Region

The Town and the Rural Economy

Boujad's immediate hinterland is relatively homogeneous. The tribesmen of the region continue to follow *genres de vie* combining pastoral transhumancy, primarily of sheep and goats, with the extensive,
seasonal cultivation of barley (*zra'*) and hard wheat (*gemh*). The
complementary ecological zones of the Boujad region are ideal for
this mix. The mountains and their forested foothills (*ghaba*) serve as
winter pastures, while the plains, after the harvest in late May or
early June, provide forage throughout most of the summer.

The only exceptions to this overall pattern of land use are isolated
patches of irrigated gardens and orchards. Prior to the protectorate,
these were almost exclusively owned by Sherqawi marabouts, although many holdings have since been sold. In many cases they continue to be cultivated by descendants of former Sherqawi slaves.
There are also occasional signs of French-inspired agricultural and
pastoral innovations, confined almost exclusively to the lands of ex-
protectorate *qaid*-s and other wealthy individuals. The French innovations date principally from the 1930's, when efforts were made to
introduce soft wheat as a cash crop. Its expense and greater risk than

traditional, hardier crops in an uncertain climate discouraged its widespread adoption. Cattle raising was also encouraged, but the large amount of capital involved in comparison to sheep raising and the greater potential loss in case of disaster limited it to a peripheral role in the rural economy of the region.

The economic activities of both townsmen and tribesmen are directly affected by vicissitudes of the climate. The most significant divisions of the year are between winter (*shta*, literally "rain") and summer (*ṣif*). Spring (*rbi'*) and autumn (*khrif*) are locally perceived as transient intercalations of the other seasons. Rains generally begin in late October and mark the onset of winter. Tribesmen try to sow their crops immediately before this period, although predicting the onset of winter involves a high element of chance. Rains fall most heavily in December and January, then gradually ease through March, when they almost entirely cease. The harvests in early June mark the return of transhumant herds to their summer pastures. The onset of each of these seasons is marked principally by the social activities associated with its typical climatic conditions, not by any fixed calendar. The most significant temporal marker is the annual festival (*musem*) of Sidi Mḥammed Sherqi, during which tribesmen make a pilgrimage (*zyara*) to Boujad to reaffirm their ties with the Sherqawa. Significantly, this celebration is tied with the annual pastoral cycle. Its timing depends upon the movement of transhumant tribal groups to their winter pastures and varies for each group. Even groups no longer transhumant continue to follow the same pattern. The lunar Muslim calendar figures in none of the activities associated with the Sherqawa.

Abrupt climatic variations constitute one of the significant factors which have always made agricultural and pastoral activities precarious in this region and throughout much of Morocco. Tribesmen see these fluctuations in terms of seven-year cycles, the content of which cannot, however, be regularly predicted. (Marabouts and miracles also frequently come in sevens, here as elsewhere in the Middle East; so use of the number should not be taken as an effort toward empirical measurement.) Many tribesmen often attribute such abrupt seasonal and microecological variations in the weather to maraboutic intervention. Winters on the Tadla Plain[1] are relatively temperate: the average temperature is 3–7° C. (38–45° F.) in the coldest months, with only rare incidence of frost and none of snow. Summers are extremely hot, with the temperature frequently as high as 40° C. (104°

F.). Precipitation records for the Tadla Plain indicate average annual variations between 286 and 480 millimeters, falling on 34 to 55 days annually (Gaussen, Debrach, and Joly, 1958). The other major factor affecting agricultural and herding activities, particularly since the protectorate, has been the fluctuating but increasingly unfavorable market conditions for traditional cultivators (M. Naṣiri 1969). Each year tribesmen try to adjust their herding and agricultural activities to anticipated economic and climatic conditions, but the extreme annual variations of both make this exceedingly difficult.

The rural economy of the Boujad region can be characterized as "traditional," although what is traditional must be considered in a temporal framework. The economic and political transformations engendered by the protectorate are particularly significant. Prior to the protectorate the pattern of transhumant pastoralism and seasonal cultivation outlined above prevailed over most of the Tadla, Shawya, and Dukkala plains (Foucauld 1939:117; Mission Scientifique du Maroc 1915:I, II). With the exception of Boujad's immediate hinterland and a few other isolated regions, the traditional *genres de vie* have been directly overshadowed in most regions by the modern economic activities introduced by the protectorate. Boujadi-s say that a sign of the divine grace (*baraka*) of Sidi Mḥammed Sherqi is that he chose to settle in a region devoid of economic interest to the French. *Colons* (French colonists) avoided the region, primarily because the soils of the Tadla Plain north of the Umm er-Rbi' are thin, calciferous, and easily eroded by intensive cultivation. Outside of a settlement at Wad Zem and a few other centers, there was minimal rural colonization on the northern half of the Tadla Plain.

There was a significant nonagricultural European presence not far from Boujad. About twenty-five kilometers to its north, phosphate deposits were discovered immediately prior to the protectorate; exploitation began in earnest toward the end of the First World War, mostly on the basis of *corvée* labor. A narrow-gauge military railroad was completed to Khuribga and Wad Zem in 1918 and by 1928 was converted to standard gauge. Wad Zem, twenty kilometers northwest of Boujad, initially became the center of mining activities. By the 1920's it was replaced by Khuribga, roughly twice the distance from Boujad. To prevent the dislocation of the local European (predominantly Spanish) population of Wad Zem, the protectorate administration allotted agricultural lands to unemployed miners. These and other efforts to expand the lands under colonization, notably an attempt in the late 1920's to establish a large commercial ranch in the region, encountered determined and effective hostility from the surrounding Sma'la tribesmen. The ranch, to be located on expropriated tribal lands, was described in the conventional language of the period as a valuable "educational" experience for the tribesmen. Local officials feared a major tribal uprising and successfully advised against the enterprise and any other major expansion of *colon* holdings (Bonjean 1928:78).[2] In 1928 *colons* formed a Comité Régional d'Etudes Economiques (Regional Committee of Economic Studies) to further colonization on the Tadla Plain, but most of its effective activity was to the south of the Umm er-Rbi'. Nothing came of the efforts of the delegation from Boujad—a Portuguese bar owner, a Polish truck driver, and a Greek grocer—to attract further *colons*.

In contrast, the rich, alluvial soils south of the Umm er-Rbi' River attracted a large number of settlers (Gadille 1958:18), especially after major irrigation schemes were implemented in the 1930's. Although for over a decade Europeans were the principal beneficiaries of these projects, by the end of the Second World War Moroccans also began to benefit on a large scale. The French intended to break the "undesirable" economic habits of traditional agriculture with technical assistance, making "the native's way of living move as fast as the tractor" (Berque and Couleau 1946:18–25). Tribesmen often resisted these schemes because the authoritarian methods by which they were undertaken and technical errors made for several major failures. Nevertheless there were initial successes in introducing new agricultural techniques to Moroccans in some areas, but these were rapidly dissipated by stiff, decisive opposition from *colons* and certain pro-*colon* protectorate officials (Julien 1972:308–310).

These various economic transformations significantly affected even peripheral regions, such as Boujad and its hinterland. Prior to and during the earliest years of the protectorate, virtually all tribesmen lived the entire year in tents (Foucauld 1939:117, 121). The spread of mining activities and agricultural colonization, coupled with administrative restrictions on transhumant movements and the use of forest lands for grazing, resulted by the late 1920's in a significant trend toward sedentarization (Bonjean 1928:86) and a marked decline in the number of livestock in the region (see Fig. 5). For most of the year tribesmen now live in stone and wattle huts (*nwala*-s). The wealthiest live in stone or concrete dwellings. Since sedentariza-

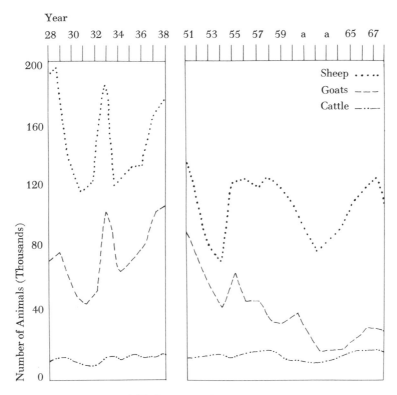

Year

^aFigures not available for 1961 and 1963.

Figure 5.
Livestock in the Boujad region, 1928–1968. (Based on Kingdom of Morocco, Ministry of Finance, Circle of Wad Zem, 1951–1968; B.)

tion occurred only after imposition of the Pax Gallica, dwellings are not clustered into villages as they generally are in the older settled regions of Morocco, but are located on individual landholdings. Tribesmen continue to live in tents only during the winter transhumant moves.

A rough index of the economic stagnation of the region is the slow rate of rural population growth over the last seventy years. Elsewhere on the Tadla Plain, the rural population has doubled from an estimated range of seventeen to twenty-six persons per square kilo-

meter around 1900 to roughly thirty-six to fifty-five at the present.
That of Boujad's immediate hinterland remains in the range of seventeen to twenty-six (Noin 1970:I, 80, 91, 251).

The "stabilization" of Boujad's hinterland had a direct impact on
Boujad. The vast economic and political hinterland which Boujad
possessed prior to the protectorate rapidly contracted. After 1912, the
town no longer served as a major caravan entrepôt for the interior
plains of western Morocco and the Middle Atlas Mountains. While
the Sherqawa of Boujad continued to receive substantial donations
from pilgrims throughout the religious hinterland of western Morocco, the remainder of the town's effective economic base rapidly contracted to its immediate, disfavored environs.

Nevertheless, Boujad as well as other settlements in the interior
of Morocco enjoyed a marked population growth at the onset of the
protectorate. This quickly leveled off, despite the continued influx of
immigrants from surrounding rural areas.[3] Of all the settlements on
the upper Tadla Plain, Boujad has experienced the least growth. As
a consequence, younger Boujadi-s tend to emigrate, given the real and
imagined possibilities for work and the attractions of "bright lights"
of the more dynamic coastal towns and nearby Khuribga. Older Boujadi merchants and men of influence who initially concentrated their
energies and investments in Boujad and its region have shifted their
activities as far as possible to such cities as Casablanca and the prosperous, irrigated plains of the nearby Bni Mellal region.

Other towns in the region, some little more than weekly markets
prior to the protectorate, became the major beneficiaries of the economic rationalization introduced by the French. In addition to Wad
Zem and Khuribga, previously discussed, Fqih ben Ṣaleh and Bni
Mellal emerged as market and administrative centers for a vast irrigation scheme, to which sugar refineries and associated industries
have recently been added. Qaṣba Tadla, little more than a ruined
fortress in the latter half of the nineteenth century (Foucauld 1939:
139–140), regained life as a major military post early in the protectorate.

Boujad: Its Organizational Frameworks

There are four major organizational frameworks through which an
outsider can begin to discern the internal ordering of the town: spa-

Table 1.
Population of Boujad, 1883–1970

Year	Total	Jews	Europeans
1883	1,700	200	0
1913	4,000–7,000	400–500	[a]
1926	8,879	1,010	138
1936	10,211	[a]	158
1951–1952	11,389	[a]	[a]
1956	[a]	336	53
1960	14,728	80[b]	[a]
1970	18,000 (est.)	2	17

Sources: Foucauld 1939:125; Cimetière 1913:282; B, 1926, 1941, 1956; municipal electoral lists, 1963; Kingdom of Morocco 1961.
[a] Not available.
[b] Based upon municipal electoral lists, 1963.

Table 2.
Population growth of Boujad compared to surrounding towns, 1936–1960

	1936	1951–1952	Growth over 1936 (%)	1960	Growth over 1951 (%)
Boujad	10,211	11,389	11.5	14,728	29.3
Qasba Tadla	7,409	8,789	18.8	11,733	33.5
Wad Zem	5,688	13,174	131.6	18,640	41.5
Bni Mellal	10,471	15,968	52.5	28,933	81.2
Fqih ben Saleh	3,187	6,654	108.8	13,484	102.6
Khuribga	8,011	20,365	154.2	40,838	100.5

Source: Kingdom of Morocco 1961:82.

tial, economic, religious, and administrative. Taken together, their value is in giving a concrete configuration of the town's major activities. To a certain extent these are also meaningful frameworks to Boujadi-s themselves. I qualify the extent to which they are meaningful "native" categories because there is a simpler, more basic set of assumptions which Boujadi-s make about the social order and which cut through the organizational frameworks presented here. Thus, in the following chapter I will present and analyze one aspect of spatial organization, the quarter system, in much more detail in order to make visible the relation between it and the more basic assumptions which are made about the social order.

One thing that I want to stress throughout the primarily ethnographic presentation of this chapter is the lack of clearly defined social roles in relation to formal economic, religious, and governmental institutions. That is, knowledge of a person's occupation, descent, or other formal statuses in itself says very little about how he normatively conducts himself in reference to other persons in society. S. F. Nadel specifies that "true" roles always entail a "halo effect." For instance, being a bureaucrat entails a significant set of "further characteristics" which hold for a variety of situational settings (Nadel 1957:28). In Morocco, knowledge that someone is a shopkeeper, government employee, or the like does not in itself give significant cues as to the role the person plays in society. This is not to argue that such formal institutions as the governmental apparatus, the "offices" provided by the mosque, the Qur'anic schools, or the economic institutions which I shall describe in this chapter are unimportant. These merely constitute components of wider fields in which particular activities—economic, political, religious—are carried out. Social action is played out between total social persons, making it difficult to conceive of persons solely or even predominantly in relation to sets of formal institutions, as is common in our own society.

Space

From a distance Boujad resembles an oasis, flanked on its western side by orchards, groves, and gardens. These yield a rich array of dates, nuts, carrots, cucumbers, olives, pears, and pomegranates. In recent decades many of those toward the north have been cleared for housing, although most toward the south remain intact. On its eastern fringe, Boujad is bordered by a rocky, barren plateau almost totally devoid of vegetation. Although in the sixteenth century Boujad was reportedly in the midst of a forest (one grove of trees, locally considered sacred, still remains), by the 1880's firewood had to be car-

ried from the foothills of the Middle Atlas Mountains, nearly ten
kilometers away at the closest point (Foucauld 1939:119).

The town possesses a certain beauty. Viewed from the west, its
whitewashed buildings are framed in the background by the peaks
of the Middle Atlas Mountains. This gleaming whiteness contrasts
dramatically with the rectangular, emerald-green tiles of the domes
of the major Sherqawi shrines. The major colonial contribution to
this image was to enclose the main market (*suq*) on three sides with
a profusion of arcades, each of which forms a portal to a merchant's
stall (*hanut*). These were designed in the late 1920's by a French
Native Affairs officer (*officier des Affaires Indigènes*), who was inspired by a photograph of the arcades surrounding the Ka'aba at
Mecca. Since Boujad is also a pilgrimage center, he felt it appropriate that it replicate the Ka'aba. Strictly speaking, tribesmen and Boujadi-s distinguish between the pilgrimage (*hajj*) to Mecca, made
during a specified season during each year, and "visits" (*zyara*-s)
made to the shrines of marabouts.[4] The analogy with Mecca which
inspired the arcades was one of the many colonial neologisms which
with varying intensity affected the roles which Sherqawi marabouts
were enabled to play in society. Nevertheless, construction of the
arcades presumably improved the view of Boujad from the Bureau
des Renseignements (Intelligence Office; now the offices of Boujad's
qaid), located on a small promontory on the other side of the market (see Fig. 6).

Unlike most traditional Moroccan towns, the older part of Boujad
is not enclosed by a defensive wall. Sherqawi *baraka* was considered
sufficient protection from surrounding tribes, almost all of which are
clients of the Sherqawa. Despite the lack of a wall, the oldest traditional part of town (*medina*) is sharply defined by the vestiges of
portals to its interior passageways—the last of the actual gates was
removed in 1965. These gates and the walls of the outermost houses
allowed the town as a whole and each of its quarters (*derb*-s)[5] to be
sealed off at night.

Much of the *medina* proper, particularly toward the north and
east, dates from the beginning of the protectorate. Its outer limits are
clearly defined, but no obvious pattern governs its internal labyrinth
of narrow, winding streets, many of which are blind alleys. Most of
these passageways, too narrow for cars, are generally cluttered with
pedestrians, donkeys, handcarts, mules, merchandise, and children

shouting and playing. In the somewhat less hectic residential quarters, women perform such household chores as drying grains on the side of the street and discreetly, or so they hope, gossip with their neighbors.

To a European, the overall impression is one of total confusion, since there is no generalizing principle which allows one to get from one place to another on the basis of abstract criteria. One only knows how to get from one point to another by having gone there before. Despite the modest size of the town, even Boujadi-s sometimes get lost in unfamiliar quarters. Similarly, the façades of houses in the *medina* give few clues to the prestige or wealth of their inhabitants. Most of the buildings are rectangular, whitewashed structures, commonly two stories high, with no open space between them. Houses open on the street only by narrow entranceways and occasionally by small, iron-grilled windows on the upper stories. From the street, only a few of the most substantial mosques and shrines are distinguishable from other buildings, either by ornate entranceways or by open doors revealing their interiors. Distinctions of wealth and prestige become evident only within the concealed interiors of most houses. Wealthy ones often have open courtyards with fountains and gardens; poorer households have only a cramped, rectangular patch of concrete with a narrow shaft for air and frequently evince varying stages of decay and disrepair.

Despite its minimal European population, the influence of the colonial experience on the overall spatial organization of Boujad is substantial. In the late 1920's and early 1930's, the protectorate's Service de l'Urbanisme (Urban Planning Service) developed plans for virtually every Moroccan town, including Boujad. Each town was explicitly divided into zones for "traditional" Moroccans, "evolved" Moroccans, and Europeans. Each zone was presumed to conform to the "mentality" of certain elements of the population. Thus the traditional *medina* was left virtually as it was, except for the eventual provision of sewers, water, and electricity.

To the west of the market, the limits of what was meant to have been Boujad's European sector are defined by a park, garden, tennis court, and swimming pool. Since only a handful of Europeans not connected with the administration ever lived in Boujad, the core of this sector remains the Bureau des Renseignements (Ar. *biru*), constructed in 1929. This building still houses most of the administrative and judicial functions of the central government. It also served as the personal quarters for Boujad's military Native Affairs officer until 1933. Military control gave way to civilian in that year, so that a succession of *contrôleurs civils* were lodged there until independence in 1956, when they, in their turn, were replaced by Moroccan *qaid*-s appointed from outside the region. Adjoining villas house the medical officer, public-works chief, and schoolteachers. Secondary schoolteachers and their families constitute the only remaining Europeans. On the principal highway behind this array of buildings are a gendarme post, a filling station, a bar-restaurant-hotel which serves as the town's roadhouse, and a soccer field, originally a landing-strip. A few buildings, mostly schools, have been added to this sector in recent years, but, as in the colonial period, only "outsiders"—non-Boujadi-s —live in it.

The third main provision in the 1931 urbanization plan was for a native housing project called New Boujad (*Bja'd Jdid*). This was initially intended to house the "evolved" Muslim bourgeoisie of the town. The streets in this zone are laid out in a monotonous rectangular grid. Houses at its core, dating from the early 1930's, follow elaborate specifications of design and material laid down by the French. This carefully regulated urbanization was progressively engulfed by adjacent, less controlled zones of growth in which governmental intervention was limited to insistence on maintaining the original rectangular pattern of the "new" town. Since the French tried to discourage immigration from rural areas in the latter years of the protectorate, much of this housing dates from the last two decades. The first years after independence saw a rapid, almost disorderly growth, followed by a period in which the former French policy of discouraging rural emigration was tacitly reintroduced and, since 1971 (as a consequence of the political climate?), again abandoned. In general, however, the main outlines of the colonial conception of forty years ago have remained intact.

The Economy

The major towns of the Tadla Plain—Boujad, Qaṣba Tadla, Wad Zem, Fqih ben Ṣaleḥ, Khuribga, and Bni Mellal—are all linked in a series of rotating markets. A market is held in each town of the cycle on one day of the week. In turn, each of these towns forms part of a cycle of smaller rural markets which rotates around the larger one. In principle, markets are not held on Fridays, the day the weekly sermon (*khoṭba*) is given to the congregation in the mosques. Nevertheless, there are at least two small rural markets on the upper Tadla Plain which are exceptions to this pattern. Tribal informants claim that once there were more Friday markets but that they were actively discouraged during the rise of mass nationalism after the Second World War.

On Thursday, its market day, Boujad's population more than trebles. The buses and trucks which carry professional traders begin arriving before dawn. Some tribesmen arrive the night before, although most appear only on the market day itself. Other buses and trucks circulate throughout the region, collecting tribesmen and the animals and crops they wish to bring to market. *Funduq*-s—caravanserais in classical Arabic but empirically better described as market-day stables which also serve as storage depots, lodging for the town's near-destitute, and, occasionally, brothels—are packed with tribesmen and their animals. Similarly the nine public baths (*hammam*-s) and the major Sherqawi shrines are crowded with tribesmen.

Boujad's merchants do most of their business on market day. Similarly, the religious and civil courts have their weekly sessions, and the *qaid* hears reports from and gives orders to the government-appointed *shaykh*-s and *mqaddem*-s responsible for tribal groups and listens to tribesmen's complaints (*shikaya*-s) and petitions. The medical clinic works to capacity, and the post office cashes money orders from overseas, distributes military pensions, and passes on to government *shaykh*-s the handful of correspondence which arrives for the rural areas.

Prior to the protectorate the entire market was held in the large open area in front of the shrine of Sidi Mhammed Sherqi. As mentioned in Chapter 2, Sherqawi marabouts collected the firearms of the tribesmen and held them until the conclusion of the market. This custodial activity ceased once the protectorate was effectively established in the area. Despite a few modifications introduced by the protectorate administration, the principle by which the market is organized remains that of competitive settlement, as throughout most of the Middle East.[6] In other words, all sellers offering similar goods or services—vegetables, spices, used tin cans, jewels, small utensils, ready-made clothes, blankets, chickens, haircuts and shaves, and so on—are grouped together in the market.

Virtually every household in the town gets caught up in the market as buyer or seller, and generally as both. In the course of the day many people shift between the two roles. Sellers can be ranged along a continuum from full-time professionals who make the rounds of markets to those who only occasionally have animals, crops, or other goods to sell. The quantity of such goods is often minute. For example, a woman might wait all morning to sell half a dozen eggs and use the proceeds to make minor purchases later in the day. Similarly, the retainer of a prestigious family, who receives only meals for his services, gets cash by purchasing small quantities of fruits wholesale before dawn, as they arrive by truck in Boujad. Later in the day he sells them at a slightly higher price. The minute capital he needs is provided by one of the wholesalers, who thus secures the man as his client.

Townsmen, especially those with capital to invest, take as active an interest as tribesmen in the livestock market.[7] Many have joint-venture arrangements (*shorka*-s) with tribesmen. These agreements are representative of the complex dyadic bonds which hold together most of the economy and the rest of society in that they are rarely based on economic considerations alone. To ensure mutual confidence, such partners are generally linked by multiple bonds, including ties of kinship and patron-client relations. Typically, the townsman puts up part of the capital for a herd. Annually, his share of the profit (*rebh*) is mutually agreed upon with his tribal partner (*saheb*). The division varies primarily by such factors as the skill and reputation of the tribesman and some of the noncontractual benefits of patronage which the townsman may be thought to offer.

Since more lucrative opportunities for major capital investment can now be found in other regions of Morocco, pastoral agreements are at present generally preferred only by townsmen with moderate amounts of capital who do not have the prestige or resources to oversee and defend investments in more distant regions. This has contributed to a further decline in the region's rural economy.

Apart from herding agreements and similar arrangements which some townsmen have for the provision of grains for their household, the tie between buyers and sellers at the Thursday market tends to be exclusively economic, with a tendency to purchase only at the most advantageous price. This holds at least for those who can make cash purchases. In contrast, shopkeepers in Boujad maintain fairly stable and complex dyadic ties with their clientele, sustained by the judicious use of credit. The advantages of extended credit and other non-economic considerations outweigh the slightly higher prices which most of these merchants charge.

Commercial and craft activities are more complex than can be assumed by the uniform appearance of most of the shops. In 1970 there were 838 craftsmen and merchants, grouped into forty-two distinct crafts and twenty-six distinct mercantile specializations, such as butchers, spicers, vegetable-sellers, salt-packers, tailors, weavers, barbers, bellowsmakers, locksmiths, carpenters, cloth merchants, and those who "buy and sell" (*biʿ u-shri*) virtually anything of value, usually in minute quantities, often literally pinches of produce.

The handful of European merchants who were in Boujad during the protectorate left soon after independence. European enterprises included a café-hotel on the main road, a bus and truck service which ran to local markets, a grocery and dry-goods store which catered primarily to Europeans, a garage, and a small cement factory. All of these businesses were purchased by Boujadi Muslims after 1956, although virtually none has been subject to any further capital investment. Similarly, Jewish shops were purchased by Muslim merchants or left to Muslim apprentices in the years immediately after independence. How these various enterprises were disposed of depended on the particular circumstances of each trade. Thus the stocks of the itinerant cloth traders were largely taken over by rural Qur'anic teachers (*fqih*-s), who used their close ties to and familiarity with the rural hinterland to their advantage.

Boujad never was a significant craft center. Even at the beginning of the protectorate, craft activities were characterized as ailing; most processed or manufactured goods came from the coastal cities (Cimetière 1913:285). Certain crafts enjoyed a temporary renaissance during the Second World War, when European goods were unavailable. Local shoemakers and tailors worked for the Vichy French and later the Allied forces. Otherwise, administrative reports throughout the protectorate reiterate the irreversible decline of most of the crafts. The ready postwar availability of superior manufactured goods, such as cheap, waterproof plastic shoes and ready-made or second-hand clothing, quickly cut the market for the locally made products of shoemakers and weavers. Only carpentry continues to thrive. The low cost of labor in Boujad encourages many coastal firms to contract piecework to Boujad.

Boujad's shops range from large depots (*ḥri*-s) owned by the town's nine major merchants to the more common merchants' stalls (*ḥanut*-s), often only six feet wide and not much deeper. The most substantial of these merchants are known as "traders" (*tajer*-s) and generally deal in a wide variety of commodities; those with more limited capital are generally known by the commodity they sell, such as "charcoal-seller" (*fekhkhar*).

Very few shops are the result of cooperative ventures. In general, men avoid as far as possible situations in which they share responsibility as equals with others or in which they are subordinate to someone else. This preference cuts through all social activities and will be discussed at length in Chapter 5. Each merchant and craftsman tends to work for his own account, although a few acquire venture capital from close relatives and other individuals who have confidence in them.

The organization of merchants and craftsmen into "guilds" (*ḥanṭa*-s) does not constitute an exception to this tendency toward personal authority. In Boujad, the formal organization of guilds is a French administrative imposition of the 1920's rather than a pre-existing form of corporate activity. Even the orientalist Louis Massignon, who asserted that craft and mercantile "guilds" were the institutional cement of Muslim cities, found little evidence for his contention in Morocco, the only country in which he essayed a sociological inquiry into the subject. In particular he singled out Boujad as the clearest representation of the "primitive" form of Moroccan guild, superficially Islamicized but still essentially "Berber," since there was no *formal* pattern of leadership. Decisions in each craft or trade were reached by informal consensus; "guilds" were not corporate organizations that had an existence independent of individuals (Massignon 1924:62). Although the forms of craft and mercantile organization in the larger cities of Morocco also failed to support his thesis that Islamic guilds were corporate, he explained this away by claiming that they too evidenced only superficially Islamic forms (1924:139). This strategy of assuming pre-existing societal forms to explain away inconsistencies between observed ethnographic reality and presuppositions concerning Islamic society is, of course, the same as that used by Bel.

There is no sharply ordered hierarchy of prestige between the various crafts and trades. Such a ranking is impossible, since all but the poorest merchants and craftsmen have many sources of income which are not reflected in the activities of their shop or craft. A

merchant who sells ready-made slippers (*belgha*-s) from Fes may
have a minimal visible turnover of goods in his shop but derive
substantial income from the rental of buildings and lands, speculation
on the animal market, and other sources. Most merchants of rural
origin similarly possess rights to land or produce which ensure them
the basic foodstuffs needed for subsistence in town. Everyone tries
to spread out his activities to insure against the hazards of any single
one. Thus occupation, taken in its common European sense, can be
a very poor indicator of a person's wealth or status.

Prestige is based primarily on the ranking of total social persons,
not on the specific economic activities which they undertake. A few
occupations, such as the dirty, nonlucrative work of tanning and
potting, unequivocally signify low income and prestige, but this is not
the case for most activities. Butchers, for example, are considered to
be engaged in an unclean trade but often are considered more prestigious than schoolteachers and government clerks, since some are
known to have more substantial incomes and higher life-styles. One
of the few effective, though not determinant, general indicators of
status is whether a merchant or craftsman is of urban or rural origin.
Rural immigrants generally cluster in those activities which require
the least capital, such as selling fruits or vegetables and "buying and
selling." Even in these cases, however, there are exceptions which
Boujadi-s are quick to point out.

Religion

Most townsmen say that the formal complex of Islamic institutions
centers around mosques, the Qur'anic schools (*mesjid*-s) generally
associated with them, pious endowments established for the support
of religious activities, and, finally, the religious court (*l-maḥkama
dyal sh-shra'*). Since the protectorate, the latter has been restricted
to adjudicating law of personal status: marriages, divorces, inheritances, and certain land transactions.

This institutional complex is characterized as being shared in principle by all members of the Muslim community (*umma*). Many
townsmen presently consider religious brotherhoods and the patterns
of clientele associated with marabouts as being apart from the formal
institutions because they are particularistic—their support comes
only from a designated membership or clientele. Such views have

Table 3.
Economic rank of Boujad's merchants and craftsmen correlated with place of birth

Economic Rank	Place of Birth							
	Boujad		Boujad's Rural Hinterland		Other		Total	
	(%)	N	(%)	N	(%)	N	(%)	N
Low	69.5	388	90.4	189	40.5	17	73.2	594
Medium	22.9	128	9.1	19	42.9	18	20.4	165
High	7.9	44	0.5	1	16.7	7	6.4	52
Total	69.1	560	25.8	209	5.2	42	100.0	811

Note: This table is based on an economic census of shopkeepers and craftsmen which I conducted in 1970. Economic rank was a judgment of informants.

become widespread only since the 1920's. Most tribesmen and many older Boujadi-s make no such distinction.

Boujad has two principal mosques in which the Friday sermon is given by a prayer-leader (*imam*) before the assembled congregation. The older of these mosques was built by Sultan Mulay Sliman in 1805 (see Fig. 6). The communal sacrifices of the Little Feast ('*Id le-Ftur*), which marks the end of Ramadan, the month of fasting, and the Great Feast ('*Id le-Kbir*), or Feast of Abraham, are held in it when the weather does not permit their being held at the communal prayer-ground (*msalla*) located on the eastern edge of the town. A second major mosque was completed in early 1973 but was already in use two years earlier. It is located on the northwestern edge of the *medina*, next to New Boujad. Once finished, this mosque began receiving formal support from the Ministry of Pious Endowments. But its construction was financed locally, primarily by wealthy non-Sherqawi merchants and a few Sherqawa. One of the latter is a leading local politician who received no substantial support from other Sherqawa in elections in the early 1960's. Consequently, he allied himself with his non-Sherqawi supporters and became prayer-leader of the new mosque.

The two principal mosques and many of the others associated with residential quarters have personnel regularly attached to them who receive stipends from the Ministry of Pious Endowments. Most of these are Qur'anic teachers (*fqih*-s). Their meager official stipend is supplemented by monthly gifts in cash and produce from the parents of the children they teach and other gifts at the graduation of the children. Qur'anic teachers at smaller quarter mosques depend entirely upon such local donations and whatever annual amount is agreed upon with the household heads of the quarter. Other personnel who receive modest official stipends include a group of elderly men who each evening recite parts of the Qur'an at the mosque of Mulay Sliman, prayer-callers (*mwedden*-s) and the prayer-leaders of the two major mosques.

The funds for these stipends and for the maintenance of certain mosques and shrines of descendants of the Prophet Muhammed are distributed locally by a deputy overseer (*na'ib*) of the Ministry of Pious Endowments. This official, who also operates a cigarette shop, collects rents from the various properties held by his ministry. In Boujad these are limited almost exclusively to the merchants' stalls built into the outside walls of the larger mosques. Elsewhere in Morocco, particularly in the regions surrounding the major traditional cities, the Ministry of Pious Endowments has more substantial urban—and, until recently, rural—properties.[8] Prior to the protectorate and up to 1927 Boujad had an overseer (*nadir*) of pious endowments who was also a Sherqawi. In 1927 this office was shifted to Wad Zem, where a wealthy Sherqawi continued to hold the position; after independence the office again shifted and fell to a non-Sherqawi in Bni Mellal.

Finally, there are a small number of descendants of the Prophet (*shorfa*; sg., *shrif*) in Boujad who have a formal spokesman (*naqib*). They have no significant collective activities, although a certain prestige adheres to their descent. In the past various material benefits accrued to them as a result of it.

Except for the collective annual prayers on the two major feast days and the Friday gatherings in the principal mosques, there are no regular gatherings which symbolize the unity of the Muslim community. Of course, formal Islamic ideology has a profound effect on the daily and annual cycle of activities. Most adult male heads of households perform the full cycle of five daily ritual prayers and regulate their activities in terms of these and other, more occasional,

Islamic obligations. Nevertheless, formal religious organization does not inherently provide a vehicle for effective social action. Individuals, such as the politician-*imam* mentioned above, can utilize a religious office to legitimize their social honor and mobilize effective followings. But again it is the configuration of attributes possessed by persons, not any particular offices they might hold, which forms the key to understanding social action.

The most significant of the religious brotherhoods in Boujad are the Tijaniya, the Qadiriya, and the Kittaniya orders. When more active in the earlier half of the protectorate, the Tijaniya attracted mostly notaries and minor Makhzen officials; the other two orders had their greatest local appeal among moderately prosperous merchants and craftsmen. In principle, each brotherhood has a leader (*mqaddem*) and a lodge (*zawya*) in Boujad. New recruits became scarce after the widening popularity of reformist ideas and the nationalist movement in the mid-1930's. The remaining adherents of these orders, who in no case currently exceed two dozen elderly men, gather each Friday afternoon after the midday prayer in their respective lodges or in each other's houses. There they recite the devotions associated with their particular order. On feast days their spokesman (*mqaddem*) takes the flag of their order to the house of the prayer-leader of the town and breakfasts with him before they proceed together to the mosque or the communal prayer ground.

There are also disciples of the various ecstatic religious orders in Boujad—the Heddawa, Derqawa, 'Issawa, and Hmadsha. These are considered by most townsmen to be much less reputable than the orders mentioned above. Their membership comes primarily from the urban *Lumpenproletariat*—beggars, charm sellers, some musicians, manual laborers, and the descendants of slaves. They gather at private houses, where they are often invited to perform exorcisms when possession by a malevolent *jinn* is suspected to be the cause of illness or misfortune. Only the Hmadsha have a *zawya*, attached to the shrine of the Sherqawi marabout Sidi l-Hafyan, who is said to have been the mystic teacher of their founder, Sidi 'Ali ben Hamdush. The local Hmadsha often have their number augmented by pilgrims coming from elsewhere, especially during a small yearly festival (*musem*) attended only by members of the order.

The most significant complex of religious activities in Boujad, as measured by offerings, sacrifices, and the number of participants, consists of those centered around the Sherqawi shrines and the

Sherqawi religious lodge (*zawya*). The latter is not a regular meeting place for clients of the Sherqawa, as are the lodges of religious brotherhoods. It is the residence of a Sherqawi who is considered by tribesmen to be a living marabout and who strives to cultivate this reputation by writing charms for supplicants and entertaining delegations of tribal clients.

Boujad has twenty-six maraboutic shrines, twenty-three of which are Sherqawi.[9] The most significant of these is that of Sidi Mhammed Sherqi. Associated with his shrine are those of several of his children, a mosque, and a recently completed hostel for pilgrims. The main shrine is lavishly, if crudely, adorned on its interior with mosaics, brass ornaments, large candles, hanging rugs, and a large collection of hand-wound European pendulum clocks. Substantial offerings are collected at this and the other principal shrines. The remaining Sherqawi shrines are more modest, with relatively bare interiors, and doorkeepers (*bewwab*-s) present only on those days when there are enough visitors to make collection of their offerings worthwhile.

The largest influx of visitors and pilgrims comes in September and early October, during the festival (*musem*) of Sidi Mhammed Sherqi. Tribesmen in the immediate region of Boujad arrive on muleback and horseback with their tents. Groups from more distant regions, such as Shawya, now arrive by bus or truck. These visits are staggered over approximately a month, with the Sherqawa often arranging for antagonistic tribal groups not to be present at the same time. Each group stays for three or four days. In September 1969 approximately twenty-five thousand tribesmen came on pilgrimage during a two-week period in which I tried to make estimates of arrivals.[10] Moreover, the Sherqawa said that the number of pilgrims was somewhat attenuated that particular year because the *qaid*-s of several regions discouraged attendance. Formally, the *qaid*-s argued that the tribes under their jurisdiction were delinquent in their taxes and that the money that would ordinarily be spent on the *musem* should go instead to their taxes. However, tax arrears are a chronic problem in rural areas. Informally, the *qaid*-s utilized the tax-arrears argument primarily against those groups that indicated displeasure with the government candidates proposed for local elections to be held that year. Some officials thought that denying tribesmen participation in the *musem* would be particularly efficacious in breaking their resistance. In 1972 the same officials, again for political reasons, sought to encourage the festival but to link it to a show of loyalty to the government. The provincial governor made a substantial contribution at the principal shrine and local officials tried to obligate the tribes present to greet the governor ceremonially upon his arrival. Most refused, saying that they came to Boujad for the marabout Sidi Mhammed Sherqi, not for the Makhzen. Even the suggestion of reprisals did not alter their position. Provincial officials, reluctant to risk a major incident, dropped the matter that year, but achieved a compromise in 1973 by which tribesmen agreed publicly to greet the governor. These actions implicitly reflect the continuing strength of maraboutism as a social force in rural Morocco.

The Makhzen

The contemporary Makhzen presence in Boujad has three foci—the local administrative bureaucracy, the courts, and the schools. Boujad was an administrative anomaly both during the protectorate and after independence. At present it is virtually the only *annexe* (*melhaqa*) in a national administrative apparatus which elsewhere begins at the higher level of *cercle* (*da'ira*). In the early protectorate, the entire Tadla Plain and part of the Middle Atlas Mountains were governed from Boujad, but it was soon relegated to a *cercle*, and finally to an *annexe*. Although the French progressively downgraded Boujad's administrative significance, they retained it as an *annexe* because of the prestige they ascribed to the Sherqawa and the role of the Sherqawa as "friends" of France. As I mentioned in the last chapter, for the duration of the protectorate the town's *qaid*-s were the marabouts of the Zawya Sherqawa. The marabouts of the other leading descent group, the 'Arbawi Sherqawa, provided the *qadi*-s. Both *qaid*-s and *qadi*-s tended to pack the subordinate positions under their influence with their supporters, although, after several scandals in the 1930's, the French began diluting Sherqawi hegemony over the subordinate local posts.

In 1913 the French briefly and unsuccessfully experimented with a Sherqawi *qaid* to administer the tribal hinterland. Four non-Sherqawi *qaid*-s drawn from the tribes they administered or from neighboring tribes soon took his place. In the 1930's the number of rural *qaid*-s was halved. All of these officials were under—or, in the fiction of the protectorate, were advised by—a French *contrôleur civil*. All communications with the Makhzen and government agencies passed through the hands of the *contrôleur*, who thus ensured that the *qaid*-s under his supervision confined themselves to eminently local affairs.

Since independence a single *qaid* for both the town and the tribal hinterland, an outsider to the region appointed by the Ministry of the Interior, has assumed all of the duties of both *contrôleur* and *qaid*, except for the judicial functions which these officials had during the protectorate. This *qaid* is directly or indirectly supported by a local bureaucratic presence which includes a clerical staff for himself and his assistant (*khalifa*) and a paramilitary force of *mokhazni*-s. There are also various specialized services which he nominally coordinates: water and electricity offices, a gendarme post, a public-works office, a post office, and a medical dispensary, downgraded from a hospital in the early 1960's. Although all local government officials and clerks are appointed from Rabat, most of the lower echelons (except for the gendarmery) are staffed by natives of Boujad or adjoining towns. Movement from these posts by promotion or transfer is minimal.

The local bureaucracy is formally complemented by an elected municipal council for Boujad and by rural communes for the surrounding region. Each of these has its own budget, with income from local market taxes, occasionally supplemented by central government subsidies. Due to administrative inexperience and the lack of personnel independent of the local Ministry of the Interior officials, these bodies are largely dependent upon the local *qaid* for their initiatives. In one recent year the only action of the municipal council of Boujad was to provide chairs for the *qaid*'s office, although since 1970 they have undertaken more substantial projects. Appointment to communal councils has been regarded in recent years principally as a sign of favor from the local and provincial officials of the Ministry of the Interior. This fact has not necessarily made such individuals dependent. One member of the municipal council was considered locally to be a "shadow *qaid*"—his intimate knowledge of the Boujad region, his general reputation for exercising influence, and his multiple contacts with government officials elsewhere gave him in effect more power than the officially designated *qaid*. Similar "shadows" are found throughout the local administrative apparatus.[11]

Since independence both the religious law court and the civil court have been under the separate jurisdiction of the Ministry of Justice and thus independent of the *qaid* and other local officials. The religious court, which in principle was autonomous throughout the protectorate, is staffed by a *qadi*, together with a staff of several clerks and notaries.[12] The civil court is staffed by a civil judge (*hakem*) and several assistants. This judge is a Sherqawi who, because of his reputation for probity, is one of the few in Morocco allowed to preside in his native town.

The most pervasive Makhzen presence in Boujad is that of the school system. In Boujad as elsewhere, this has since independence undergone a massive expansion in both personnel and students, if not in quality. Prior to the Second World War, the French policy was to educate only those Muslims who in any case would tradition-ally have been educated. In the last decade of the protectorate the educational system expanded considerably but still enrolled only a fraction of the school-age population, predominantly urban and male. For Morocco as a whole in 1938, 1.7 percent of school-age children were enrolled in primary schools and 0.1 percent in secondary schools. The respective figures for 1955 were 11.2 percent and 1.2 percent, with 90 percent of elementary-school children dropping out before attaining a certificate of primary education (Cerych 1964: 297–299). There was a similar drop-out rate for secondary educa-tion, since only 530 Muslims acquired the *baccalauréat* in Morocco during forty-four years of French rule (Waterbury 1970:84). In Boujad, those Muslims enrolled in school were at first exclusively the children of prominent Sherqawa, rural *qaid*-s, and a few pros-perous merchants, although recruitment was somewhat widened by the 1950's. In contrast, nearly all of Boujad's Christian and Jewish school-age population received schooling, the latter through an Al-liance Israélite school established in 1931. In addition, a limited number of students were educated in a private "free school" (*medrasa hurra*), set up in 1947 by local nationalists interested in providing for a truly Muslim education, primarily in Arabic. This school was assimilated into the government system shortly after independence.

Since independence the number of students has dramatically in-creased. Some 38 percent of the school-age population was enrolled in primary schools throughout Morocco in 1966–1967 (Tiano 1968:115). Presently more than half the children of school age receive some primary schooling, and roughly 6 percent go on to at least the first few years of secondary schooling. For Boujad, this means that almost all the sons of townsmen and a fair number of their daughters enter the primary schools. There are a few rural schools as well, but access to education in rural areas remains difficult and the quality low.

Literacy can now be assumed for younger townsmen. In 1969, 181 teachers were employed locally at the primary and secondary levels. There were approximately 5,500 elementary-school students and 1,200 in the first three years of secondary school. Students wishing to complete the remaining three years of the secondary cycle must at present go to other towns, although additional years of the six-year secondary cycle are to be made locally available shortly.

Almost all of the primary schoolteachers are Boujadi-s, including the school directors. Boujadi-s also predominate in the secondary schools, although outsiders are also employed. These included a dozen French instructors in mathematics, science, and history in 1969; nine remained in 1973. In recent years there have been modest efforts to place a few instructors from other parts of Morocco. But throughout their educational careers, most students continue to experience the same multiplex bonds linking them and their families with their instructors as pervade all other social activities.

Summary

This chapter has introduced some of the key institutional frameworks for social action in Boujad. By *institution*, I mean primarily a field identified with specific conventions or accepted ways of accomplishing certain sorts of social action. I have also tried to provide a concrete ethnographic representation of the town and its region in relation to recent historical developments. The account of economic institutions pointed directly to how persons relate to each other in the market setting. The accounts of government and religious institutions were more formal. How these and other institutions work or are thought to work will become clear only after the account of the social structure. By *social structure*, I mean the principles by which the units constituting a given society—persons or groups of persons—are defined and related to each other. The next chapter specifies these principles and elaborates them, first in an urban, then in a tribal, setting.

4
Social Structure

A Definition

Given its dominant association with the Sherqawi marabouts, Boujad is hardly the Moroccan equivalent of Middletown. Only two other towns in Morocco, Wezzan and Mulay Idriss, have such a singular importance as pilgrimage centers. However, the strategy of looking for a Middletown on the basis of a "lowest-common-denominator" typicality has contributed significantly to the present impasse in the characterization of social structure in North Africa, particularly in Morocco. Efforts to abstract a notion of social structure from superficial patterns and characteristics have resulted in a bewildering array of apparent local and regional structures in which tribes and localities are perceived as what Jacques Berque, in another context, has called "little monsters of social ingenuity" (*petits monstres d'ingéniosité sociale*) (cited in Lacouture and Lacouture 1958:80).

A review of recent attempts to characterize North African society has pointed to the fact that it is "not blocked out into large, well-organized permanent groupings—parties, classes, tribes, races—engaged in a long-term struggle for ascendance. . . . Structure after structure—family, village, clan, class, sect, army, party, elite, state—

turns out, when more narrowly looked at, to be an *ad hoc* constellation of miniature systems of power, a cloud of unstable micropolitics, which compete, ally, gather strength, and, very soon overextended, fragment again" (C. Geertz 1971:20).

One reason for the difficulty in perceiving structure in North African society, and perhaps to a certain extent elsewhere in the Arab world, is that many standard definitions of social structure are narrowly conceived to account only for situations in which *groups* of persons are ordered in positions and statuses (e.g., Evans-Pritchard 1940:262; Turner 1969:125–126; Gellner 1969:35–69). In many parts of the Islamic Middle East and elsewhere it is increasingly apparent that social structure can also be conceived with *persons* as the fundamental units of social structure, rather than their attributes or statuses as members of groups. This is the case for Morocco, where, moreover, persons are not arranged in layer-cake strata in which broad groups of persons are seen as essentially equal. Instead, they are linked in dyadic bonds of subordinance and domination. Moreover, these ties are characteristically dissolved and re-formed rapidly and significantly. The relatively stable element in this type of social structure is not the patterning of relations between persons or groups of persons, as is suggested by many definitions of social structure. Rather, it is the culturally accepted *means* by which persons contract and maintain dyadic bonds and obligations with one another.[1]

This conception of social structure is implicit in the way Boujadi-s perceive regularities in the social order and proceed to act on these assumptions. Like other Moroccans, they discriminate with considerable subtlety between variations in wealth, power, the prestige of descent, patronage and clientship, and the effectiveness with which persons can utilize such attributes. The aggregate of influence a person possesses with respect to others is frequently expressed by the terms *kelma* "word" and *wejh* "face." The assessment of who has these qualities is continually affected by the outcome of social action and is never taken for granted. Given the various resources available, each person is necessarily a *bricoleur*, or social handyman, viewing society less as definitely structured than as capable of being re-formed so as to maintain or increase his own standing in it. The dominant image of society is a constellation of interpersonal ties, not any arrangement of groups—since groups, from the point of view of Moroccans, tend to have an ephemeral protoplasmic quality, from national political parties to the most informal local association.

Persons achieve social honor, in Weber's sense of the term, on the basis of varying, experimental combinations of their attributes— wealth, political office, residence in a quarter, maraboutic descent or descent from the Prophet, etc.—in no case can the social honor of a person be determined from an abstract knowledge of his attributes or statuses alone. Some of these statuses, such as those of kinship, might be relatively stable, even permanent in the case of blood relations, but the obligations and expectations which persons hold as a result of them are still a matter of significant variation and amenable to a wide latitude of revalorization. As already discussed, few Moroccans make any assumption about the social honor of a person solely on the basis of any formal status or office which he may possess. For instance, the attributes *marabout* and *Sherqawi descent* in themselves say little of the social status of the persons holding them. Like other bases of prestige, their significance has shifted significantly with the social and economic transformation of the last sixty years.

The Spatial Representation of Social Structure

The concept of social structure is inherently linked to how Boujadi-s conceive the spatial organization of their town. Like other units of society, the quarter (*derb*) is a cultural construct which for Boujadi-s is not defined in terms of an *ad hoc* listing of formal features. These serve only as indices of the underlying cultural concept.

An earlier generation of colonial ethnographers recorded the formal arrangements of quarters and, accepting the then popular theories of Lévy-Bruhl on the nature of "primitive" mentalities, concluded that the evident protoplasmic disorder of quarters was a direct physical projection of the "alogical" disorder of the "indigenous" mind (e.g., Louis Brunot, cited in Hardy 1926:21). Lacking an adequate conception of social structure as based on culturally accepted means by which dyadic bonds between persons are contracted and maintained, ethnographers instead sought, and failed to find, order at the level of "on-the-ground" social relations and the use of physical space.

Boujadi-s presently divide their own town into anything from thirty to approximately forty-three quarters (see Fig. 6 and Table 4). The differences in perception are related to what informants know of the social history of the town, which varies with generation and experience, and how they have experienced it, which varies with

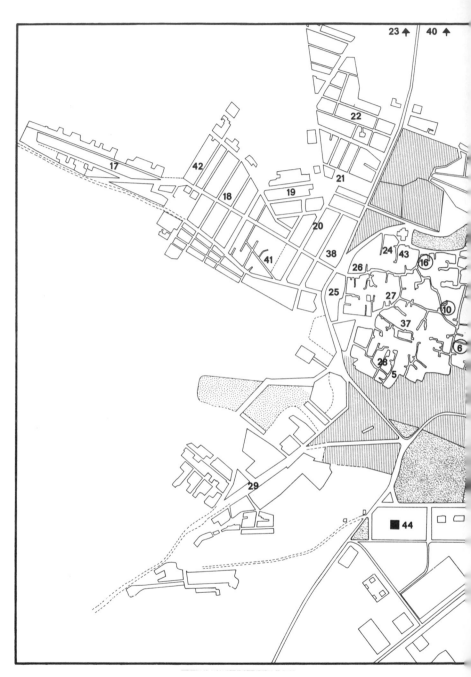

Figure 6.
Boujad, 1970. Numbers on the figure are keyed to Table 4.

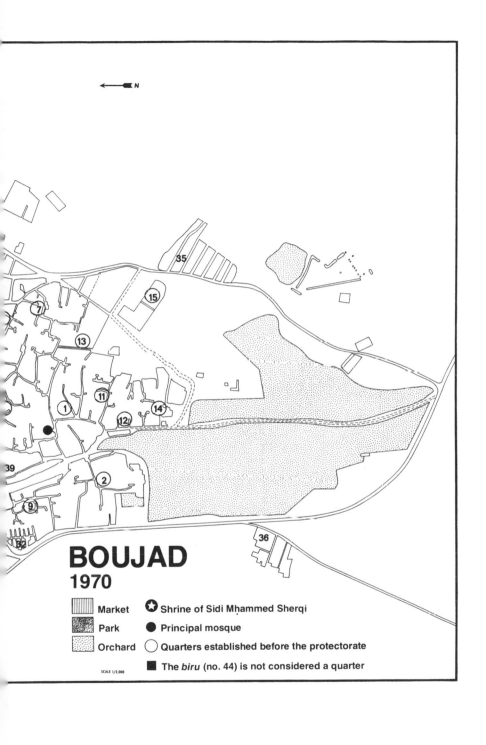

N

BOUJAD
1970

Market	⭐ Shrine of Sidi Mḥammed Sherqi
Park	● Principal mosque
Orchard	○ Quarters established before the protectorate

■ The *biru* (no. 44) is not considered a quarter

SCALE 1/2,000

Table 4.
Population of principal quarters of Boujad and birthplaces of adult residents

Quarter	Total Adults	Total Residents (estimate)	Birthplace of Adult Residents		
			Boujad (%)	Boujad Region (%)	Elsewhere in Morocco (%)
1. 'Arbawi	152	304	86	5	9
2. Zawya (ca. 1850)	286	572	64	19	17
3. Mkansa	94	188	83	11	6
4. Old Sellamiyin	215	430	64	26	10
5. New Sellamiyin (ca. 1930)	a	a	a	a	a
6. Ghazawna	136	272	75	14	11
7. 'Allaliyin	197	394	64	21	15
8. Qadiriyin	293	586	74	15	11
9. Qsayra	192	384	54	26	20
10. 'Aziziyin	a	a	a	a	a
11. Ghrari	73	146	67	23	10
12. Zalaghi (1900)	119	238	62	24	14
13. 'Aysha Haddu	a	a	a	a	a
14. Hmid	224	448	63	21	16
15. Bni Musa	61	122	75	15	10
16. Ayt Stur	a	a	a	a	a
17. Shbuki (Lahuna) (post-1956)	193	386	20	71	9
18. Qaid Mhammed	a	a	a	a	a
19. Gahda (post-1956)	77	154	26	68	6
20. Khaluqiyin (Smuniyin) (1935)	159	318	66	25	9
21. Kamun (1958)	177	354	34	50	16
22. Mimuna (post-1956)	161	322	27	52	21
23. Warezzin (1960)	66	132	11	73	16
24. Mulay Driss (1935)	108	216	70	24	6
25. "Burdil"[b] (1930)	a	a	a	a	a

26. Gar'a	138	276	53	41	6
27. Ghalem	123	246	58	35	7
28. S'idiyin	28	56	a	a	a
29. Qṭater (1950)	416	832	29	61	11
30. Muludi	221	442	69	24	7
31. Sqaqi	a	a	a	a	a
32. Dăwwar le-Makhazniya					
(1950)	19	38	a	a	a
33. Fridiyat					
(post-1956)	285	570	44	45	11
34. Khuribga	63	126	73	19	8
35. Sanya	141	282	40	40	20
36. Sulṭan (Drawsh)					
(1950)	78	156	40	18	42
37. Bni Meskin	97	194	74	19	6
38. Hasan	44	88	a	a	a
39. Nwaser	133	266	66	14	20
40. Kuwwasha	48	96	a	a	a
41. Jdid	59	118	44	49	7
42. 'Amir	68	136	44	38	18
43. Sid l-Ḥafyan	103	206	49	39	13
44. *Biru* (government offices and official residences)					

Notes: The figures for adult residents are based on the registration forms for the 1963 municipal elections. An adult is defined for electoral purposes as a person 21 years of age or older.

Because of the rounding off of decimals, percentages do not always total 100%.

Names of Sherqawi quarters are italicized. Identification numbers of quarters established prior to the protectorate are in italic type. Dates in parentheses are those of the founding of the indicated quarters.

a No data available.

b A direct borrowing from French *bordel* ("brothel"). The quarter was an official red-light district under the protectorate.

social position. Only those clusters of households evaluated as sustaining a particular quality of life are known as quarters; thus some Boujadi-s do not consider certain sections of the town to constitute "real" quarters.

Ideally the households of a quarter are considered to be bound together by multiple personal ties and common interests. These complex ties are said to symbolize *qaraba*, a key concept which literally means "closeness." As used by urban and rural Moroccans, *qaraba* carries contextual meanings which range imperceptibly from asserted and recognized ties of kinship to participation in factional alliances, ties of patronage and clientship, and—the facet which will be developed here—common bonds developed out of residential propinquity. "Closeness" is acting *as if* ties of obligation exist with another person which are so compelling that they are generally expressed in the idiom of kinship. This is because kinship ties, especially those of blood, symbolize bonds which, however they are valorized, are considered permanent and cannot be broken. Most quarters have a cluster of households which claim relation to each other in this way.

In many respects "closeness" in present-day Morocco resembles the concept of "group feeling" (*'aṣabiya*) presented over five hundred years earlier by the North African philosopher and protosociologist Ibn Khaldun. In his exposition of the concept, Ibn Khaldun indicates the multiple bases on which "group feeling" can be asserted among both townsmen and tribesmen but ultimately opts for the ideological position that the "naturalness" of blood ties makes them superior to all other modalities as a basis for "group feeling" (Ibn Khaldun 1967:249–310, esp. 264). Present-day urban and rural Moroccans make the same claim. Such a position does not distinguish between "closeness" using kinship as an idiom in which social relations can be expressed and "closeness" as the presence of "actual" ties of kinship.

A quarter, then, can be defined as the extension of "closeness" in contiguous physical space. It can be said to have prestige in relation to the strength of the *qaraba* attributed to it by its component households and by other townsmen. A quarter should be able to assume a certain moral unity so that in some respects social space in it can be regarded as an extension of that of its component households. A household can belong to only one quarter, but there is flexibility over time as to which this can be, especially among households of lesser prestige.

"Closeness" in a quarter—just as between kinsmen, factional allies, and patrons and clients, in towns or elsewhere—can be symbolized by the exchange of visits on feast days and on other occasions, by assistance and participation in the activities connected with births, circumcision, weddings, funerals, graduation from school, and memorization of the Qur'an. The heads of households of a quarter (*mwalin ed-derb*) share certain minimal collective responsibilities; they often construct and maintain a mosque, hire a Qur'anic teacher (*fqih*) for it, and congregate there the night of Laylet l-Qadr (the 27th of Ramaḍan) to listen to the recitation of the Qur'an until sunrise. They may also hire a night watchman (*'assas*).

Because of the multiple ties which link the residents of a quarter, respectable women who never venture to the main market can circulate discreetly within it, since the residents are "known" (*me'ruf*) to each other. For this reason, quarter residents are concerned with any scandal which may affect their own reputation and may occasionally try to force the departure of undesirable households or persons.

Even when "closeness" is maintained by overlapping ties of residential propinquity and kinship, as in certain Sherqawi quarters in Boujad, informants emphasize that the obligations between persons are not fixed. As stated previously, there is an existential realism toward "the way things are" which permeates their conception of the social order. Thus one elderly Sherqawi illustrated as follows the flexibility of alliances in blood feuds involving his quarter prior to the protectorate: "How can you say that it was always your brothers or your father's brother's sons who would help you in a fight? They might live far from you and, besides, they have their own household and affairs to look after. Why should they risk their lives for you as well?" The same informant made a similar point using the concept of *hbab* (sg., *hbib*) which literally means "loved ones" but which frequently is used to specify persons linked by blood relations. When necessary for context, the meaning of such terms is more strictly delimited. For example, Boujadi-s speak of some persons as being *qrab* (sg., *qrib*) or *hbab be-sh shra'*, to indicate those who are kinsmen within the definitions of Islamic law concerning marriage and inheritance. The rights ensuing from such ties are fixed in Islamic law, but in the context of Moroccan society these rights, like any others, are a matter of negotiation in light of the total social context.

Thus in the Moroccan context, kinship, including close blood relationships, constitutes a class of relations upon which specified social roles can be developed rather than a set of relationships with specified, fixed obligations attached to them. This is in substantial contrast with, for instance, the specific obligations attached to kinship ties in southern Iraq and some other parts of the Arab world (e.g.,

Salim 1962). In Morocco the presence of "actual" kinship relations between persons is not in itself a specific indication of the actual contours of the relationship.

For "closeness" to be said to exist in a quarter, it must be capable of mobilizing for effective social action in some contexts. An external parameter can be noted here. Most quarters are composed of two hundred to six hundred inhabitants. Those residential clusters considerably smaller or larger than this range tend to be the ones which are not regarded as quarters by all informants. Such a guide is very rough but suggests that, for bonds of "closeness" to be effective in terms of physical propinquity, there is an optimal quantitative range, above and below which such ties become untenable. Census figures (Kingdom of Morocco 1961) suggest a similar range for rural local communities (*ḍǎwwar*-s).

In addition, each quarter has one or several "big men" (*kobbar*), or men with "word" (*kelma*), who in some contexts act for the common interests of the quarter and can mobilize households within it. Quarters lacking persons with "word" are usually incapable of mobilization and are regarded by many as not being quarters at all.

Residential areas with a high proportion of rural immigrants are generally said to lack "closeness." These immigrants settle wherever there is suitable accommodation available, rather than cluster by origin, and have a tendency to move frequently. Residents of such areas are said by older townsmen to be "unknown" to each other, even if they consider themselves a quarter. Generally they are unable to mobilize as an effective group, since they lack the economic resources and leadership to establish such signs of prestige as a quarter mosque. Since no one in them has "word," such quarters tend to be the last to acquire such urban amenities as sewers, water, and paved passages or (for the "new" quarters) roads.

Given the past competitive advantages of the Sherqawa, including education as "sons of notables" (*fils de notables*) in the early days of the protectorate and preferment in official positions, some have been able to maintain local and even national prominence by converting the waning power of maraboutism into assets more viable in altered social and economic positions. This is reflected by the continuing existence and prestige of several (not all) Sherqawi quarters over the last sixty years, especially the 'Arbawi and Zawya quarters, inhabited by those claiming descent from the most prominent Sherqawi marabouts of the last two centuries. In these quarters more than others, the ties of residence, faction, and descent tend to coincide, although these identities are still amenable to considerable manipulation. Many residents hold rights in the undivided estates of their maraboutic ancestors in addition to shares of offerings made to the shrine of their founding ancestor. Residents of both quarters can point to numerous occasions in the recent past when effective alliances have been formed on a quarter-wide basis.

Sherqawi and other quarters unable to maintain such prestige are liable to dissociation—since the Second World War, prosperous Sherqawi merchants in some of the less prestigious quarters have moved to New Boujad and have downplayed their Sherqawi identity. Rural immigrants moving into such quarters then try to claim Sherqawi descent as one means of upgrading their own prestige. The "closeness" of the remaining original inhabitants can no longer be expressed in social action. Not infrequently, entire quarters disappear over relatively brief spans of time as a consequence of this process.[2]

In contrast, there are a number of quarters formed over the last few decades which now attempt to claim prestige equal or superior to that of the leading Sherqawi quarters. The Khaluqiyin quarter (6-20) has at its core the sons of a non-Sherqawi merchant who before and after the protectorate engaged in trade with Khnifra, in the Middle Atlas highlands. They became prosperous and early in the 1930's purchased adjoining plots in the original French-designed New Boujad. Later, two of the brothers became active in nationalist politics and, publicly at least, were the leaders of rival parties. Most residents of the quarter claim links with these core households. These, in turn, have begun claiming descent from 'Ali Ṣmuni, a "rediscovered" brother of Sidi Mḥammed Sherqi who, they assert, unlike the marabout, was a "progressive" ahead of his time. Thus they claim the prestige of distinguished ancestry without its supposed encumbrances. Quarters founded by rural *qaid*-s during the protectorate had a similar rapid ascendancy —and, in some cases, a precipitate fall.

Establishing "Closeness": An Example

The rise and fall of quarters is related to their ability to sustain "closeness" based at least in part upon residential association. This section will outine the mechanics by which the claim to "closeness" was made in one particular quarter.

The Qsayra quarter (6-9), "The Little Fortress," is so named because it adjoins the fortified, high-walled Sherqawi religious lodge
which forms the nucleus of the Zawya quarter and, in fact, looks like
a scaled-down version of that quarter.

Qsayra's residents tend to claim "closeness" to each other by descent and marriage, although, as is also the case for Sherqawi quarters, in most cases no exact genealogical links can be demonstrated.
Most residents of the quarter claim that they or their ancestors came
from Ait Saleh, the tribal grouping to the immediate west of Boujad.
Without denying Ait Saleh origins, others prefer to stress their relations with one Hajj Bu Bakr, himself reputedly of Ait Saleh, who
founded the quarter at the turn of the century and whose household
serves as the "core" with which other households claim affinity.

Bu Bakr was a tannery owner and grain merchant when the
French arrived in 1913. Not long after this event, he made a fortune
by selling grain in exchange for land and houses during a period of
extensive drought.[3] Bu Bakr soon converted his fortune into social
honor by making the pilgrimage to Mecca and thus acquiring the
title Hajj, constructing an imposing house for himself, and marrying
a second wife. As his sons matured and married, he built adjacent
houses for them, in the manner of other men of prestige. He also
constructed a small mosque for the quarter and made the major contribution toward paying the *fqih* hired to teach in it. He died shortly
after the Second World War, although his sons and widows continue
to reside in the quarter.

The means by which residents of the quarter claim "closeness"
with Hajj Bu Bakr deserve some attention. There are some thirty
dwellings in the quarter, although when I asked informants to enu-
merate them for me they invariably excluded several. These turned
out to be those living units which somehow did not qualify as households—men sleeping in shops; the dwellings of several poor, childless
couples; and all those excluded from the circle of "closeness" for
some assumed moral defect. These "nonhouseholds" did not share
the visiting patterns of the "counted" households of the quarter or
engage in their multiple reciprocal exchanges.

The asserted ties of one informant will be examined in detail, since
they orchestrate virtually the entire range of means by which "closeness" can be asserted. At first Ma'ti (7-1), a shopkeeper who had
attended the local *collège*, claimed that Bu Bakr was of his "blood"
(*men demmi*). This he elaborated by claiming that the relation was

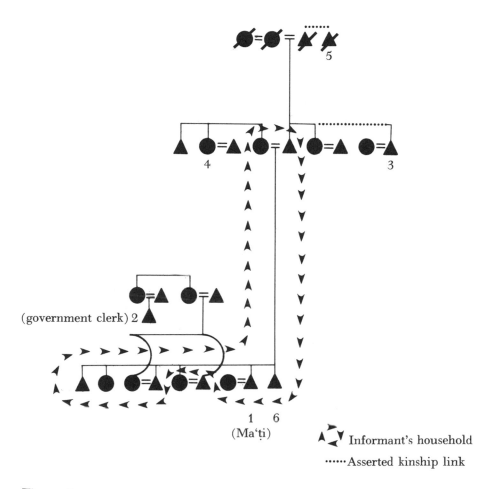

Figure 7.
Kinship ties of an informant in Qṣayṛa quarter.

through his "father's brother" (7-3), who had married a woman of
Ḥajj Bu Bakr's household.

In another context some months earlier I had asked Ma'ti to tell
me whom he considered his kinsmen, so that I had a means of check-
ing his statements. When I reminded him that previously he had said
his father had no brothers, he replied that, since he was "close"
(*qrib*) to Ḥajj Bu Bakr, then it must be through a half-brother of his
father that he had never met or perhaps through a brother of his
grandfather (7-5). In other words, "closeness" came first, then its

ideological justification. He continued that there "probably" was a second link through the marriage of his mother's sister (7-4), who also lived in Qsayra. Again, this tie could not be demonstrated. Finally, Ma'ti said that Bu Bakr's people act *as if* (*b-ḥal*) they are related (*qrib*); so they must be; and he cited at length the informal visiting patterns which prevailed between their households. No one can remember such ties clearly, he said; and since—in perfectly comprehensible *Catch-22* reasoning—no one can verify them in any exact way, they must exist. He went on to link himself in a similar manner with a minor, but significant, local government official who figures prominently in the incident which is discussed below.[4]

The Great Shrine Incident

The perseverance of a quarter or any other group is contingent upon its effectiveness in ongoing social situations. Ties of kinship, occupation, and residence, among others, may form the base of active alliances. The emphasis placed on these ties varies with the situations in which they are used.

For many years residents of Qsayra regarded themselves as a quarter and were seen as such by other townsmen. But only after an incident in 1969, which involved effective collective action on the basis of quarter identity, was it commonly regarded as a quarter of high prestige. This event, which I have labeled the Great Shrine Incident, precipitated a shift in the boundaries of commonly accepted social categories by legitimizing the fusion of residence and kinship claimed by residents of the quarter. In the process, the Sherqawi prerogative of building shrines for their ancestors was effectively challenged.

The Great Shrine Incident began with the death in France of a man called Sherqawi, an artist who had emigrated to France some years earlier. Informants from the Qsayra quarter claimed that despite his name he was not a Sherqawi but of "their blood." Moroccan friends of the artist in France had his body returned to Boujad, where at first it was placed in the common cemetery. When some of them later visited Boujad, they left money for a more "fitting" memorial with a minor local official who was a resident of Qsayra. He quickly consulted with other residents of the quarter—it is significant that he chose to pursue action along its lines rather than some other —and decided to erect a shrine (*qobba*) for the artist. As one Qsayra resident later said: "After all, he was *like* [*b-ḥal*] a saint [*wali*]. I

don't say he is, but how else do you distinguish a man except by
building a shrine over his head?"

All informants agreed that it takes more than the construction of
a shrine to make a marabout, but all shrines are regarded nonetheless as those of marabouts:

> After you die [said another supporter of the shrine] your
> sons begin talking about how great you are and build a
> shrine over your head. Then they say that you have a
> high rank [*daraja kbira*] with God. Some people visit the
> shrine, kiss it, and ask for things. However, those that ask
> the most are the descendants of the *shaykh* [i.e., the person
> in the shrine]. They ask for animals and grain from the
> pilgrims. Then, as the descendants of the *shaykh* increase
> in number, some continue to collect gifts and intercede
> with their ancestor; others become merchants and teachers
> and so on. That's all there is to it.

For residents of the Qsayra quarter, support for construction of
the shrine was a means of upgrading their own social honor. A shrine
would allow them to point to an "exemplary" ancestor in the manner of the Sherqawa and, moreover, distinguish them from other
commoners. A successful mobilization against the Sherqawa would
effectively validate their claim to "closeness."

The local official from Qsayra managed to supplement the initial
contribution with funds from the municipal treasury on the grounds
that the artist was an international figure and that the construction
of a shrine for him would enhance Boujad as a tourist attraction.
The site chosen was a promontory to the immediate north of the
town, next to the main highway, where there already were five
shrines for sons of Sidi Mhammed Sherqi. A construction permit was
obtained from the *qaid*, and a delegation from Qsayra went to Rabat
informally to see persons in and out of government who might con-
ceivably affect events in Boujad. This move indicated, of course, a
sensitivity to informal constellations of power as opposed to the formal distribution of authority. Municipal work crews were used, and,
by the end of the summer of 1969, construction of the shrine was almost completed. In fact, pilgrims began making small offerings despite attempts to stop them by Sherqawa who collected offerings at
the adjoining shrines.

By now, a few Sherqawa had become concerned. As one of the active opponents of the Qsayṛa quarter later said, if the shrine were allowed to be completed, then others could claim that they, too, were descendants of Sidi Mhammed Sherqi. The "real" Sherqawa would lose "word" by an inability to act effectively. At least some Sherqawa also stood to lose income from traffic with pilgrims.

The first men with "word" to act were two Sherqawi notaries from the prominent 'Arbawi quarter. Both were engaged in overseeing the collection and distribution of offerings at the main shrine and regularly emerged as spokesmen for Sherqawi interests. They tried to halt construction of the new shrine first by asking the local *qaid*, not a native of the region, to intervene. He refused (the local official from Qsayṛa was one of his close collaborators) on the grounds that the matter was internal to the Sherqawa and that the Makhzen was not about to intervene in their "family" affairs. The regional overseer of the Ministry of Pious Endowments, an early supporter of the Istiqlal (Independence) party and a reformist (Salafi) Muslim, also declined to intervene, arguing quite correctly that, since the Sherqawi shrines were not among his holdings, the matter was extraneous to his office.

The next move of the notaries was to prepare a petition in the name of "all" Sherqawa, only to find that, because of several recent and some not so recent disputes among Sherqawa, there was considerable resistance to its signing. Clearly, social action did not coalesce along simple, arbitrary lines of kinship or residence but depended upon each person's weighing the various alternatives for action open to him.

Eventually some sixty signatures were collected for the petition. Significantly, the most influential of the signers were prosperous Sherqawi merchants who had resided for years in Casablanca and thus were removed from local factional alliances. Armed with their petition, the two notaries went first to a minister in Rabat. According to one of those present at the interview, his reply was markedly unsympathetic. "Once dead all Muslims are equal," he replied, and would have nothing to do with the prerogatives claimed by a maraboutic descent group. The notaries tried to argue that the shrines were "historical," not "religious," monuments, but this also fell on deaf ears.

Their next visit, to an influential private individual, was more successful. A single telephone call was placed to the *qaid* of Boujad, who immediately rode out to the shrine and forbade further work on it.

Informants from both sides of the dispute stressed that their formal arguments were much less decisive than the fact that someone with influence had acted.

Supporters of the shrine from the Qsayra quarter congratulated themselves that it took months for a mere stalemate to be effected against them—the nearly completed shrine was left standing—and regarded their setback as temporary: "We will stay quiet for a few years and then start building again. By that time even the Sherqawa will forget whether or not Sherqawi is a descendant of Sidi Mhammed Sherqi and will only remember his name."

It would be misleading to interpret this incident primarily in terms of the successful attempt of nonmarabouts to acquire for themselves the symbols of maraboutic prestige. This would be perhaps too "traditional" a view of "traditional" Morocco in the light of the frequency of such occurrences in the past (e.g., Bel 1938:376–382). More to the point is the fact that a successful alliance was formed along the lines of residential propinquity, was sustained, and thus legitimized the assertion of quarter "closeness" as a social reality.

Social Structure: The Tribal Setting

The same underlying pattern of social structure which I have depicted in an urban setting applies equally to rural Morocco. To show this, I will describe in detail the social organization of the Sma'la and Bni Zemmur "tribes"[5] of the upper Tadla Plain, both in the present and in the historically known past. These two tribes are no more representative of rural Morocco in general than is Boujad of Moroccan towns, at least in terms of formal characteristics. But, as I indicated earlier, it is pointless to make comparisons or determinations of typicality based on such characteristics. Since the question of personal and group identity is closely related to the conception of marabouts, it is worth discussing it in some detail. In describing tribal social structure, I want to distinguish two separate perspectives, a sociological one and that of native ideology. The latter can further be divided between "official" representations offered by rural strong-men, especially those who dealt most regularly with the precolonial Makhzen and the protectorate government, and those of ordinary tribesmen.

The Sma'la and Bni Zemmur employ the idiom of agnation to describe relations between persons and groups of persons. This, of course, is one of the two features that are necessary for a society to be described in terms of segmentary lineage organization. The other feature is not present: segmentation is not the only idiom in which political relations are conceptualized; groups of persons do not primarily align themselves along the lines provided by asserted agnatic ties. Tribesmen are explicitly aware of this and, at least on the Tadla Plain, do not assert that the precolonial past was different from the present in this respect.[6]

Members of both tribes that I am here concerned with use the metaphors of a tree and the human body to describe their internal divisions. For example, one tribesman spoke of the Bni Battu as the trunk of a tree, which in turn was divided into branches. The word used to indicate branches of a tree (*'ersh*) is not used, but rather several interchangeable terms—tribesmen are not immune to mixing metaphors. Among these terms are "group" (*farqa*), "thigh" (*făkhda*), and "piece" (*tarf*). For convenience, I translate all these as "section." Sections are further divided into *dăwwar*-s, a term which I translate as "local communities." These, in turn, are composed of household units which, depending upon their economic and ecological circumstances, are called either "houses" (*dar*-s) or "tents" (*khayma*-s). The relationships within and between these various groups are spoken of as *qaraba* and are symbolized in terms of blood. Thus the Sma'la maintain that all members of their tribe are linked by blood, but *explicitly* deny that this tie obliges them to act in specified ways with regard to each other. Such a denial firmly excludes these tribes from the Procrustean bed of segmentation. As one tribesman said: "We are like the branches of a tree, but each section is on its own [*koll farqa b-uhedha*]." In other words, social and political action flows along numerous lines: residential propinquity, herding arrangements, kinship, patron-client relations, and other bonds of necessity or mutual interest. None of these ties, of course, is specific to the tribal milieu. The ecological, economic, and political conditions of rural society vary widely, although the latitude within which tribesmen can valorize actual or potential ties tends to be more limited than that available in an urban milieu.

How far the component of assumed blood relations is allowed to determine political action is a complex matter. It is not simply a question of relative autonomy from government or outside "interference," as has sometimes been maintained. To the contrary, as will be elaborated below, the coming of the protectorate to the upper Tadla

Plain, and presumably elsewhere, appears to have strengthened the notion of the formal agnatic ideology of groups as a blueprint for political action. Second, the use of the ideology of agnatic relationships varies markedly with the role informants play in tribal society. This is an aspect rarely elaborated in anthropological accounts of such ideologies. Members of the rural elite are those who, by reason of their wealth or prestige, command a following and often act as spokesmen with the administration and other nontribesmen. It is these persons who are most capable of manipulating and describing the conceptual grid provided by agnatic relationships. The mark of a tribal strong-man is his ability to manipulate this grid and all other available ties to accumulate personal wealth and power. The only clear difference between the preprotectorate and the protectorate in this respect seems to be that, prior to the protectorate, a plurality of persons commonly acted as such an elite within each tribal group, while the protectorate enhanced the fortunes of a few by giving them the protection of official sinecures. When asking about tribal social organization, I was usually referred to such strong-men or to older men who "knew" such things. In many cases these informants turned out to be the nucleus of de facto clients and allies and expected such referrals to be made to them.

The agnatic conceptual grid elaborated by the tribal elite centers less upon the relations of local communities with each other or their role in higher organizational units than upon the relations among tribes and tribal sections. This grid, or variants of it, forms a potential base upon which relations among various groups can be legitimated and as such constitutes an "official" native representation of the social structure (Bourdieu 1972:113). An example of such a conceptualization is presented in Figure 8. It is a version current among several elderly Sma'la who were government *shaykh*-s during the protectorate (and who, by reason of wealth and clientele, continue to be "shadows" to younger tribesmen who now officially exercise the same functions). In it, the Sma'la are descended from the Bni Jabir, an eponymous Arab tribe from which many tribal groups in western Morocco claim descent. Most of the other tribal groups of the upper Tadla Plain are made to have a similar origin: Werdigha, Bni Meskin, Bni Musa, Bni 'Amir, and Bni Mellal.[7] However, my informants knew only their own tribe and the neighboring Werdigha with any exactitude. Contact with the other tribal groups of the upper Tadla Plain is presently almost nonexistent. In fact, the existence of

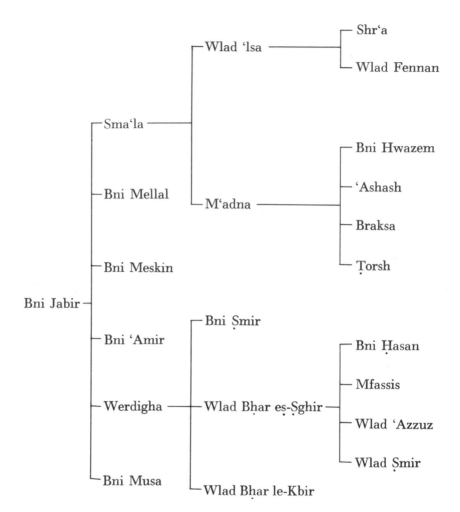

Figure 8.
Tribes of the Tadla Plain: a version of the tribal elite.

some of them as groups which ever formed the basis for united action is questionable, outside of the assumptions made by early protectorate administrators. Nonetheless, it was this set of concepts which was given administrative reality by the French: *qāid*-s were set up over each of these groups early in the protectorate. These administrative categories were not entirely artificial, since the French determined tribal groups and boundaries early in the protectorate by meeting with those who convincingly portrayed themselves as "notables" for the groups involved and appeared capable of imposing their "word" on other tribesmen. Since many of the same notables became incorporated into the protectorate administration, it is reasonable to assume that they had an interest in sustaining this particular macrogenealogical framework.[8]

A Commoner Perspective: The Local Community

In contrast to the elaborate genealogical representations of the tribal elite, the perception of social organization of ordinary tribesmen is less comprehensive and differs considerably in emphasis. Most tribesmen can offer only a truncated outline of intra- and intertribal relationships. Thus, since Sma'la is the plural of Isma'il, ordinary Sma'la tribesmen assured me that they claimed descent from an individual of that name. Similarly, all tribesmen could name the tribal sections of their own tribe, as well as the local communities of their own section and local communities from adjacent sections that were contiguous to their own or with which they had herding agreements. The enumerations of such units by different tribesmen never completely tally: the variant conceptual maps possessed by tribesmen of the rural social order are somewhat analogous to the townsmen's delineation of urban quarters. The major difference is that, unlike town dwellers, all rural tribesmen belong to a local community, although their membership in specified local communities may shift in time. The analogy was probably more direct in the preprotectorate era when, for reasons of security, membership in an urban quarter was essential.

Most ordinary tribesmen describe their social organization first in terms of their local community, the group which most impinges upon their daily activities. This group relates in various ways to "higher" levels of organization.

Literally, the term *ḍǎwwar* means "circle." In the insecurity of preprotectorate days, herding units of a local community pitched their tents in a circle during transhumance, kept their herds in the middle for safety, mutually agreed upon their movements, and, to a certain extent, negotiated collectively the tenor of their relations with other groups. Such spatial representations of social order are now less clear. For one thing, local communities are not distinguished by clustered settlements. As I have already mentioned, sedentarization occurred quite late on the upper Tadla Plain, so that households settled on their lands rather than in villages. Nor is the ownership of or right to land in this region a direct clue. Local communities own no land collectively. The rights to certain pasture lands are vested administratively in tribal sections, continuing (although in a much less flexible manner) a convention which existed prior to the arrival of the French. In contrast to some other regions of Morocco, virtually all agricultural land on the upper Tadla Plain is held by individuals and in principle is transferred according to what is locally understood and enforced of Islamic law. The value placed upon agriculture was much less intense prior to the protectorate but operated by the same principles. Although most landowners now possess formal, written deeds (*resm*-s), preprotectorate usage was generally based upon tacit verbal understandings and conventions. Tribesmen often purchased land rights in other local communities or acquired them by inheritance and marriage. Similar principles of land use existed elsewhere, for instance in the Berber-speaking region of Bzu. Only a few ex-protectorate *qaid*-s have taken advantage of the Torrens system of land registration, introduced under the protectorate, to obtain a title (*titre*) which fully removes their land from the jurisdiction of the Islamic law courts.

Members of local communities conceive of relations to each other in much the same way as do residents of urban quarters. They claim agnatic ties but are unable to demonstrate specifically that such ties encompass all members of their group. When asked to trace such relations in detail, tribal informants invariably responded that only someone older could do so. In turn, elderly informants vaguely referred to "earlier times" (*bekri*) as the period when the local community was entirely composed of traceable agnatic relations. Parenthetically, *bekri* is a temporal category used for all social action thought to have some effect upon the present social order but for which no specific context or verification can be provided. In actuality, local communities commonly consist of several agnatic cores, none of which necessarily predominates, which are interlinked by complex affinal and contractual ties.

For purposes of kinship and inheritance, a narrower, more precise range of relationships is specified. Most tribesmen are aware that by Islamic law, relationships (*qaraba*) are constituted exclusively by designated agnatic ties and by marriage. Nonetheless, even these evidence considerable latitude. As one tribesman said, the *qadi* is in town, not in the country. By implication, even for purposes of inheritance, the legal definition of *qaraba* is not necessarily the decisive one in social reality.

In rural local communities, as in urban quarters, the significant criteria of group membership are a general support of its members in mutual interests and the capacity to act together with other members on certain ritual and political occasions. Contrary to Durkheim, it is not just performance of a ritual (or other collective action) which creates a feeling of solidarity. There is also a pre-existing community of interests which makes such action possible. There is a dialectical, mutually reinforcing relationship between ritual and social action. In the case of Morocco, the ensuing solidarity is symbolized by the notion of *qaraba* as sustained among its members.

Each local community has a council (*jma'a*), not to be confused with the governmental councils present at the level of tribal sections (which in governmental neologism are considered to be rural communes). Participants in the council of a local community are not formally designated. Any adult male head of a household who has an interest in the issues at hand participates, although the opinions of those who are economically or politically weak tend to be discounted or ignored in favor of those with more substantial material interests and skills. Such councils discuss the direction of movements during the winter months of transhumancy and agree when necessary on a spokesman (*mqaddem*) to represent them collectively. Frequently the same men are repeatedly selected as spokesmen, but they cannot as a consequence be said to hold formal "office." The decisive factor is what local community members consider the most efficacious representation of their interests, as well as internal constellations of wealth and power. Dissidents always have the option of breaking away and forming new local communities or, in some cases, of shifting their allegiance to other groups with which they have pre-existing ties.

There are a number of parallels between the performance of collective actions associated with urban quarters and those associated with rural local communities. Each local community constructs a mosque, although this may be no more than a tent or hut (*nwala*) almost indistinguishable from other dwellings. The council of each local community usually contracts on an annual basis for a Qur'anic teacher to instruct its children in the rudiments of reading, writing, and the Qur'an. The mosque often serves as the sleeping quarters for this teacher (*fqih*). One inhabitant of each local community, usually self-selected, serves as prayer-caller.[9]

Each local community also has associated with it the tomb of a marabout, although this is usually only a sporadically maintained, derelict, rectangular structure in the midst of their communal burial ground. Only rarely are new ones constructed. These marabouts generally are called *fqih*-s by tribesmen and are often compared to the impoverished, transient Qur'anic teachers, also called *fqih*-s, with whom tribesmen are familiar. Sacrifices are never offered at these tombs, although women occasionally offer candle stubs or coins, which children promptly pick up. In contrast with the leading Sherqawi marabouts, little is known of these *fqih*-s beyond their names, nor do they have claimed descendants. Occasionally such marabouts are drawn out of anonymity by having compelling or unusual dreams and other uncanny events attributed to their inspiration. In another case, a maraboutic shrine gained prestige when the brother of an ex-*qaid* restored a tomb near his lands and encouraged offerings to be made to it. He then persuaded some Sma'la to visit it each fall on their way to the *musem* of Sidi Mhammed Sherqi in Boujad. As a consequence, two local communities began leaving token offerings of grain at harvest time, assuming that the tomb housed a "forgotten" Sherqawi. "Closeness" to the Sherqawi was attributed by the tribesmen to the *qaid*'s brother because of the care he bestowed on the tomb.

Although each local community usually is associated with a maraboutic tomb, there is no one-to-one correlation. There are many more tombs than local communities. This allows for shifts in boundaries and identities. On the plains to the north of Boujad there are eighty-nine such tombs, an average of one for every six square kilometers and 150 persons. These maraboutic tombs constitute a framework in which aspects of the social order can be concretely symbolized as groups shift in their composition. Most local communities also maintain covenants with a major marabout, such as Sidi Mhammed Sherqi and jointly make offerings to certain of his descendants, called "visitors" (*zewwar*-s), who are thought to constitute particularly efficacious links between the group and the marabout. These will be discussed in detail in Chapter 6.

Each household or tent in the countryside belongs to only one local community, just as an urban household belongs to only one quarter at any time. The refusal or inability of a household to contribute to any of its collective obligations does not in itself serve as a sign of dissociation from the local community, although it generally affects its capacity to have a say in the collectivity's affairs. When breaks occur, a household unit or group of them may decide to form a separate local community. This will be identified by a separate marabout's tomb, burial ground, mosque, and other indications of collective identity. A particularly useful means of tracing the realignments both of local communities and of tribal sections is their conduct at the annual festival of Sidi Mhammed Sherqi in Boujad. Conduct at this festival constitutes a form of publication of new social alignments. These are perceived by the arrangement of tents and the part taken by local communities and tribal sections in "powder plays" (*tehrăk*-s), competitive displays of horsemanship in which riders try to gallop in a line abreast and fire their muskets in unison on a given signal. Such "powder plays" are always accompanied by heavy, serious betting between the groups involved. Differences that develop during these contests often themselves engender new lines of social demarcation.

Tribal Sections and Alliances

The identity of tribal sections is more stable over time than that of local communities. In part this is because both the protectorate and the independent Moroccan administration invested what are administratively considered to be tribal sections (often "tribes" to tribesmen themselves) with collective rights and obligations. These included rights to collective pasture lands, permits for transhumant movements, taxes, and other administratively imposed obligations. To a certain extent the protectorate "froze" the lines of political maneuver by recognizing these units, although there still was considerable flexibility as to how rights and obligations were construed, allocated, and defended. Prior to the protectorate, sections also fulfilled defensive functions. The upper Tadla Plain is dotted with the ruins of fortified compounds (*dshar*-s), generally located on promontories, which served as places of refuge from which sections could defend themselves and their flocks. No similar enclosures existed at the level of local communities or, in general, at the level of tribes.

Arrangements for the use of grazing land are currently the best indication of the flexibility with which idioms of group relationships are interpreted. An informant from Bni Baṭṭu, one of the most "traditional" tribes in its *genre de vie*, stressed that the most important factor in such arrangements was that both parties be mutually "known" (*meʿruf*) to each other and confident of each other's trustworthiness. This was considered more important than abstract considerations of tribal and sectional allegiance. Asserted ties of agnatic descent or affinity, common bonds with Sherqawi marabouts, contractual ritual alliances (*ṭaṭa*) (see below), and simple de facto agreements of cooperation are all regarded as sufficient for such confidence to exist.

Grazing agreements were not limited to negotiations between groups. They also occurred between individual herd owners who were not necessarily from the same tribal section or tribe. I use the past tense because of the marked decline in the size of herds and transhumancy since the end of the Second World War. Presently, transhumancy is confined to administratively approved seasonal movements among neighboring groups and shows little yearly variation. Such agreements were often not ordered within the formal structure of intergroup agnatic relationships, although for administrative reasons the French in the early years of the protectorate encouraged such a conception. Some French administrators in the 1920's and 1930's argued, without providing specific examples, that collective, tribe-wide pastoral agreements were "traditional," while other types of arrangements were recent, spurious accretions. A *contrôleur civil* stationed in Boujad during this period, basing himself upon specific ethnographic data, argued in opposition that arrangements made by individuals and local communities appeared equally "traditional" (B.1331, 4 July 1935).[10]

In many ways, the lines of authority of the French tribal administration were a more perfect representation of the principle of segmentation and the encapsulation of smaller political units in larger ones than the conceptions employed by the tribesmen themselves. The assumption that agreements were concluded only between large collectivities appealed to popular French understandings of how tribal men ought to act (and undoubtedly did in some parts of Morocco) and, more concretely, had the advantage of being administratively tidy: *transhumance* was bureaucratically defined as the passage of herds between administrative districts. When such movements led to

intertribal clashes, settlement was complicated by the fact that local
French administrative posts had to communicate indirectly with each
other through hierarchical channels. Such communication was
particularly onerous in the Boujad region. Boujad and the tribes attached to it were in the zone of civil administration after 1931. The
mountainous zone to the east, traditionally used for transhumance,
was a "Berber" region and under military control. In fact, to solve
the administrative problem and at the same time maintain a clear
separation between "Berber" and "Arab" tribesmen, a military administrator in 1935 seriously proposed the ban of all pastoral transhumancy in the region. The Boujad *contrôleur* pointed out in reply
that such a decision would bring economic disaster to the tribes of
the Boujad region that were dependent upon access to the complementary ecological zone of the mountains.

The modalities of grazing agreements depended upon a range of
political and economic factors. For instance, the Sma'la tended to
deal with the Berber-speaking Zayyan in tribal sections. This was
partly because long-range transhumance required a large number
of personnel to be effective. Zayyan territory was also potentially
hostile. In contrast, most Sma'la dealt with the Bni Khiran and Werdigha tribesmen to their west as individual heads of residential units
(*khayma*-s). These tribes occupied complementary ecological zones.
One herder might possess rights to land more suitable for grazing in
humid years; another, land more suitable for dry years. Depending
on the total complex of relations existing between the two parties,
such arrangements varied from direct reciprocal exchanges or generalized mutual aid, accompanied by no more than symbolic gifts,
to the payment of cash or a specified number of animals of the herd
in exchange for grazing rights (B.1331, 4 July 1935; Bonjean 1928:
74–78).

The formality attached to such agreements varied widely. Two
tribesmen, even of different tribes, who had such arrangements of
mutual trust were descriptively called "companions" (*saheb*-s). The
same term often applies to local communities with mutually sup-
portive relationships. In a terminological variation, the Bni 'Isa section of Bni Battu (Bni Zemmur) call their relation with the Wlad
Khellu, also of Bni Battu (see Fig. 9), one of "brotherhood" (*khawwa*). These two sections share the same pasture land, together with
the other sections of the Bni Battu, and are distinguished by having
pragmatically supported each other's interests in grazing and admin-

Tribe	Section	Local Community

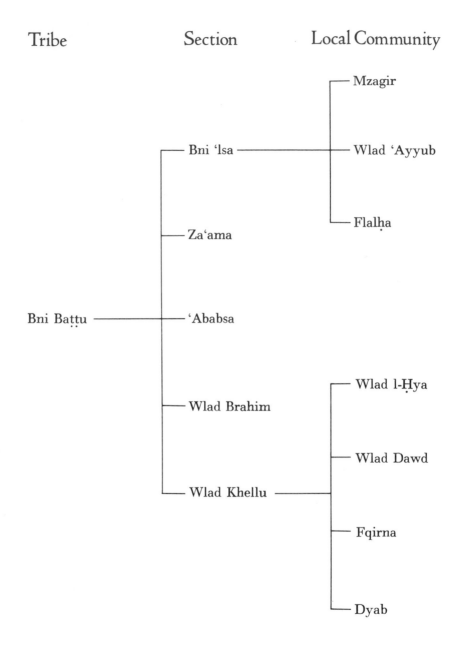

Figure 9.
Bni Baṭṭu. (Based on information from Wlad l-Ḥya tribesmen, 1970.)

istrative disputes over several decades. This relationship, however, entails no ritual or formal contractual alliance. Members of both tribal sections explained that a *khawwa* relationship simply implied that they tended to act in each other's interests over a prolonged period. None of the other sections of the tribe had any similar record of sustained mutual support.

Prior to the protectorate, local communities and sections could formally symbolize mutual support through a "contractual ritual alliance" (*tata*). This type of alliance existed in various forms in many other parts of Morocco (Bruno and Bousquet 1946; Vinogradov 1973; Hart 1973). On the upper Tadla Plain, such alliances were generally made between local communities or sections of different tribes, although I have recorded several instances of intratribal alliances. The contracting parties agreed to refrain from fighting and raiding each other and, in general, to aid each other against external threats. Informants explained that such alliances were like the existence of milk brotherhood except that intermarriage was permitted.[11] Such alliances were temporally too remote from my informants for them to describe in detail how they actually operated. In principle, one was supposed to treat a *tata* ally as a brother. I have already indicated some of the contingencies which effectively allow such obligations to be variously interpreted.

Tata was contracted in formal rituals. For instance, the Flalha local community of Bni 'Isa section (see Fig. 9), concluded an alliance with the 'Ababsa *section* of the same tribe.[12] The councils (*jma'a-s*) of the two groups met in Boujad at the shrine of the Sherqawi marabout Ma'ti ben Saleh (2-6), clasped hands over his cenotaph, and swore their alliance.

The Wlad Khellu section of Bni Battu concluded a *tata* alliance in a different way. They have—or, strictly speaking, had—alliances with three tribal sections. Two of these had territory contiguous to theirs: the Arab-speaking Wlad 'Ayyad (Bni Zrantel) and the Berber-speaking Ait Bu Haddu. The tie to a group spatially distant from them was with the Jriyyat section of Shegran. In one instance, *tata* was concluded by a communal meal between the councils of both sections. Afterward, each man present removed one of his slippers (*belgha-s*) and placed it in a pile along with those of other men of his section. These were then matched at random. All members of the two groups were henceforth in a *tata* relation, and those whose slippers were paired generally approached the other group through their counterpart. In another case, lactating women of the two sections nursed each other's children after the communal meal of the two councils. In the final case, a *cous-cous* eaten by the councils had in it milk from the women of both groups.[13]

Once *tata* was contracted, any violation of it, such as theft, was thought to incur supernatural retribution. Since French pacification, no new alliances have been contracted. As one tribesman said: "Now we are all in *tata* with the Makhzen." Existing relationships, however, continue to be recognized, and the term is now used metaphorically. For instance, tribesmen ask for the price of *tata* (i.e., a low price) from Boujadi merchants who are by origin from a group in *tata* with their own.

Knowledge of such alliances tends to be highly concentric. Each tribesman tends to have knowledge only of the *tata* relations of his own section. Those of other groups are not systematically known. Such alliances involve only the two contracting parties, so that a group called upon to come to the aid of a *tata* ally could not call for the support of groups which in turn were allied to it.

The Evidence of the Past

It can be argued that the political and economic transformations of the last sixty years have been so substantial that tribal organization described primarily from contemporary ethnographic evidence or the contemporary remembrance of things past differs fundamentally from that of the preprotectorate era. Of course, some very basic shifts have occurred. Since the protectorate, government intervention has greatly restricted the possibilities of intergroup hostilities. Matters previously settled among the tribes themselves or through maraboutic mediation now almost inevitably involve government intervention. Under current conditions, tribesmen can be more flexible in contracting and honoring alliances. Nevertheless, as I have tried to indicate, the available evidence suggests a continuity in the fundamental assumptions about the social order, rather than a sudden and marked discontinuity.

There exists fragmentary but nevertheless significant evidence in addition to that which I have already cited for the tribal social organization of the upper Tadla immediately prior to the protectorate. This is the Journal Politique of the military intelligence unit of the

French Corps de Débarquement for western Morocco, covering the period 1908–1912 (JP). These reports tend to confirm the description of tribal organization which I am presenting here. Only after the administrative machinery of the protectorate was set in place were tribes and their subdivisions assumed to be sharply delineated groups—whose form and capacity for alliance with other groups corresponded exactly, and curiously, with the assumptions implicit in the rural administrative apparatus.

Particularly relevant is the manner in which resistance was organized against the French on the upper Tadla Plain. It indicates a flexible, even entrepreneurial perception of the mechanics of alliance formation. For example, in the summer of 1910, one Shaykh Mḥa l-'Aṭṭawi recruited tribesmen of the upper Tadla to form a raiding party against tribes in the Shawya that failed to resist the French.[14] He was initially joined by two to three thousand men on foot and five hundred horsemen from Bni 'Amir, Ait Rba', and several sections of the Bni Meskin. His method of recruitment on the upper Tadla Plain was to proceed with his followers from one local community to another. In the best tradition of pyramid sales tempered with extortion, he demanded a "contribution" for his holy war (*jihad*) and threatened confiscation of the herds and grain supplies of recalcitrant groups. "Contributors" then were allowed to join the raiding party and take a share of future exactions (JP, August 1910). There is no evidence that any formal apparatus based upon agnatic intergroup relations had any effect upon Shaykh Mḥa's operations.

French reports suggest a similar situation with Weld Karda. vaguely described as a "war chief" of the Sma'la, who later became one of the first protectorate *qaid*-s. His recruiting strategy resembled that of Shaykh Mḥa except that it was on a smaller scale. Most of his following was from the Sma'la, and raids were limited to the contiguous Werdigha tribe, who at that time were reported to be "conciliatory" toward the French (JP, September–December 1910).

An incident particularly indicative of the latitude of options available to tribesmen in forming alliances occurred during the struggle for the sultanate between the brothers Mulay 'Abd l-'Aziz and Mulay Hafeḍ which began in 1907. Bitter fighting broke out between supporters for the two contenders among the Bni Zemmur and Sma'la, resulting in a large number of deaths. To the discomfiture of the French, support for the two contenders was determined not only by what the French considered "political" factors, which for them meant the contest for the sultanate, but also by what they considered "ordinary" (i.e., apolitical) local disputes. Thus, an October 1909 entry in the Journal Politique states: "The Ait Saleh section [*fraction*] of Bni Zemmur . . . is fighting with the Wlad Gwawsh section of the same tribe [over water rights—a dispute which persisted into the 1930's]. The former, being more directly under the influence of [the Sherqawi marabout who supported 'Abd l-'Aziz], professes sympathies for Mulay 'Abd l-'Aziz. Nothing more is necessary for the opposing section to place its cause in care of Mulay Hafed and to contract an alliance with the Hafedist Sma'la tribe." Three months later the author of the report corrected his assessment of the composition of the two factions and reported that the marabout of the Sherqawi lodge[15] had concluded a truce between the Sma'la and the Bni Zemmur, "or rather between the Hafedist and Azizist leaders of these two tribes" (JP, January 1910). Tribal alliances clearly suggest a much more complex pattern than that allowed by the formal ideology of agnation.

I have tried to make two major points in this chapter. The first is to show that social structure in Morocco, both urban and tribal/rural, is based upon the ordered relationships not of groups of persons, but of persons. Moroccans do not conceive of the social order as consisting of groups in structured relationships. Emphasis is placed on managing personal networks of dyadic relationships. This is enough of a departure from accepted sociological understandings of North African society, particularly that element designated as "tribal," that I have presented my ethnographic account in detail. Tribes, tribal sections, local communities, quarters, agnatic descent, and so on merely constitute frameworks by means of which persons relate to each other. The constant element in this type of social structure is the means by which persons contract and maintain ties with each other. This is implicit in the concept of "closeness" (*qaraba*), by means of which Moroccans describe such relationships.

Second, in specifying that this underlying notion of social structure is relatively constant over time—at least over the period of roughly a century that is my chief concern—I am not proposing an unchanging metaphysical formula. Nonetheless, because of the inherent flexibility of this type of social structure, it is capable of accounting for a wide range of patterns of social action in Morocco, including the transformations engendered by the protectorate. This becomes more apparent when attention is shifted from the sociological description of social structure, the concern of this chapter, to the matrix of social definitions of reality through which everyday life and actions become subjectively meaningful to Moroccans themselves.

5

Impermanence and Inequality: The Common-Sense Understanding of the Social Order

The Common-Sense Foundations of Social Experience

Social institutions are subjectively held ideas about social relations shared by members of a given society. The existing social order is a manifestation of this texture of meaning. Whatever specialized knowledge members of a society possess or whatever activities they perform, they share a "natural" attitude toward the social world (Schutz 1967). This attitude is made up of everyday, unsystematized, common-sense symbolic understandings of how the world "really" is. Under ordinary conditions, these basic assumptions about the social order are so taken for granted that they are not articulated by members of a society. But they form the implicit background against which social action is planned and carried out. Special frames of reference, such as formal religious ideologies, are elaborated against the background of such understandings.

World views, or "natural" attitudes toward the world, are made up of a number of key concepts that have a "logico-meaningful" (Sorokin 1937:18–28) fit to one another. Like the parts of the jigsaw puzzle, the concepts that compose a world view have no uniformity in direct relation to one another. Karl Mannheim compared the presentation of a world view to that of biography, in which the "inner world" of the subject must be reconstituted from fragments of meaning contained in outward actions or statements. Each of these fragments actualizes an underlying pattern of meaning and serves as a "document" of it (1952:73). The ultimate test of an adequate description of a world view, therefore, is not quantitative or statistical but consists of the description's ability to render behavior intelligible in a given society.

In this chapter I present five of the key concepts through which Moroccans comprehend social experience. I deliberately say "Moroccans" rather than "Boujadi-s." This study is primarily based on fieldwork in Boujad and its region, but subsequent work elsewhere in Morocco suggests that the same underlying assumptions inform comprehension of the social order throughout the country. Significantly, Boujadi-s (and other Moroccans) also make this presumption, although they are sensitive to regional nuances. I do not intend to argue that the assumptions of the nature of the social order described here stop abruptly at Morocco's national frontiers. As I indicate below, many of these assumptions are expressed in terms of Islamic ideas that are hardly unique to Morocco or to North Africa. Had I worked near Morocco's frontiers, the issue of cultural boundaries would probably have been more immediate, but for most Moroccans the significant others with whom they come in contact are thought to share the same assumptions.

These five key concepts are God's will (*l-mektub*; *l-mqayyed*; *qodret Allah*), reason (*'qal*), propriety (*theshshem*; *hshumiya*), obligation (*hăqq*), and compulsion (*'ar*). To describe them briefly, the concept of *God's will* focuses man's attention on the empirical social order by attenuating speculation on other possible orders. *Reason* enables men to perceive this order and discern what is in their best interest. *Propriety* is possession of the self-control which enables men to act properly in the social order, while the nature of *obligations* contracted by men determines and maintains their social honor in relation to other men. Finally, *compulsion* is a means of restoring serious breaks in the web of obligations which bind men together. The emphasis given to these five concepts is admittedly arbitrary, but this is inherently the case in any attempt to describe a world view. Any such description is largely shaped by the range of social action that it attempts to render meaningful. For the problems of social identity and religious belief that form the core of this book, the five concepts that I present here are particularly significant. In passing, however, I mention a number of other related concepts. Were my primary concern with other ranges of social action, such as sexuality and sexual comportment (which figure in this chapter only as subsidiary issues), then my emphasis in describing aspects of the world view would shift as well.

The five concepts are not in a rigid, fixed relation with one another. They are maintained only insofar as they are actualized by individuals and seem to explain meaningfully and render coherent action in the social world. When they cease to do so, they tend to shift in emphasis, since men strive to perceive their social world coherently. Their interconnection can be compared to Edmund Leach's now-renowned elastic rubber sheet (1966:7). As they are used in different settings and by different persons, these key concepts are elaborated in different ways. Since they are interconnected, a change in the meaning of one leads to shifts in the meanings of the others. This flexibility accounts for their ability to accommodate and account for the major shifts in the loci of economic and political power over the last seventy years.

Certain of the Moroccan concepts that I will describe also have rich historical layers of meaning and are used elsewhere in the Muslim world. This is especially true of *God's will* and *reason*. Both of these terms occur in the Qur'an and have been the subject of an interesting study of the world view of seventh-century Arabs (Izutsu 1964). They also appear in James Siegel's account of changing perceptions of the world in northern Sumatra (1969: esp. 98–133). I am interested in seeing the elaboration and integration of these concepts principally in their Moroccan context, but I point out their uses elsewhere to show the range of variations attached to them. Popular uses of these terms in Morocco vary from those implicit in formal Islamic texts, including the Qur'an. Such divergences are not the concern of this study, for the simple reason that in ordinary situations most informants never considered the possibility that these terms could be understood in any way but theirs. The fact that these concepts are tacitly construed by Moroccans as Islamic, if not human, universals, makes their resulting vision of the world all the more reasonable and compelling.

God's Will and the Social Order

The inequality of men in this world (*ed-denya*) is too matter-of-fact to be a matter of speculation to most Moroccans. These inequalities are attributed to God's will, a concept which explains the present state of affairs as well as the outcome of any future sequence of events. *God's will* (*qodret Allah*) is a term from classical Arabic, although it is used by almost all informants, including tribesmen, as synonymous with "that which is recorded or written" (*l-mqayyed* or *l-mektub*). Perhaps the most common expression of this concept occurs in the phrase "if God wills" (*in sha Allah*), which invariably prefaces any expression of future action or events. These concepts have often been glossed in colonial ethnography as Islamic "fatalism," a term so ambiguous as to have minimal explanatory utility. Much of French colonial ethnography eagerly represented Moroccan society as frozen in time and incapable of meaningful internal change (e.g., Lévi-Provençal 1922:11). The equation of "God's will" with "fatalism" fit the colonizer's vision of the native better than it did the Moroccan's assumptions about "the way things are."

For Boujadi-s and other Moroccans, the notion of God's will implies quite the contrary of popular French colonial ethnography: men are free to take the world as it is and to determine action on the basis of their empirical observations. The actual state of affairs is an expression of God's will. Being inevitable it cannot be questioned.

God's will legitimates the present—and ephemeral—distribution of social honor as the God-given state of affairs. The ranking of individuals in relation to one another is never taken for granted but is constantly empirically tested. Provisionality is the very essence of the cosmos. Consequently, attention is focused upon assessing exact differentials of wealth, success, power, and social honor among *particular* men as a prelude to effective, specific social action, not upon speculation over the general order of the world. God reveals his will through what happens in the world, and men of reason constantly modify their own courses of action to accommodate this will.

Far from providing cosmological ballast to an ossified status quo and discouraging the planning of future action, the concept of God's will attenuates speculation on why particular projects succeed or fail and blocks metaphysical reflection on the fate of man in this world. The wide-awake man is thus much more concerned with adjusting to circumstances as they come along than with considering how things might have been or should be. An elderly, salaried Qur'an-reader, who formerly collected offerings at the shrine of Sidi Mḥam-med Sherqi, explained the concept in the following manner:

> God created the world. He decides and knows everything. You have a car and I don't. That's God's will [*qodret Al-lah*]. One day it might be taken away from you. That's also God's will. If you are a shopkeeper, how you treat people doesn't always affect your business. There are bad-tempered traders like M—— who are still rich and successful. God decides whose affairs prosper.[1]

A Boujadi shoemaker articulated the same concept in explaining what he would do if someone told him his sons had been seen drinking:

> If [my sons] had heads they would realize what other people were saying and leave off their conduct. As a father I would tell them to stop. If they didn't, then they would show no respect for their father. That is written [*mqay-yed*]. If they continued, that also would be written. Similarly, I tell my sons to study and beat them. The younger boy is always playing in the streets, but he is better at school. Should I ask him why he is playing [i.e., get him to stop]? He knows his lessons. The older boy always reads his lessons aloud in front of me but he is worse in school. How can I judge who is the better of the two? That is God's affair.

He applied the same concept to explain the ethos of competitive settlement among merchants and craftsmen:

> If there are five ironsmiths next to each other and a tribesman comes wanting his plough fixed, no one calls out for the client to come to him. That would be improper [*hshu-ma*]. You say nothing and the person will come to whomever God has chosen. Of course if you know the way things are done [*qaʿida*] and deal fairly and politely with people they may do the same with you. But whether they actually do so is also God's affair.

In Morocco, the concept of God's will also emphasizes the limits of responsibility of one man for the moral and economic fate of others. Their fate is God's; and each man looks after himself (*ydebber raṣu*).

> God created differences among people. And of many who are young [he referred to some nephews in their twenties], they still have time; they will learn. Let people do as they want. God distinguishes between them. A Muslim's duty is just to show people the path to those who wish to be with God, and that is that. Either they take it or leave it. The Prophets allow them the choice. There is paradise and there is hell, and God will select who goes to each. (A Makhzen official)

Men are bound together by multiple social obligations, but these tend to be particularistic. There are abstract, normative obligations incumbent upon each member of the Muslim community (*umma*) to aid other Muslims, but these obligations tend to be stylized. Thus, almsgiving (*ṣadaqa*), an obligatory precept of Islam, tends to be performed on such occasions as the day of 'Ashura, a feast day in the Muslim lunar calendar on which a tithe is given to the poor, on market days when beggars make the rounds of merchants, and frequently when one is about to undertake a long and arduous journey. The limit of men's responsibility toward one another is illustrated by the fact that many rich merchants and notaries in Boujad, all considered pious Muslims, made fortunes in the famine of 1945 by purchasing land from tribesmen and houses from townsmen for a few measures of grain, turning tribesmen into sharecroppers and townsmen into tenants. Since the allocation of men's fate is God's affair, no Boujadi-s suggested that this sort of action was ruthless or morally objectionable.

At least on occasion, many Boujadi-s recognize incongruities between what they perceive as fundamental Muslim ideals and "the way things are" (*qaʿida*), but this perception does not lead to any significant tension between ideal and real. Even in the interior of the mosque, where informants insist on the absence of inequalities of Muslims before God, men of prestige tend to have their customary places of prayer, which men of lesser prestige avoid. In small quarter mosques, the presence of a man of stature during evening prayers often causes the mosque to be avoided by men of lesser stature. On one such occasion, I asked a Boujadi I knew well why he abruptly turned away from a small quarter mosque he regularly attended without saying his evening prayers. He simply denied that the incident could have taken place, since normatively it should not have. Emphatically, however, the incongruity between norm and conduct constituted no dilemma for my informant.

There are several ways in which incongruities between "the way things are" and Islamic ideals are made reasonable. One is to say that the world at present is defective or corrupt (*khayba*):

> These times are rotten [*had l-weqt mkhasser*]. No one wants religion now. Everyone wants the path of money. Once a notary ['*adel*] was a learned man; now he is just anyone with connections and money to buy the post. It is a game. (A Makhzen official)

> Everyone wants to show his influence [*kelma*]. The Minister [*wazir*] has a sofa as high as your knee; so the *qaid* wants one as high as your chest. This has been the state of the world since Adam. (A broommaker)

Such complaints reverberate throughout the writings of centuries of Moroccan historiographers, indicating that they are not peculiar to the last few decades (Lévi-Provençal 1922).

A complementary explanation of incongruities is to claim that some professed Muslims are ignorant of what Islam "really" entails. *Islam* literally means "submission," and an "ignorant" person (*jahel*) is one who is uncontrolled and unsubmissive, a slave to his passions.[2] Sometimes individuals are so characterized, but just as often the term is applied to entire categories of persons. The assertion that many do not abide by the Islamic code of conduct then makes comprehensible the present imperfect state of the world:

> Those people in the countryside, those ignorant people, what do they know of Islam? They don't pray or fast. They just live like animals: sleep, eat and work, and give grain and animals to any con man [*gheddar*] from the *zawya* or a brotherhood. (A merchant, once prominent in the Istiqlal [Independence] party)

Another educated informant made the following comment about
the widespread belief in marabouts:

> These stories of the marabouts bringing Islam to the Magh-
> reb, they are all lies. People use them just to collect money
> from the ignorant. Islam came to the Maghreb with 'Uqba
> ben Nafi.[3] People converted, but they did not remain Mus-
> lims. 'Uqba was near Tangier when a soothsayer [*kahen*,
> "one who practices magic"] approached him and killed
> him. People did not stay Muslim until after the time of
> Mulay Driss.[4] But most men are still ignorant. They do
> not know what is and is not Islam and what their ancestors
> did and did not do. So they are happy for someone to tell
> them stories about marabouts.

Those who assert that they really "know" Islam feel under no obligation to dispel the ignorance of others. If others want to change
their way of thinking and acting, that is God's and their own concern. Each man looks after his own interests and takes the world as
it is. Islamic precepts are acknowledged as ideals but are peripheral
to social action in this world because they are unattainable. A man's
attention is directed away from an ideal normative state of affairs:
"God has given that which is [*had esh-shi lli 'ta Allah, had esh-shi lli
kayn*]."

Reason as a Social Concept

Since the pattern of events of any given moment is divinely ordained,
the "reasonable" man sets about perceiving the multiple empirical
ties between persons and adapting them to his interests as best he can.
All formal roles—kinship, political, religious, and economic—are
open to a wide range of negotiation as to their exact parameters and
contents.

Reason (*'qal*) is the capacity to discern the meaning of social action and, on the basis of this perception, to engage in effective social
action. It signifies adroitness or cleverness, without the pejorative
English connotations of the latter word, more than a capacity for
dealing with abstract rational phenomena. Its possession assumes an
empirical knowledge of and capacity to manipulate the shared code
of conduct called the *qa'ida*, "the way things are done."

Reason enables a man to perceive what will pass as acceptable and approved conduct in the management of his various social obligations to kinsmen, neighbors, merchants, and clients, men of influence and men without, and how to weigh these various commitments in relation to one another. The classical Arabic verb from which 'qal is derived can carry the meaning "to hobble a camel" and in other contexts can signify "confinement" or "control." These original meanings vividly parallel the contemporary Moroccan usage. Reason provides a man control over his nature (*ṭbi'a*) and passions (*shehwat*; sg., *shehwa*) within the precepts of Islam. Several informants explained this by citing a popularly known Qur'anic aphorism: "Man has reason. He distinguishes between that which harms him and that which doesn't."[5] Ordinarily the *qa'ida* provides a rough guide to "proper" behavior.

A majority of Boujadi-s ordinarily assume that the *qa'ida* is based upon, if not identical to, Islamic law (*shra'*) in both its jural and its moral sense. In its jural sense, Islamic law is composed of those rules of conduct which in principle are enforced in a *qauli*'s court: contracts and procedures related to marriage, divorce, inheritance, and certain property transactions. In its moral sense the Islamic law also prescribes the obligations of a Muslim: the five "pillars" of ritual prayer, fasting, pilgrimage to Mecca, alms, and the confession of faith that there is no God but God and Muhammed is his Prophet. In scholarly texts there exists a complex set of prescriptions for conduct, many based upon the Prophet's life. Few Moroccans know these in any detail. In its more popular sense as a code of conduct, Islamic law as popularly understood glides imperceptibly into "the way things are done" (*qa'ida*). For Boujadi-s who distinguish between them, *shra'* usually refers to specific, known precepts of Islam, while *qa'ida* refers to more generalized patterns of acceptable conduct: styles of greeting, bargaining, and other expected forms of deference and civility in the conduct of social relations. Most Boujadi-s, however, tacitly assume that Islam is what Muslims do, or should be expected to do, and thus merge the two concepts.

The *shra'* and *qa'ida* as popularly understood together provide "recipe" prescriptions for acceptable social action. The *shra'* is considered ideologically to be immutable, and many Boujadi-s will make similar claims of the *qa'ida*. Since the latter is unwritten and the former is inaccessible in written form to virtually all Boujadi-s, there are, however, no effective criteria by which the claim of immutability can be demonstrated. Thus, from an analytical point of view the code of conduct is responsive to the shared, constantly renegotiated universe of meaning within which Moroccans live and is amenable to transformation.

Men acquire reason as they assume a greater autonomy in the social world. Thus, at birth a child has no reason at all and in this respect is indistinguishable from animals.

> How could a child have [reason]? When he is born he has absolutely nothing. How could he know the *shra'*? Islamic law doesn't rule [*tă-yhkem*] over him; it doesn't control his conduct. Reason grows in the child when he learns to distinguish, to weigh [his actions]. When he is small he will put his hand in the fire because he doesn't know it will burn. When he grows older—by Islamic law when he is eighteen [*sic*]—he has reason. But God gives reason earlier to many children.
>
> To have reason means that you must know the Islamic law. You must pray and fast. A good father will teach these things to his son beginning at the age of seven—take him to the mosque, encourage him to fast at least part of the day during Ramadan.
>
> First you try to lead him by words, later with beatings if he doesn't listen. If he disobeys you and doesn't begin praying and fasting, then people will say of the father as well that he doesn't have reason. (A shoemaker)

Reason is considered more likely to be fully developed in men than in women. This is not due to any innate masculine capacity, but to the fact that the activities of a woman are confined primarily to her household and quarter. Hence a woman's reason, or ability to engage effectively in a wide range of social relations, is, like that of children, considered to be less than that of men. Some women are cited as exceptions, but the general rule is unquestioned. This is not to say that women lack power. Within their own sphere they are recognized as having formidable capacities for action. Women are often thought to be familiar with magical acts and other practices only dimly known by ordinary men. Being less restrained by reason, women are fully able to draw upon these resources in pursuit of their interests.

Men have reason and know how to get what they want.
They are not quick to run to the Makhzen and to the
street when their child gets a bloody nose. If a woman sees
her child fighting in the street, she joins in without asking
what has happened and is ready to fight another woman.
They don't have heads. (A Sherqawi grain merchant)

A man will think. He sees the quarrel leading to the
Makhzen; he knows the other man has more "pull"
[*shoqa*] with the Makhzen than he does. He knows how
to deal with people bigger and weaker than he is. A woman
is light-headed [*khfifa*]. She doesn't know how to do these
things. If she goes to the *biru* [French *bureau*, government
offices], who pays attention to her? Better that she stay at
home, where she can teach her daughters to cook and sew.
They don't know Islam like men do; they even have tricks
to avoid fasting. (A vegetable-seller)

You must keep a close watch on your women and children,
because their reasoning is weak. If you don't want to see
a man and you tell your wife and children to say you're
not at home, they will say to the man that you are home
but told them to say that you aren't. Or if you want them
to keep quiet about a fight, they won't be able to. (A schoolteacher)

From the vantage point of townsmen, tribesmen are another category of persons deficient in reason. Since reason is judged by the ability of a person to demonstrate knowledge of "how things are done"
in relevant social contexts, tribesmen often are somewhat handicapped in town settings. While most have multiple ties with kinsmen
and others who have migrated to towns, these ties are usually less
effective than those available to townsmen in facilitating commercial, legal, and administrative transactions.

Since most tribesmen are illiterate, it is easier to deceive them and
to make them act in an "unreasonable" manner in urban settings.
Especially bewildering are the mechanics of court procedure. Parts
of the court sessions are in classical Arabic (as when the judge dic-
tates to his clerk). Most townsmen also find classical Arabic hard to

follow, but they can anticipate actions in court more successfully. In
the Islamic law courts, plaintiffs and defendants must have depositions prepared on their behalf. Even the rare literate tribesman has
difficulty in understanding these documents. Since notaries are paid
for each document they prepare, they often knowingly allow tribesmen to commission and bring before the court documents that are
without judicial merit. The entire process is seen as unpredictable by
tribesmen, and tempers flare in the courtroom. One *qadi* said: "Most
of the cases in my court are from the country, because country people
have less '*qal* than townsmen. They don't know how to deal with each
other; so they fight openly and end up in court."

Another sign of men who lack reason is a futile public display of
anger. In court, for instance, tribesmen often challenge the judge to
throw them in prison after they have been ordered to support a divorced wife. After one such outburst a *qadi* said: "What do I care if
he goes to prison or not? If he had reason he wouldn't say that." The
implication is that a man with reason would recognize the futility
of his loss of self-control.

Reason concerns the "inner" state of a man only in so far as he has
the ability to exercise control over his impulses. Proper conduct is
linked principally to efficacious performance in the social order, not
to one's inner state or to abstract moral or ethical principles. Emphasis
is placed on the ability of a man to control whatever "natural" impulses he might have and to present a "wide-awake" alertness toward
social obligations and social action. The conduct of a reasonable man
shows "balance" (*mizan*), the ability to calculate a course of social
action in relation to its consequences for a total network of social
relations.

For example, by Islamic law certain individuals have fixed rights
in inheritance from certain relatives. One Boujadi, in a client relation
to an elder brother much more prosperous than he, described how he
acted at the division of his father's estate:

> I did not demand my share of the inheritance and choose
> which of his possessions I wanted. So that we would remain
> on good terms [*bqa 'qalu*], I told my brother to leave my
> share in a corner, and I would come and pick it up later.
> If I fought or tried to have influence [*kelma*], I might get
> a larger share, but my brother would no longer help me.

Ideally, the reasonable man is taciturn and not prone to listen to gossip or allow "everything in the market" to enter his head. Nevertheless he keeps close tabs on the actions of others while giving the impression of a man who keeps his own counsel and weighs the consequences of his actions. Again, he is in full control of himself and never acts impulsively:

> If a reasonable man is in a group of ten or twelve people he will say only a few words, but each of these words will be weighed. You talk of high things. You do not say that Fulan [the Moroccan equivalent of "Jones"] was here and Fulan was there and he said this and that. You speak, but within the code for conduct [*qa'ida*]. A green-headed person [*kheddar*]⁶ who runs from one shop to another carrying stories of what people are doing is without value. After all, how do you know whether that person is saying what he has heard or not? What is his objective [*gharad*]? If you act on what he says and later find out that he lied, he will deny his words. It is another matter if you always deal [*te-tsaref*] with another person, and drink tea with him. Then a man is more likely to tell you something reasonable. Which is better, something you buy for ten *ryal*-s, or for fifteen? People are like that too. (A grain-trader)

> If you say everything you know to a man who is your friend, that is fine as long as he remains your friend. But you might quarrel tomorrow, and then he will harm you with his knowledge. Do you know the story of the dove? She had her babies in a nest high in a tree. She cooed and a snake heard her, climbed the tree, and ate the children. (A carpenter)

A shoemaker described a situation in which a local government clerk paid less than the generally understood price (*qa'ida*) for some repairs:

> I did not tell him directly that he owed me more. If I did he would have been embarrassed [*tă-yhshem*]. He would

have paid, but the next time I went to the Makhzen to ask for something, he would have remembered. I might have had to wait for days to get his attention. Instead when he next came to me I said I had no leather. Then from another shoemaker he learned the price and realized why I said I had no leather. Then he paid my due. So he was not embarrassed, I got my price, and there is nothing [i.e., no friction] between us. He knows me as a reasonable man.

Since open disagreement or the direct refusal to comply with someone's request both have the effect of challenging his status, the reasonable man attempts such a challenge only after careful calculation:

If you want me to go to the other side of town I will agree when you ask me, but will then go and sit in the house or at the market where I always sit. The next day you will ask me why I didn't go. I will tell you that my brother came, my legs hurt, or some other such thing. You know that my brother did not come and that my legs are good, but you will understand that I had some reason for not going. I want you to be well-disposed to me and was embarrassed to say "no" to your face. I say "yes" to avoid friction [*le-mhakka*], and thus your "reason" is not "broken." (Owner of a public oven)

Reasonable men do not stand on absolute rights or wrongs. They accommodate themselves to social realities. They make themselves aware of ongoing changes in the shared cognitive map of the social universe and realize that the "rules of the game" call for constant, active negotiation over the content and contours of that map. This understanding of the world should by no means be taken for the amoral opportunism by which Edward C. Banfield characterizes the world view of Sicilians (1967). Moroccans place a great value upon maintaining the proprieties of the social order. Thus, to "break" the reason of another person, as in the above quote, is to challenge the assumptions of social ranking implicit in his conduct. Even when such challenges are deliberate, the reasonable course is to proceed whenever possible by indirection, leaving room for face-saving maneuvers on the part of those who stand to lose. As social positions are changed, the attempt is made to do this with minimal overt confrontation.

Since social honor is ephemeral, one's situation is easily liable to reversal.

The most significant expression of reason and its relation to the Islamic code of conduct is in the complex symbolism associated with the month of fasting, Ramadan. Ramadan and the rituals associated with it are thought to sum up much of what it means to be a Muslim. For most Moroccans, it is the period in which Islam is most consciously brought to play in daily routines.

Some neo-orthodox modernists (Salafi-s) erroneously claim that Ramadan separates those who deal with marabouts from those who "know [formal] Islam." This is empirically false. For the majority of tribesmen and many older townsmen, dealing with marabouts and participating in formal Islamic rituals present them with no intellectual or moral contradiction. Moreover, fasting is as widespread in the countryside as in the towns. Equally misleading are the interpretations of the nationalist press, which carries articles, curiously taken mainly from the writings of an earlier generation of European orientalists, which view Ramadan foremost as a diacritical mark distinguishing between Muslims and Christians, or justify the fast by its supposed medical virtues. Neither of these interpretations, however, is particularly widespread.

For most Moroccans, the celebration of Ramadan distinguishes men with reason.[7] Throughout the year there is, of course, an elaborate Islamic ritual cycle which includes five daily prayers, communal prayers on Friday, a feast marking the end of Ramadan ('Id es-Sghir or 'Id le-Ftur), and the Great Feast ('Id le-Kbir, the Feast of Abraham), among others. In principle, the Muslim community as a whole participates in these various rituals, although in practice they are primarily activities of adult, urban males and some members of the rural elite. In contrast, the rituals associated with Ramadan are performed by the entire Muslim community, except children, pregnant women, and others excused for reasons of health.

To Boujadi-s, the fast implicitly symbolizes the capacity of man to regulate his nature and live by the rules of society which God has revealed through his Prophet. During Ramadan, as at other times, there is no denial of man's passions or appetites. Between sunset and early morning, life is carried on much as usual, except that those who ordinarily drink alcoholic beverages cease to do so for the entire month.[8] Those who smoke will abstain during the day. Fasting during the day dramatically symbolizes man's ability to discipline his desires in accordance with the arbitrary code of conduct laid down by God. Men's capacity to follow the divine model reaffirms that they are not bound by their passions to live in a totally anarchic world. Daily prayers also symbolize the divine template for conduct, but Ramadan is recognized as a more intensive, sustained discipline of human nature. Although work habits are modified to alleviate the physiological tensions which accompany fasting, tempers often run short. Most people will, however, try to show their reason, and hence their capacity to follow the Islamic code of conduct, by avoiding situations in which they lose their self-control.

Deference and Propriety

Reason grows in a person with his ability to perceive the social order and to discipline himself to act effectively within it. Proper social comportment within this framework is symbolized by the concept of *theshsham*, or *hshumiya*. These terms approximate the English concept of *propriety* (which is the translation I give to the terms when used in the abstract), although they are also used in contexts where the English terms *deference, respect, circumspection*, and occasionally *embarrassment* would be fitting.

The locus of propriety is not so much the inner moral consciousness of a person as his public comportment with respect to those with whom he has regular face-to-face relations. A person is said to lack propriety when he is caught outside the image which he is expected to project of himself before "significant others." Maintenance of "proper" comportment reflects one's possession of reason.

Like reason, propriety is a quality which persons acquire as they mature. It is inculcated by parents, especially the father, and to a certain extent by other relatives and outsiders. This is achieved both by suggestion and, on occasion, by the use of physical force. As a son acquires reason, he is expected increasingly to show deference toward his father in the household and in public.

Before boys are taken to the mosque and initiated in the fast, fathers as well as mothers play with their sons and show affection and tenderness (*hanana*) toward them.[9] As a boy matures, only the women of the household, especially his mother, continue manifestly to display affection toward him. Mothers and sons develop strong, expressed ties of affection: widowed or divorced mothers frequently live with their sons and look to them for moral and economic support. It is believed that if a father were to continue to be affectionate with his son as he matured, the son "would become soft like a woman, allowing others to dominate him [st'ămaru]." Thus the father increasingly assumes a greater formality with his son and becomes hard (qaṣeḥ) with him.

As a boy matures, he increasingly strives to avoid situations in which his father or other persons can exercise domination over him. This often entails tacit public avoidance of the father, even when the son continues to live in the same household. This avoidance continues after a son becomes economically autonomous and establishes his own household. It does not indicate active hostility so much as a desire to avoid situations in which the son, himself the head of a household, is placed in a position in which his own "word" must be circumscribed. On the marriage of a son, the father avoids those aspects of the celebration which would bring him into direct contact with his son. He generally sits with his friends in a separate room, away from the female dancers (shikha-s) and musicians usually called in for the celebration. Direct contact between father and son on such an occasion is thought to be highly improper.

Propriety is similarly related to subordination and restraint outside of the household. Among examples of impropriety are acts of adultery, homosexuality, or other illicit sexual exploits, at least if they become publicly known; fighting in the street; being caught in the act of stealing; and various forms of deceit and exploitation .These are considered less as "immoral" than as "improper" acts. It is their public knowledge which is the subject of greatest concern, since, as one Boujadi said, only God knows the true motivation of a person's actions.

In women, modesty (le-ḥya), obedience to her husband, and the avoidance of any behavior which would publicly imply that she is not subordinate to her husband are principal elements of proper conduct. Sexuality in this case is, of course, heavily symbolic of patterns of deference.

As indicated in the above account of father-son relations, impropriety often arises when the will of one person is openly challenged or blocked by that of another, or when a person assumes a social role which others are not willing to accord him. Thus it is embarrassing to ask for something from a relative, associate, or stranger and to have the request refused. Considerable intellectual energy, especially involving the use of intermediaries, is spent constructing situations so as to avoid such overt confrontations.

As an illustration of the attention paid to such tactics, one informant explained why he never entered the house of a higher-ranking neighbor on his own initiative:

> I was embarrassed [*kont te-nehshem*] [to do so]. He's a big man in the Makhzen. He might insult a less influential man or push him around if he doesn't restrain his conduct in front of him. If you call at his house without being asked to come, he gets a bad idea of you and says that you're no good or "uppity" [*fik sentiha*]. Then he will push you around. That's how big men [*le-kobbar*] are, especially if they don't know you. You must be respectful [*heshman*] with them.[10]

The nuances of propriety are elaborated in numerous ways. These include spatial hierarchies—from sitting at a distance from social superiors and avoiding unnecessary encounters with them, to being at an intimate distance to men of prestige. The seating patterns of guests at a meal and the order in which they are served give subtle nuances of hierarchy. The most precisely calibrated patterns of deference emerge in styles of greetings. Most informants are uncomfortable about explicitly discussing their implications, particularly those which reflect the most pronounced inequality. Ignoring a deferential greeting or unceremoniously rebuffing one underlines extreme social distance. Kissing the feet, or the hem or sleeve of another's *jellaba* (a type of North African robe with a hood), similarly expresses extreme social difference. Sons kiss the hands of their father, uncles, and guests as an act of deference. The same greeting is also offered to certain officials. Some informants justify this by saying that officials are representatives of the king and emphasize the latter's role as God's deputy (*khalifet Allah fel-l-ard*). Submission, they claim, is to the office, not the individual. Actual practice, however, goes far beyond deference to persons in their official capacities. It is extended to anyone to whom it is felt that deference is necessary or useful. To use an appropriate American colloquialism, you kiss the hand you can't cut off. As relations of equality are approximated, reciprocal handshakes and embraces become common. Public acknowledgment of one's place in the social order and proper conduct toward significant others implies primarily a circumspection and cleverness designed to avoid censure and heighten one's chances of success in the social order.

To summarize the argument so far, the concept of God's will directs attention to what actually happens in social relations and away from abstract considerations of why things are the way they are. Reason is the capacity to discern realistically existing, if ephemeral, patterns of dominance and deference in the social order and to act appropriately. Propriety entails the circumspection necessary to act within the shared code of conduct. The next concept that I will describe, obligation, indicates more clearly how these preceding concepts articulate with the social order.

Obligation

The particularistic social ties which constitute the fabric of the social order are contracted and maintained by the exchange of obligations (*hăqq*-s). Men cannot control God's allocation of success, but they can render the actions of other men, including marabouts, more predictable by contracting and maintaining ties of obligation. The nature of these obligations and the persons with whom they are held provide an index of social honor, although since the totality of anyone's ties is rarely known, these indices must always be approximate. *Hăqq* is a polysemic term which, according to context in colloquial Arabic, can mean "share," "privilege," or "obligation."[11] One speaks of having an obligation "over" or "in" someone else (*fih l-hăqq*, *'lik l-hăqq*). Some obligations are minimally prescribed by Islamic law and "the way things are done" (*qa'ida*), such as certain obligations toward kinsmen and communal religious ties. Even these obligations can be fulfilled within a wide latitude of acceptable conduct.

A number of actions can initiate a relationship of obligation: an invitation to a meal, performance as a go-between, or any other service or assistance. An obligation contracted by one means, such as service as an intermediary, need not necessarily be reciprocated in the same form. Obligations can also be contracted by omission: a missed appointment (at least between individuals of nearly equal social honor) creates an obligation on the part of the person who failed to keep the appointment. The mere offer of a service or support imposes obligations as effectively as an action actually performed. Even exchanges of greetings, by their complex code of gestures and manners, impose obligations, since they publicly assert what one person would like the other, and observers, to think regarding their relations.

Obligations are not directly convertible into cash. In the context of a regular, multifaceted social relationship, such an insinuation would be considered base and vile (*duni*). However, if there is no viable bond with the person being approached, a "sweetener" (*hlawa*) or bribe (*reshwa*) is part of accepted, even if not condoned, social practice. The term *reshwa*, for example, also designates the nonreturnable gift, which, apart from the bridewealth (*sdaq*), is given by the groom to his bride's father in order to expedite consent for the marriage. In themselves, such cash transactions are not considered immoral. Theoretically they can be considered to be the limit case of *ḥăqq* relationships in that they imply a one-time reciprocity. Baseness is generally attributed to such transactions only when the price exacted is considered abusive in light of the resources of the person making a request or when that person is capable of performing a reciprocal service of value at some later time. In the latter case, it would be considered both brash and lacking in reason to demand cash. There is a moral component here, but most informants emphasized the propriety, not the morality, of such situations. Another form of one-time exchange is the immediate reciprocation of an obligation, such as an invitation to a meal, with one of equal value. Such action often signals a desire not to enter into an ongoing relationship. An overt display of this intention is regarded as improper.

A category of transaction that falls outside the sphere of obligations is called *fabor*, which literally signifies a gratuitous act. The term *fabor* probably derives from Mediterranean port *sabir*, or lingua franca, rather than directly from the Spanish *favor* (see Lanly 1970). Its foreignness suggests that it is peripheral to the conduct of social relations in Morocco. The term *fabor* is often used in requesting alms from foreigners or in demanding services which the supplicant cannot reciprocate. Ideologically, the giving and receiving of alms (*sadaqa*) between Moroccans are also outside of the calculation of obligation. Nonetheless, an implicitly triangular reciprocity is involved. Beggars ask God or a marabout to repay the donor on their behalf. The same sort of triangular relationship is initiated in making a request to a person of much greater prestige.

Similarly, a man to whom God has allocated prosperity is supposed to be generous (*krim*), taking what God has given him and willingly distributing it to others. Such generosity (*karama*) manifests itself in largesse to guests, in such pious works (*ihsan*) as the construction and maintenance of mosques or orphanages, or—to indicate the flexibility of the concept—in provision for the salary of a trainer for the local soccer team. Such acts directly contribute to a man's social honor by legitimating his wealth but are not considered to entail specific reciprocal obligations on the part of those who benefit by them. "There is no bill for *karama* in this world," as informants say, but *karama*, while not explicitly considered by Moroccans as an obligation, follows the same principles. To accept the generosity of someone without being able to reciprocate is to confirm the superior status of the donor.

The complex web of personally contracted bonds of obligation by which society is knit together is always asymmetrical. All relationships impose obligations of calculable intensity. The dominant partner in such a tie is said to have "word" (*kelma*) over the other. The relation is that of patron-client if it is fairly regular and marked by such pronounced inequality that the client cannot reciprocate with services of equal magnitude. "Word" exists even when the relationship is much more finely tuned. There is a carefully nuanced vocabulary and repertoire of gestures for the discussion of these gradations, which depend on a wide range of such factors as education, wealth, kinship ties, and networks of obligations held or thought to be held with others.

The reason why dominance is so coveted in this system is that it allows a man to be autonomous, to assert his claim to be a full social person. In so far as a person is obliged to defer to the wishes of others, his autonomy and social honor are diminished. All members of the society utilize the skills and resources available to them to compete for dominance. Thus, the head of a household wants formally to assert his dominance over its other members. The comportment of wives, sons, daughters, kinsmen, and servants associated with his household affects to a certain extent his own social honor. The comportment of these individuals is expected to be orchestrated as far as possible with his own interests or at least (especially in the case of adult married sons in his household or already living apart) not publicly discordant with them.

There is a specific avoidance whenever possible of relationships which entail a sharing of authority or of responsibility with other persons, such as partnerships in a business enterprise or the sharing between certain relatives of a household. The popular proverb "A thousand debts before I become anyone's partner [*alf medyanin u-la meshruk*]" is to a large extent borne out in social reality.[12] The reason for this avoidance of partnerships is that, in relations of near equality, the "word" (*kelma*) of a person is more easily called into question. Since each person strives to have "word" in social relations and at the same time tries to minimize situations in which he is obligated to others, the near-egalitarian relations of obligation contain a continual, inherent tension. Necessity often demands that a person enter into definite relations of deference to others, although in some circumstances such a tie (as when a person is known as factotum for someone of much higher prestige) can be a means of advancing social honor.

In general, the reasonable individual strives for flexibility in relations in which he is under obligation to others, while at the same time fixing as firmly as possible relations in which he holds obligations "over" other individuals. Since by God's will "the way things are" is constantly in flux, an individual strives to be as free as possible to change the weight of obligations within his personal network, yet to remain within the bounds of propriety.

The vocabulary used in speaking of relationships of obligation implies this ledger concept of exchange. One term frequently used to indicate a contractual relationship of obligation literally means "to exchange" (*tsaref*; n., *msarfa*). Persons who "exchange" with each other are called "companions" or "associates" (*shab*; sg., *saheb*), a term which in itself carries no connotation of affective relations. It simply describes persons who regularly deal with each other. This is not to argue that affective relations are nonexistent or unimportant in Moroccan society. They are, however, decidedly subordinate to relations of obligation. A person who jeopardizes his own interests in steadfastly supporting another is often considered "unreasonable" or, in other words, defective in his cognitive map of the realities of the social world.

Below is a typical example of how obligations are contracted, slightly edited, from my field notes. It is so commonplace, undramatic, and "trivial" to Moroccans that none of the actions described needs explanation to be intelligible. It is remarkable, however, in that one of the participants in the events, here called Ḥmed, was aware of my work and willing to interpret what he understood of his own role in the incident and those of the other actors.

> In [a town adjoining Boujad] I was in the large American car of a wealthy local official, Ḥajj Ṣaleḥ, who made his fortune by buying land during the famine of 1945. With us was a recently arrived official, Ḥajj Ḥmed, who in the Makhzen was the immediate superior of the car-owner, but inferior in wealth and—at least for the moment—local influence. Also in the car was Bu 'Azza, a moderately prosperous tribesman who had come to seek the advice of Ḥajj Ḥmed. Near the market, we passed a man with a few chickens. Ḥmed asked Ṣaleḥ to stop the car so that Bu 'Azza could run out and buy him a chicken. "These [name of tribe] really know how to buy chickens," Ḥmed said as he watched the transaction from the car. When Bu 'Azza returned, a scruffy-looking individual followed him, put his head in the window, and said to no one in particular that Bu 'Azza owed him 80 *ryal*-s. Bu 'Azza said nothing. Ṣaleḥ, ignoring the intruder, told his driver to proceed. The driver sounded the car's deafening bus horn to clear the road of carts and pedestrians and began to move. No one in the car made any overt sign of being aware that the man's head was still in the window in an effort to keep the car from moving and settle the transaction. Then Ḥmed asked Ṣaleḥ to stop the car, said to Bu 'Azza's alleged creditor: "Here's 20 *ryal*-s of the debt," and diffidently threw the money out the window. Again the car started, but this time Bu 'Azza asked for a halt so that he could pay his creditor the other 60 *ryal*-s.

According to Ḥmed, Bu 'Azza, the tribesman, was sent to bargain for the chicken, because at the time he was in a relation of obligation to Ḥmed. Since Bu 'Azza did not know whether Ḥmed would pay, he could be trusted to argue for the lowest price possible. (Ḥmed repaid Bu 'Azza for the chicken shortly afterward.)

In paying Bu 'Azza's debt, Ḥmed did not know anything of its nature or whether a debt existed at all. The individual to whom the money was given was in his eyes a beggar, one unable to reciprocate. The money given to him was thus *karama*, that is, the passing on of God's bounty with no anticipation of repayment. Such an act gives a man a claim to high social honor in the eyes of other Muslims.

Later my informant, Ḥmed, spoke of his relations with his subordinate official, Ṣaleḥ. There was no question that Ṣaleḥ could manipulate officials to his advantage both locally and in Rabat. Ḥmed, as Ṣaleḥ's bureaucratic superior, faced the delicate problem of having to treat Ṣaleḥ as a person of the same level of prestige. Ḥmed's tone and gestures never became peremptory with Ṣaleḥ, as they did with other subordinates. No direct assertion of "word" was possible; informally Ṣaleḥ, while not as well educated or as smooth in his etiquette, dress, or speech, was decidedly more influential. The fact that Ḥmed was riding in Ṣaleḥ's car rather than his own reflected this. Significantly, however, he performed an act of *karama* in front of Ṣaleḥ and other witnesses, while Ṣaleḥ attempted no such gesture. Ḥmed, by performing an act which Ṣaleḥ showed no sign of undertaking, tacitly asserted a higher social honor.

The action reported above had another meaning in relation to Bu 'Azza. For him, the payment on his behalf put him in a further relation of obligation (*ḥăqq*) to Ḥmed. By asking something of Ḥmed and later having a part of a debt paid on his behalf, he became Ḥmed's client, under obligation to perform a service for him in the indefinite future. At the time of the incident, Ḥmed had no such clients locally and needed them to ensure the flow of information necessary to perform his functions.

The modalities of initiating ties of obligation are particularly clear in the case of encounters between individuals from different parts of Morocco, where mutual knowledge of social networks and individual abilities is incomplete or only circumstantial. A local Makhzen official spoke of how, when he first arrived in Boujad, some Sherqawa tried to put him in a relation of obligation.

> They invited me to a meal. I could not refuse. They, and others later, would kill one sheep, sometimes two. A few days later they came to me and asked that some documents be changed. Another time they brought an entire tribal council [*jmaʻa*] and grain and sheep for me. I didn't even

> know for certain how much "word" they had. They tried
> to embarrass me [*t-ḥashemni*] into helping them get what-
> ever they wanted.

Persons are expected to reaffirm continually those ties which they
want to maintain. Some key occasions when such reaffirmations are
expected include marriages, births, and deaths; the graduation of a
son or daughter from school; completion of a child's studies at the
mosque; departure for and return from the pilgrimage to Mecca; and
religious feast days. Neighbors, associates, relatives, and anyone with
whom there is an ongoing social tie are expected to acknowledge such
occasions by congratulations, a gift, or attendance at the celebration.
Receptions for such occasions invoved nuanced indications of the
guest's prestige: whether a meal is offered or simply tea, seating arrangements, the order of eating (often there are several sittings), and
marks of attention from the host. Merchants and others also stay at
or near their shops for part of the day in order to exchange greetings
on the street with persons more distant to them.

All occasions except death are accompanied by the giving of gifts
(*hdiyya*-s). Depending on the prestige claimed by the household, the
gifts are paraded through the streets on trays on the heads of women,
on carts, or on an open truck. Women, children, and, for wealthier
households, musicians join the procession. In the case of marriage,
the formal justification for this display is that the gifts indicate the
standing of the households involved. Prestige is reflected in several
ways—the size of the gifts, the identity of the donors, and where the
procession is allowed to circulate. On the marriage of his son, a powerful landowner arranged for a procession which passed through all the
town's main streets and lasted for hours.[13] Less distinguished processions are generally confined to one or two adjoining quarters. A wider
circulation for modest processions is considered improper (*ḥshuma*).
It would suggest the lack of reason on the part of the head of the
household, who would be subject to ridicule for such pretension.

In the contracting of obligations, men take care to avoid situations
which might call into question or limit their claims to prestige. A
direct, open refusal to a request characteristically signals an indiffer-
ence to or open challenge of the tie of obligation which links two persons. Hence a premium is placed on the use of intermediaries
(*wasiṭa*-s) in order to avoid such situations.

The selection of intermediaries depends on the issues to be negotiated and the stature of the parties involved. For instance, matters publicly supposed to be beneath one's attention. such as delayed rent payments by a tenant, minor disputes over prices, or negotiations for which the outcome is uncertain. are managed by entrusting them to a servant or client. Should there be a refusal or lack of direct compliance for any reason, both parties (depending on their relative standing) can deny their original messages and produce more suitable ones.

Some examples can indicate the range of choice involved. In dealings with the Makhzen, there is often a grey area in practice (as opposed to law, in which there is a strict separation of powers) between local officials of the Ministry of Justice and those of the Ministry of the Interior. Interior officials are present at each rural market, while *qadi*-s and civil judges are located only in the larger towns. Many tribesmen fail to distinguish between the formal authority of the two ministries, since in the protectorate *qaid*-s also had the authority of civil judges. In addition, court cases often involve considerable travel and expense. since they take place only in town. Hence tribesmen frequently submit judicial disputes to agents of the Ministry of the Interior, who deliberately set their fees lower than the cost of formally presenting cases to the courts. Such decisions are legally unenforceable, and the Interior officials often err in interpretation of the law. Particularly when they fear that disgruntled litigants might later bring their case before a court, Interior officials who administer such informal justice send go-betweens of no formal standing to the judges with "hypothetical" cases to determine the law. This avoids direct friction (*mahakka*) between the officials involved and direct challenges to their authority. Judges usually refuse to cooperate, but, if a go-between is carefully chosen, they sometimes feel compelled to give advice.

Negotiations over marriage similarly require careful selection of intermediaries. Occasionally, when only kinsmen are involved, the suitor asks the father of a girl directly. However, women are most frequently used as intermediaries in such negotiations. since any messages they communicate can be conveniently denied by both parties involved.

Failure as an intermediary in such an enterprise constitutes an obligation that must be repaid. When a local school official wanted to marry the daughter of a prosperous local merchant, a friend offered to secure the consent of the girl's father and assured the school official that he would not be refused. He later was refused. When other townsmen learned of this, the school official was severely embarrassed. Because of the public knowledge of his failure, the intermediary owed a major obligation to the official. He settled it by offering his own daughter and settling for a token bridewealth. Not to have settled the debt would have led to a break in relations between the two men.

Compulsion

A serious breach in relations of obligation, such as described above, or the need to oblige a person to come to one's aid or serious threats to social honor can lead to placing a "compulsion" (*'ar*) upon the person responsible for creating the situation or capable of restoring satisfactory relations. Metaphorically, compulsion is thought of as a weight which can be "thrown" on a person or group. Once "thrown," this weight can be "lifted" only by performance of the action requested.

Westermarck in *Ritual and Belief in Morocco* defines *'ar* as a "conditional curse" with supernatural sanctions (1926:I, 518). Supernaturally inspired disasters are thought to occur to persons or individuals who do not respond appropriately to a request placed in the form of *'ar*. Because of the serious consequences thought to follow its use, the *'ar* is not lightly invoked. Proverbs justify the use of indirection so as to avoid such situations: "Deceit is better than the *'ar* [*l-ḥila ḥsen men l-'ar*]" and "Cleverness conquers the lion [*l-ḥila ta-teghleb s-sbe'*]."

There are two types of compulsion, the "great compulsion" (*'ar kbir*) and the "lesser compulsion" (*'ar sghir*). The *'ar kbir*, which virtually disappeared upon the establishment of French control, involved the mediation by marabouts or their descendants of disputes between tribes, tribal sections, or local communities. The prestige of the marabout called upon was commensurate with the gravity of the dispute involved. At least ideally, marabouts even interposed themselves between contesting groups to bring about a cessation of hostilities. Alternatively, the flag from a "dead" marabout's sanctuary or the cloth shroud (*ghoṭa*) of his tomb, carried by one of his descendants, could be used to compel a truce or settlement. The *'ar kbir* was also invoked if a caravan escorted by a Sherqawi was attacked.

"Lesser" 'ar, the only form which presently exists, involves individuals placing each other in situations of compulsion. Compulsion invoked by a descendant of the Prophet or a marabout is considered especially serious, but other persons can use it as well. It is often used to bring an end to disputes involving divorce, court actions, and major threats to social honor. Serious cases of compulsion may involve the public sacrifice of a sheep at the door of the person being compelled or the placing of one's daughter in his protection. Less dramatic but nevertheless effective forms of compulsion include public gifts of large amounts of sugar or a public request on the supplicant's behalf by a respected descendant of a marabout or the Prophet.[14] The same principle of compulsion is implied in the carefully constructed phrases of deference and flattery (*isti'ar*)[15] employed in the opening lines of written letters and requests. The intent of such phrases is to compel an individual to respond favorably to whatever the supplicant requests by reminding him of his social honor and implicitly suggesting that a refusal would be beneath the station of the one being so compelled. This practice also has its face-to-face equivalent.

'*Ar* can be construed as an extreme form of obligation (*hăqq*) which is employed only after other forms of obligation fail. '*Ar* merely compels the restoration of relations or the performance of a requested action; its imposition implies no judgment on the rights and wrongs of the situation which led to its use in the first place.

Like obligations, '*ar* can be invoked only for situations which fall within the limits of propriety. It cannot be "thrown" for trivial reasons or for goals not sanctioned by "the way things are done." Within these limits, it is considered against reason and improper to resist a request made by '*ar*. A Boujadi informant raised in a nearby town gave an example of '*ar* which occurred in the late 1920's:

> My father [a pious notary] was regarded by the neighboring tribes as a marabout, although he was not. Because of his reputation the French got my elder brother [also a notary at the time] to help them establish the rural tax [*tertib*] in the region. The tribes brought it to our house, thinking it was the tithe ['*shur*].[16]
>
> Then the French appointed [an in-law of Pasha Hajj Thami l-Glawi, *pasha* of Marrakesh] as *qaid* of the region.

He was a rough, ignorant man. One day at the market, the *qaid* slapped my father on the face before everyone, when my father refused to listen to his words. Later a friend of the *qaid* told him of my father's reputation and warned him that the tribes might rise up against him.

At the next market the *qaid* brought his daughter. Before everyone he went to my elder brother and said, "She is yours. Take [i.e., marry] her. She will never return to my house."

That was '*ar*. The *qaid* asked for no bridewealth, although later my brother paid something so that there would be a marriage by Islamic law.

An essential component of using compulsion is that it must be done publicly, as in the above case. The person initiating compulsion must be fairly certain of approbation for his activities. Refusal of such a request indicates a heedlessness toward potential disaster and a serious breach of the social order.

The following example of the use of '*ar*, taken from my field notes, is more mundane but exhibits in fuller detail the circumstances leading to its use.

Two teen-age girls got into a fight on the street and began hitting one another. A third girl from a neighboring house intervened, trying to break up the quarrel. The young brother of one of the girls came by and immediately rushed to the aid of his sister. He entered the house of the girl who had tried to break up the quarrel and struck her in the stomach. Then he dragged his sister home, slapping her for getting involved in a street fight in the first place. Meanwhile, the girl whom he had struck had fainted. Neighboring women came to sit with her and brought small gifts. When her father returned, his first act was to take his daughter to the doctor to get a certificate confirming that she had been injured. Since there were no injuries, he was unsuccessful. Further, the gendarmes refused to intervene without such proof of physical harm.

The morning after the fight, the father gathered witnesses to make depositions with the *qaid*. This was the first step in bringing the matter before the civil court. The charges deposed were assault and *siba*,[17] which in this case meant entering another man's house without his permission, a very serious matter, since it affects his honor and that of his women. Some of the witnesses, all women, dropped out on pressure from their men, who feared being caught in the middle of a protracted conflict between neighbors.

Weeks passed, with the father of the struck girl trying to line up everyone who could potentially intervene on his side (the judge was one of his distant kinsmen).[18] The other girl in the original fight, the servant of an important household, was beaten for getting involved in the first place. Her master, of much higher social rank than the father of the girl struck by the boy, refused to lend his support on the ground that the quarrel was none of his affair and that, since it was a woman's quarrel, no one could tell what really were the issues. (He would also have lost prestige in lending support to the minor quarrel of a client household.)

After the case was finally docketed, the father of the boy then came to the door of the girl's father at sunup, together with some of his friends and a gift of several cones of sugar. He asked for a suspension of hostilities [*sulh*]. Without opening his door to confront his opponent face-to-face, the girl's father refused settlement on the grounds that the court date was already set. The first attempt at '*ar* was unsuccessful.

Several days later an old, influential Sherqawi, a distant relation of the girl's father, came, together with some friends of the boy's father, on behalf of the latter (who was a commoner). The Sherqawi intermediary kissed the girl's father on both shoulders. He again offered the gift of sugar, asking that the matter be dropped. This time it was. The girl's father later told me it would have been improper [*hshuma*] for him not to have done so. The intermediary was carefully chosen by the supplicant as being in the social network of the girl's father and higher in "word." A refusal by the girl's father to drop the dispute would have asserted that the intermediary who came to him was insignificant and thus would have created a formal, open challenge to this other individual as well.

Common Sense and Religious Sense

The common-sense perspective toward "the way things are" is the overall one through which social experience is shaped and interpreted. As I have already indicated, some of the key concepts which make up the core of this perspective are explicitly thought to be Islamic and thus serve further to legitimate it. Despite the incorporation of some religious symbols into the common-sense perspective, religious beliefs can by no means be seen as just a symbolic expression of the social order. But the two perspectives are interdependent. It is doubtful whether a religious understanding of the world could exist in a given society if it were totally alien to the prevailing everyday orientation toward social reality. As Clifford Geertz has written, "religious symbols formulate a basic congruence between a particular style of life and a specific (if, most often, implicit) metaphysic, and in so doing sustain each with the borrowed authority of the other" (1966:4). Thus at least part of the religious perspective moves beyond the realities of everyday life.

It is important, I think, to recognize degrees of separation of the religious and common-sense perspectives, a point that is further discussed in the next chapter. I suggest that implicit ideologies show a much greater congruence with the everyday perspective than those which are consciously articulated. In a civilization-wide religion, such as Islam, many permutations of explicit and implicit ideologies are copresent and affect each other. Maraboutism, of course, is essentially an implicit ideology. Nineteenth- and early twentieth-century sources almost unanimously attest to the significance of marabouts. Lacking the concept of world view or other devices to explore implicit ideological patterns, ethnographers of this period were unable to account for why marabouts were so highly regarded in any but such broad formulae as Bel's assertion of the "traditional" reverence for "human fetishes." Contemporary maraboutism is a pale reflection of an ideology which once was given a much fuller expression and which was a template for a much more significant range of activities than is presently the case. Still, it gives an idea of the earlier ideological bases of marabouts.

My intention in the following chapters is not simply to detail the partial congruence between maraboutism and everyday assumptions about the social world. Studies documenting such a relationship have been an ethnographic staple for several decades, even if not for the Muslim world. It is important to see just how this seeming convergence is accomplished, but it is even more significant to examine where it fails.

6

The Ideology of Maraboutism

Max Weber began his study on the sociology of religion by proposing to examine "the conditions and effects of a particular type of social action" (1968:399); he explicitly avoided a definition of religion for two reasons. In the first place, he saw no analytical utility in formulating a definition so broad as to encompass the wide diversity of behavior labeled as religious by actors in various societies. Second, he did not want to assume a priori that the religious was in all cases set apart from everyday purposive conduct or that behavior could be meaningfully classified into such analytic categories as *religion* and *magic* on the basis of our own notions of causality.

As suggested earlier, whatever else religion might entail, it is a set of beliefs, more often implicit than explicit, that are understood by members of a society against the background of tacit, shared assumptions about the nature and conduct of everyday life. Religious ideologies may not be entirely derivative from these common-sense assumptions, especially in the case of such "universal" religions as Islam and Christianity, but they are necessarily understood in their context.

Weber's caution about defining religion is rarely reflected in later, protracted debates among anthropologists and sociologists over whether religion should be defined in terms of the nature of beliefs as labeled (e.g., Durkheim's distinction between "sacred" and "profane") or their content (e.g., Tylor's "spiritual beings"). As the neo-Weberian W. G. Runciman has recently argued, neither of these basic approaches (or subsequent refinements of them) has been entirely satisfactory (1970:59–62). His own contribution to the debate has been to reiterate Weber's implicit point of over half a century earlier that any attempt to distinguish "religious" from other forms of belief presumes that it is already known "what exactly people *do* believe" (Runciman 1970:61). Only once beliefs have been identified in the categories of the actors themselves is it possible to ask which are religious. He argues that sociologists and anthropologists generally use the term *religion*

> in the sense where "ideology" would do almost as well—
> that is, in denoting those distinctive combinations of factual
> with ethical beliefs which constitute the "religion" of the
> Nuer, Dinka, Tokugawa Japanese, Homeric Greeks,
> Roman Catholics . . . and all the rest. In other words, if
> there is a general distinction to be retained between "non-
> religious" and "religious" beliefs, it is merely a distinction
> between what may be loosely called "matter-of-fact"
> beliefs on one side and beliefs about the conduct of life on
> the other. The latter may stand in many different sorts of
> relation to the matter-of-fact beliefs about the cosmos which
> the people in question also hold. But they are a universal
> and unambiguous category—all cultures have *some* [such]
> beliefs. (Runciman 1970:75–76)

Much recent work on the concept of religion tacitly adopts a similar position. The "definition" of religion offered by Clifford Geertz in "Religion as a Cultural System" (1966:4) is to him less a definition than a five-point paradigm for the exploration of the systems of meanings embodied in certain types of symbols. The paradigm recognizes the futility of rigorously setting apart a religious component from other systems of meaning in all societies.

To be sure, in some contexts the term *religion* can be employed clearly and unambiguously, as where it delineates nothing more than declared membership in a formally organized religion (e.g., Lenski 1963). But such uses clearly take for granted the more interesting issues of definition. Most uses of the term *religion* are much more complex. For example, Wilfred Cantwell Smith's *The Meaning and End of Religion* subtly interrelates religion with sociohistorical context in documenting the historical trend toward reification of the concept of religion in both the Christian and the Islamic traditions. He sees increasing use of the term in both traditions as symptomatic of an increasing fragmentation of man's social and personal life, so that the religious, instead of being central to a coherent, generally implicit, vision of the world, emerges as merely one facet of a person's life alongside many others (1963:124). Clearly what is considered religious in these traditions cannot be encapsulated in a definition devoid of social or temporal context.

The identification of the "properly religious" is facilitated when one of its elements is an articulated, bounded ideology, as opposed to a merely implicit system of belief. However, the presence of such ideologies in the "universal" religions, such as Islam, does not automatically indicate the roles they play in the local contexts in which they are received and understood. Of course, within these major traditions there are a wide range of explicitness of belief and significant variations in patterns of belief (cf. Weber 1968:388–401). Thus the reformist and modernist movements in North Africa, of which more will be said later, possess fairly coherent doctrines based on clearly stated, universalistic grounds. Despite the significance of these movements over the last half century in North Africa, their ideologies are far from being popularly accepted, especially in Morocco. In general, their largest impact has been among an educated urban minority. The traditional maraboutic belief system, on the other hand, is almost entirely particularistic and, as I shall indicate, ordinarily an unquestioned, taken-for-granted part of the social order. Reformist doctrines are radical in the sense that they seek to alter established patterns of belief (cf. Harris 1971:208–214). They call into question the taken-for-granted assumptions about the cosmos and the social order and thus must necessarily be explicit. To a limited extent their adoption by many of the urban bourgeoisie has compelled an explicit, but generally ineffective, articulation of maraboutism. Nonetheless, one of the strengths of maraboutism is that even at the present it does not have to be consciously articulated or explicitly defended in order to be maintained by the vast majority of Morocco's rural population. While aware of the disrepute into which maraboutism has fallen in the eyes of most of the urban bourgeoisie, the rural majority and some townsmen continue to act as if they accept its fundamental tenets.

The Clients' View

How do the clients conceive of marabouts? The assumptions implicit in maraboutism are not systematically articulated by them. Nor, for that matter, are they by the Sherqawa, whose identification with maraboutism is discussed in the next chapter. Ties with marabouts and what they indicate of the social and political alignments of those who hold them are so integral a part of their world that no explanation of them is considered necessary. But the assumptions behind these ties can be discerned in how persons act and in how they describe their relations with marabouts. The meanings implicit in statements and ritual acts are systematically patterned into a social logic, even if it is only fleetingly perceived, if at all, by their carriers. As in any social group, some people are naïve or even cynical about its ideology, although most manage to take it for granted (cf. Bendix 1963:341–343). Skepticism is generally confined to the assessment of individual marabouts, not to the underlying conception of how the supernatural intervenes in the affairs of this world.

The key to understanding the ideology implicit in maraboutism is in the cultural conception of *baraka* as a form of causality and the means by which it can be appropriated to sustain one's own activities. *Baraka* in Morocco and, for that matter, throughout the Muslim world is considered "a mysterious wonder-working force which is looked upon as a blessing from God" (Westermarck 1926:I,35). How this is elaborated depends upon social context, but in Morocco *baraka* is often invoked as an explanation for uncanny events, extraordinary political sagacity, and a range of mundane situations indicating well-being, abundance, or merely sufficiency of any quality or material. Westermarck's extensive, if itemistic, listing of instances of *baraka* half a century ago still largely holds for rural Morocco (1926:I,35–251). It is associated with a multitude of gestures and acts in daily life, words, places, animals, plants, foods, writing, descent from the Prophet or from Sidi 'Umar, times of the year, events in personal life cycles, and, of course, marabouts. Thus, for most Moroccans, *baraka* is as much a part of the everyday world as is witchcraft among the Azande. It is a concrete manifestation of God's will and is invoked as an explanation of why some things happen while others do not. Marabouts are conceived by their clients as having the ability to transmit this *baraka* and thus are concrete symbols within the social system of the pervasiveness of the supernatural in mundane affairs.

One way of understanding the significance of such a concept is in relation to the dominant patterns of the social structure, as Mary Douglas has suggested (1966:107, 111). The fact that Sherqawi marabouts and certain other powerful maraboutic descent groups have maintained a pre-eminence throughout four centuries of major political realignments indicates that *baraka* does not operate in a freely competitive system in Morocco, although marabouts and their descendants frequently represent the concept in this way. Maraboutic ideology as held by marabouts and their descendants, to be discussed in the following chapter, differs significantly in emphasis from that of their clients. Both ideological variants are influenced by a second factor that Douglas fails to consider, or assumes not to exist, in order to highlight her argument on the relation of ideology to social structure. This is the influence of competing patterns of belief. Perhaps in "simpler" societies one can assume that ordinarily such a factor need not be taken into account. At least many social anthropological monographs, including those written after decades of colonial domination of the society under study, make such a presumption. But Morocco, even preprotectorate Morocco, including the tribes of the Middle and High Atlas mountains, is no more a "simple" society than were the tribes of ancient Palestine, whose ideological fermentation has been so ably described by William Robertson Smith (1919). Both marabouts and their clients are, and have been in the past, aware of nonmaraboutic conceptions of Islam, and this awareness has had an impact on their own ideological tenets and ritual behavior. I shall discuss the consequences of this awareness later at greater length but think it important to emphasize for the present discussion as well.

Moroccans place maraboutism in the following context. Some townsmen explain that all Muslims believe in the existence of saints (*wali*-s), since the Qur'an specifically mentions them. A *wali*, in classical Arabic, is simply an individual who is close to God. Strictly speaking, as educated Muslims do, only God knows who is a saint, just as only he knows those who are sincerely devoted to him, "the pious ones" (*salihin*; sg., *saleh*). In ordinary usage both *wali* and *saleh* refer to anyone popularly considered to have "a certain rank with God" (*sh-daraja l-'end Allah*). This conception implies, of course, a hierarchy among Muslims before God, a notion emphatically denied by reformist Muslims and even by many clients of marabouts, but still at the base of popular Sufism.

The concept of *marabout* (*mrabeṭ*) overlaps with that of *saint*. Essentially a marabout is "one who is tied to God." The word comes from a root meaning "to bind, to tie, to fasten," as one would a camel to a stake. What clients of marabouts and many other Moroccans assume, and what is not textually justified by the Qur'an as now interpreted by most educated, urban Muslims, is that marabouts are endowed with a special relation toward God which makes them particularly well placed to serve as intermediaries to him. Marabouts are regarded as "close" (*qrib*) to God. The meaning of "closeness" here is modeled upon, and to some extent constitutes a pattern for, relations among men.

Those who believe in marabouts further assume that marabouts can be "tied" to men. The creation and maintenance of such ties are regarded as essential or, in some contemporary contexts, simply advantageous, because nothing ever just happens. All events are the result of the active intervention of God's will, even if by maraboutic proxy. The problem for individual believers is how to ensure the flow of grace to sustain their particular concerns. This ideology is concretely symbolized in many ways. One is for client tribesmen to bring some of their seeds for fall planting to Sherqawi marabouts or their descendants, asking for an invocation (*da'wa*) to be said over them. These are later mixed with other seeds. When asked for an explanation of their action, tribesmen reply that "grain does not grow by itself." In the past, when Sherqawa are said to have provided all the seeds necessary for planting, the representation of this underlying belief was considerably more explicit. *Baraka* in such contexts is often referred to as a physical substance (e.g., "a little bread" [*sh-khbiza*]) which can be gleaned by physical contact with a marabout or his shrine, and even taken away from clients again if they reveal their acquisition of *baraka* to others. This is one of the reasons why tribesmen are often reluctant to speak openly of their dealings with marabouts and their descendants. Knowledge of these ties by hostile third parties (including other marabouts) can threaten their efficacy.

Thus the core of belief in maraboutism is quite simple. It postulates that relations between men and the supernatural operate in nearly the same way as do relations between men only.[1] For those who

believe in marabouts, the dyadic, personally contracted bonds of in-
feriority and superiority which are thought to structure the Moroccan social order hold equally for relations toward the supernatural.
The major difference is that the supernatural is thought to be con-
sistently stronger than men and much more difficult to predict. All
such ties are maintained by ongoing exchanges of obligations (*hăqq*-s).
In so far as possible, men contract and maintain ties with those persons they consider capable of sustaining or enhancing their interests
and reassess these ties as economic and political circumstances shift.
Depite the formal ideological claim that only God knows those who
are "close" to him, clients of marabouts seek this-worldly signs which
indicate who such persons might be.

As I stated in the introduction, this conception of man's relation to
the supernatural is incongruent with the formalist notion of Islam
without any intermediaries, but the two are not mutually exclusive.
The opposition of these conceptions is logical, not sociological. Those
Muslims who tacitly accept the concept of maraboutism, or who act
as though they do, also claim to accept the tenets of formal Islam,
which are generally known to them at least in broad outline. They
often say the daily prayers, attend Friday mosques, fast, and accept
in principle all formal obligations incumbent upon Muslims. However, they implicitly act as though these formal tenets of Islam, the
way relations with God are supposed to work, are peripheral to a
"way of thinking and feeling about reality in general" (Bellah 1970:
146) which is directly linked to their immediate social world. At least
for some Moroccans, the reality of belief in marabouts is confirmed
by the nature of the social world, "the way things are," even if other
Moroccans regard the extension of the patterns of conduct that
pervade the social order to encompass the supernatural as erroneous.

The coexistence of the ideology of maraboutism with variations of
formal, explicit Islam is clear from the following statement, in which
a townsman contrasted what "everyone else" believed and what he
claimed was his own position, which he claimed was identical to that
of the lectures on Islam broadcast on the radio (*radyo shra'*):

> Of course the radio says that everything comes directly
> from God. But just as the king has his ministers, God has
> his [marabouts]. If you need a paper from the govern-
> ment office, which is better? Do you go straight to the
> official and ask for it? You might wait a long time and

> never receive it. Or do you go to someone who knows you
> and also knows the official? Of course, you go to the friend,
> who presents the case to the official. Same thing with
> *baraka*. If you want something from God, you go to [the
> marabout]. He is just like us. The only difference is that
> he works with God [*khdem m'a Allah*] and has a high
> rank [*daraja kbira*] with him. If the marabout is too great
> [to directly approach], you go to his children. (A barber)

Although marabouts are thought to have a "high rank" with God,
their clients are not assured that their requests will be granted. A
woman who serves as custodian at one of the shrines in Boujad explained why: "The marabout is close [*qrib*] to God, but only has his
turn to make his requests [*itlob l-ḥăqq*]. Have you seen how we stand
in line in front of the butcher's and the hospital and take turns?
Even the marabout is like that with God." The principal concern
of clients of marabouts is not the implicit criticism of maraboutism
by those opposed to it, but the ability to secure ties with the most
capable marabouts disposed to act on their behalf.

The abilities attributed to marabouts vary greatly. Only a few,
such as the principal Sherqawi marabouts, have an extensive clientele
and a reputation for efficacy over a wide range of activities. These
have a regular clientele of tribal groups and attract individual
pilgrims from most of the regions of Morocco. In contrast, a much
larger number of marabouts have developed a reputation for specified
ranges of action, such as the ability to cure throat ailments (Sidi
Shegdal of Bni 'Amir) or skin diseases and syphilis (Sid et-Tunsi of
Shawya). The clientele of such specialist marabouts tends to consist
entirely of individual pilgrims seeking cures for these specific
maladies. Finally, there are the minor marabouts connected with
specific *dăwwar*-s, mentioned in Chapter 4. These may not be
regarded as particularly efficacious in any field. On occasion their aid
will be sought, without much hope of success. For that matter, tribesmen do not offer them much to show faith in them. Some of these
enshrined country marabouts are even approached, as are some of the
less reputable country *fqih*-s, with requests for magic—to further an
amorous adventure or bring disaster upon a personal enemy. Most
persons dread approaching major marabouts or intercessors to them
with such requests.

The reputations of these marginal marabouts often are quickly forgotten. In contrast, prominent marabouts like those of the Sherqawa are legitimated by attributes which in principle reflect the permanency and continuity of *baraka* and the ability to communicate it. These include the claim to mystical insight, transmitted along an unbroken chain (*silsila*) of powerful marabouts ultimately linked to the Prophet Muhammed, and patrilineal descent from the Prophet Muhammed or his second caliph, 'Umar ben l-Khaṭṭab (d. 644). The Sherqawa, collectively known as the "children of the *shaykh*" (*wlad esh-shaykh*) are thought to possess these enduring characteristics. Those Sherqawa who effectively control the resources of the *zawya* are considered to be marabouts, particularly as this is symbolized by their apparent wealth, their ability to secure the support of other Sherqawa, and the size, strength, and faith (*niya*) of their client groups as measured by offerings and sacrifices. Only two living Sherqawa presently enjoy such a reputation. The power of en-shrined marabouts is manifested in a similar fashion—the lavishness of their shrines, the respect accorded them by living Sherqawa, and the strength and intensity of their clientele. Such enshrined mara-bouts are almost exclusively those who in the past were lords of the *zawya* or sons of the founding marabout.

Not all of the internal differentiation among the Sherqawa is lost on their clients, but there is a tendency to impute to all of the descendants of Sidi Mhammed Sherqi the attributes of the best known. Thus the Sherqawa are collectively considered to be better off and more prosperous than the non-Sherqawa of Boujad. The implicit as-sumption is that the *shaykh*'s descendants prosper because of their "closeness" to their maraboutic ancestor. Many of the Sherqawa had the advantage of education in the colonial past, when access to it was much more restricted than is presently the case. They also held until recently all significant local administrative posts and continue to hold several. Regionally and nationally prominent Sherqawa also are seen from the viewpoint of clients of marabouts as deriving power and social honor from the *baraka* of their maraboutic ancestors.

Marabouts and Clients: The Symbolism of "Closeness"

The reputation and prestige of a marabout are only part of the con-cern of his clients. As with other social ties, those sustained over a period of time and in multiple diffuse ways are considered to be the most efficacious. Thus, most of the tribal groups of the Tadla Plain and neighboring regions claim covenants (*'ahd*-s; *bay'a*-s) with the Sherqawa which were sealed in "early times" (*bekri*). *Bekri* is that range of time which forms a backdrop to the ordinary social horizon. The ordinary social horizon is composed of those events impinging upon the lives of tribesmen which can be placed in their full social context. Events which happened in "early times" are also thought to have a significant effect upon the present, but their context is not fully known or is thought to differ from that of the present. Myths are thought to portray "early" events. As in myths elsewhere, some of the events and transformations portrayed in them do not occur in other contexts; the myths also refer dramatically to origins and transformations (Cohen 1969:337). In so far as they affect the present, the covenants portrayed in myths are regarded as "true" events and constitute a part of the universe taken for granted by tribesmen of the Tadla. Such covenants, maintained and regularly renewed, are considered to be the strongest tie that can exist between marabouts and their clientele. Even individual pilgrims often try to claim "closeness" with the Sherqawa through membership in one of the many groups mentioned in the myths current on the Tadla and elsewhere in Morocco.

Such myths serve as "charters" through which individuals and groups of individuals legitimate their ties with the Sherqawa. This Malinowskian facet of maraboutic myths does not exhaust their rich and complex symbolism, but it is the only aspect of the myths that imposes itself upon the consciousness of the clients of marabouts and thus is an aspect closely related to the social context of maraboutism.[2]

Because orientalists and ethnographers have long presumed that such myths do not exist in the Muslim world, at least outside the corpus of formal Islamic rituals, they have been almost entirely neglected by scholars interested in the Muslim world. As an example, I present one of them below. It is a short "origin" myth, depicting how Sidi Mhammed Sherqi came to Boujad and called upon the tribes to settle in the region.[3] Like most of the others, this myth is known to all tribesmen of the region and most townsmen. This particular version is taken from a caretaker at one of the Sherqawi shrines. Such Sherqawa know the most elaborate versions of such myths and recite them regularly to pilgrims.

> Why did Sidi Mhammed Sherqi settle there? It was because of that boy, Sid l-Ḥajj l-Meknasi.[4] He used to go on

pilgrimages to Mecca. He made seven pilgrimages and on the seventh he died atop Mount 'Arafa.[5] That camel which carried him living [to Mecca], by Sidi Mhammed Sherqi's covenant with it, returned him dead.

When the camel returned his son dead, Shaykh Sidi Mhammed Sherqi went into his wife's room and said to her, "O Khelfiya!" She replied, "Yes?" He asked her, "Wasn't there something of value given to us? Today shall we give it back or not?"[6] She answered, "By God, Sidi Mhammed Sherqi, we'll return it in the same condition it was given to us." He said to her, "Whoever is like me can find strength in destiny. Death is hot, acrid. She gave me a cup of bitterness. Go on, O Hajj l-Meknasi, O my son, we meet in the next world."[7]

His wife didn't restrain herself, fell to the ground, and rolled in convulsions in front of Shaykh Sidi Mhammed Sherqi. He asked her, "Why don't you forbear over [the loss of Sid l-Hajj l-Meknasi],[8] who belongs to God? Look at what we have done because of that loss. What will happen when the next comes?[9] Go on!" Khelfiya will never again bear one who gave her joy like Sid l-Hajj l-Meknasi.[10]

When Shaykh Sidi Mhammed Sherqi's wife did not contain her grief at that place where they were [living], he said to her, "I'm not going to stay in this land which disturbs my praising of God. I'm going to settle in that place which is free [of the thought] of Sid l-Hajj l-Meknasi." Shaykh Sidi Mhammed Sherqi went down there, lived in that land, and began looking for water. He came to 'Ayn Shaykh.[11] He struck his walking stick against the spring, water gushed forth by the will of God, and he said, "There will be a settlement here."

When Shaykh Sidi Mhammed Sherqi settled, he needed people to fill the land with him. He called for seven from Bni Zemmur, seven from Bni Shegdal, and seven from Sma'la. He said to them, "Who wants to sacrifice?" He picked up the knife, went into trance, and the knife dripped with blood. He said to the tribesmen, "Who wants to sacrifice?" They replied, "We will sacrifice." The marabout said, "Come! I'll take your sacrifices in turn: [first]

a Sem'li, [then] a Shegdali."[12] When he went out,[13] he
called, "Bring your necks for the sacrifice." The Sem'li
came forward, but the Shegdali fell back, until all seven
[of the Sma'la] had sacrificed. [When the marabout came
out of trance] he asked, "Who entered and who remained
[outside]?" Someone replied, "O Sidi, the Sma'la went in
and the Bni Shegdal remained outside." [Then] the marabout said, "The Sma'la will be watered[14] [with *baraka*],
but Bni Shegdal will remain without."

The 'Umariya[15] whom Shaykh Sidi Mhammed Sherqi
had married said to him, "Here is my neck, O Sidi
Mhammed Sherqi, on behalf of Bni Shegdal."[16] Then
Shaykh Sidi Mhammed Sherqi said to the Bni Shegdal,
"Since the woman offered her neck on your behalf, you
are now milk brothers of the Sma'la." She gave her two
breasts: that for the Sma'la overflowed with milk; that
for the Bni Shegdal overflowed with water. The marabout
said to them, "Go, O Sma'la! Whatever I break, you can
mend; but that which you break, no one can mend."

Those are the people who filled the land with Shaykh
Sidi Mhammed Sherqi and who remain in it to this day.

This myth forms part of a cluster of some sixty that I have collected
on the Tadla Plain concerning the Sherqawa and other marabouts.
I use the term *cluster*, rather than *cycle*, to describe these myths collectively because, like the social groups from which they emanate,
they do not form closed, bounded entities. Those collected in Boujad
and its region link Sidi Mhammed Sherqi and his sons (but not later
descendants, about whom there are only miracle stories, *karama*-s,
not myths) with client groups and marabouts throughout Morocco.
Conversely, myths from the shrines of other marabouts on the Tadla
Plain and adjacent regions articulate with the maraboutic myths of
the Sherqawa. For instance, a myth of the Hmadsha religious order
near Meknes has their founder, Sidi 'Ali ben Hamdush, receiving his
baraka from Sidi Mhammed Sherqi (Crapanzano 1973:30–56).[17]
The Sherqawa are not aware of this myth, although they believe that
Sidi 'Ali obtained his *baraka* from Sid l-Hafyan, possibly a grandson
of Sidi Mhammed Sherqi, whose shrine is in Boujad and is visited
regularly by Hmadsha pilgrims. Later Sherqawi marabouts are also
said to have had complex ties with their contemporaries (some of

whom are known from written historical sources) or those currently thought to have been their contemporaries. Were such interconnections fully traced out, I think they could be shown to link all the major marabouts of Morocco and North Africa (cf. Gellner 1969: 275–278; Depont and Coppolani 1897; Rinn 1884). The clients of the Sherqawa, in any case, see themselves as tied through their marabouts to the wider society of Islam.

Tribesmen and Sherqawa are aware that at one level these myths concern the nature of obligations in social groups and between such groups and marabouts. Because of their concrete, compact imagery and particularistic references, the symbolism of these myths can be comprehended only with difficulty by those unfamiliar with the social milieu in which they are known. Several implications of the myth presented above are obvious. In the first place, the marabout, Sidi Mḥammed Sherqi, makes the land fertile so that its settlement becomes possible. This sequence of events presumes *baraka,* as described earlier, as a causal power transmitted through specifically contracted social ties. The second crucial aspect of the myth is its presentation of the contrasting forms of relation possible with the marabout, including the logical possibility of no relation (the Bni Zemmur).[18] Links are established in the myth both by sacrifice of the seven animals and the offer, not the consummation, of a woman for sacrifice as the substitute for an animal.[19] Her offering in the myth explicitly establishes (for Bni Shegdal) a kinship relation with the marabout and with other social groups that are in a client relationship to him. These possibilities are depicted in the myth by combinations of ties of milk, blood, and water. Tribesmen do not comment upon these possibilities except to say, in response to the ethnographer's queries, that some of the combinations—ties of blood and milk, milk alone, blood alone, and those not secured by either blood or milk (those of water?)—are replicated in actual social relations. Both the Sherqawa and their clients claim that the covenant represented in the myth fixes mutual obligations between them. These are depicted by the symbolism of sacrifices and marriages, which create irrevocable ties of blood and revocable ones of "closeness" between the parties.

Other myths known to the Sherqawa and all tribesmen of the region explore the same theme. In one, Sidi Mḥammed Sherqi takes a woman from the Bni 'Amir and has a son by her, Sid l-Ghazwani. This marriage places the Bni 'Amir in the relation of maternal uncles (*khal*-s) to Sid l-Ghazwani and, by common metaphorical usage of

the term, to all the Sherqawa. Later, when the Bni 'Amir are op-
pressed by a ruthless sultan, Sidi Mhammed Sherqi sends Sid
l-Ghazwani to their aid (see Eickelman and Draioui 1973). Among
other themes, the myth stresses the obligation of the Sherqawa to aid
the Bni 'Amir because of their *khal* relationship. In another myth,
concerning the Bni Wra (Shawya), Ghazwani changes the tribe from
the form of birds into humans and makes them Muslim at the same
time. A malevolent sultan had earlier cursed the tribe and changed
them into birds. From the time of their retransformation, they
regularly maintained their covenant with the Sherqawa.

Although tribesmen themselves suggest the partial replication of
certain relations portrayed in the myths with actual social relations,
it would be an error to assume a priori the role these texts play in
tribesmen's conceptions of themselves and of their relation with
marabouts. Although in part these myths are consciously construed
by tribesmen to be a sort of Malinowskian social charter, they are
not correlated in a one-to-one way with assumptions about social
conduct in the everyday world any more than the ideological use of
the concept of agnation among tribesmen directly reflects the sociological principles underlying actual conduct. These myths provide
symbolic statements of the role of marabouts in tying men to given
regions and to each other. Marabouts make possible order within
society and thus metaphorically constitute concrete, localized manifes-
tations of Islam, submission to God's will.

In regard to the distinction between maraboutism as a cultural
idiom and as a pattern for actual social relations, it is crucial to note
that the "level" at which the covenant is concluded in the myths, that
of tribes, is not matched by ritual activities of those units acting as
groups. Collective ties with the Sherqawa are maintained and reaffirmed at the "level" of tribal sections and local communities. Moreover, many collectivities have covenants with the Sherqawa which
are not represented in myths, and tribes linked to the marabout may
be in hostile relation with one another. Thus there is considerable
leeway in how such covenants are realized. Contrary to the suggestion
of some tribesmen that such covenants have "always" existed, they
actually fall somewhere between Sir Henry Maine's categories of
"status" and "contract." Tribesmen often refer to their relations with
the Sherqawa as ascribed, but both the myths and relations in the
actual social world indicate achieved, contractual relations on the
part of the persons and groups involved.

Remaining Connected

Sherqawa and client tribesmen claim that the original covenants between Sidi Mhammed Sherqi and their ancestors have been renewed
in an unbroken parallel chain of descendants on both sides which has
kept them "connected" (*mettaslin*). These links are maintained in
three ways. One is through offerings to and communal meals with
those living descendants of Sidi Mhammed Sherqi who claim special
relationships with certain tribes, tribal sections, or local communities.
These descendants are called "visitors" (*zewwar*-s), because they visit
the tribesmen at intervals throughout the year to collect the *zyara*,
which in this context means the offering made to a marabout or his
descendants. Another way is by annual sacrifices at the shrines of
Sidi Mhammed Sherqi and certain of his descendants, in the presence
of living Sherqawa. A few groups, such as the Sma'la until recently,
maintain their links in both these ways. A much larger number of
groups regularly maintain their covenant only through offerings and
communal meals with nonmaraboutic Sherqawa, omitting the annual
sacrifice at the main shrine. A third way to remain "connected" is
through offerings and communal meals with living marabouts, but
this practice is rapidly disappearing. It is presently much more
difficult for living marabouts to maintain their reputations than for
those who are enshrined. Only one of the two Sherqawa currently
considered to be living marabouts actively fosters this belief by entertaining pilgrims and accepting offerings from them individually
and collectively. Links through Sherqawi "visitors" are consequently
much more common. The majority of such visitors belong to the two
Sherqawi descent groups that have dominated the affairs of the
religious lodge over the last century, the 'Arbawi and Zawya groups.
Others are scattered throughout the remaining descent groups.

The relation of Sherqawi visitors to their clients is generally
diffuse. Often, visitors are among the very few townsmen with
whom tribesmen have regular contact. When they come to the weekly
market, they often seek out their visitors to give them small offerings
and to ask for personal invocations on their behalf. Clients also call
upon other forms of expertise from their Sherqawi visitors, whose
occupations include those of carpenter, tailor, shopkeeper, caravan-
serai operator, and notary. Beyond such particular skills, visitors can
relay requests to other Sherqawa or townsmen. Even if such intervention is not efficacious, it is in the interest of visitors to allow their

clients to think it is in order to enhance their own prestige. Each visitor is spoken of as "working" the local communities with which he is particularly regarded as an intermediary.[20] Most work five or six local communities, not necessarily in the same tribal sections. This "work" is generally passed from father to son or other close relations among the Sherqawa, including women on occasion. With the rapid spread of urban-based, formal Islam and diminished revenues and prestige from "visiting," many younger Sherqawa decline to carry on the activity. Even tribesmen now consider many visitors to be beggars, emphasizing their need to use donations for their own subsistence, although still respecting their maraboutic descent. Consequently these ties are rapidly being eroded, although there are still a large number of middle-aged visitors who derive enough income to want to continue the practice despite unfavorable comments from other townsmen. Moreover, the extent of attrition is difficult to determine because many Sherqawa and tribesmen prefer, for reasons previously mentioned, to dissimulate their links.

The major collective contacts between the Sherqawa active in the affairs of the lodge and their tribal clients occur on three annual occasions. On two of these, Sherqawi visitors go out to the local communities tied to them. The first visit is in early spring, generally in March, when pastoral contracts expire and the profits of the preceding year are traditionally divided. Some Sherqawa even buy horses for these rounds, which they then sell after the June harvests. Visitors again "work" their local communities immediately after the harvests in late May and early June. On both occasions, Sherqawa extract offerings in exchange for invocations to their ancestor to provide *baraka* for the supplicant group. This quid pro quo is often punctuated by heated, acrimonious protests. Although the tribesmen feel they need the invocations of the visitors for their well-being, many regard their demands as extortionate and openly say so. Arrangements for the collection of offerings on these occasions are usually made not by the visitor himself—only the poorest and least effective are reduced to that extreme—but by an "associate" (*saheb*) in each local community. This associate serves as the channel through which demands are made upon the group involved by the Sherqawi visitor and requests are made to him in turn. Generally such tribal associates are men of influence in their local community. Most are moderately wealthy, and many, in the hierarchy of oligarchy enhanced by the protectorate, served as government *shaykh*-s. In independent Morocco these same persons also generally play a prominent role in all representations of the tribal group with the outside world.

Living marabouts commonly made visits to their clientele until the 1930's. They ceased this practice as the size of offerings diminished. It became clear to marabouts that they were exposed on such occasions to open opposition from an emerging group of reformist Muslims and from tribesmen themselves. In such circumstances the marabout, not having full control over the conditions of his public exposure, risked substantial losses of prestige and hence of his reputation for *baraka. Baraka* may have, as Mary Douglas claims, a "snowball" bias toward success (1966:109), but it can also work just as quickly in reverse.

The importance of the intermediary role of the Sherqawi visitors with their maraboutic ancestors and the wider Muslim community is still stressed by tribesmen, although the status of such visitors is often played down. The offerings which most visitors collect are now used for their personal benefit, although they are still known by the names of *zakat* and *'ashur*. The *zakat* is the tax incumbent upon all Muslims able to pay it and used for the benefit of the Muslim community. In the preprotectorate era, when most visitors seem to have served as messengers for and intermediaries toward their maraboutic kinsmen, there are indications that some of the revenues really were used in such a fashion, particularly in years of drought. *'Ashur* means "tithe," but is not to be taken literally. It is a descriptive term which traditionally has signified taxes paid to the Makhzen or any other regular levy. Tribesmen designate offerings to marabouts or visitors as the "share of the *shaykh*" (*l-ḥăqq dyal esh-shaykh*). Upon making them, tribesmen say to the visitor that they are given "in the face of God" and "for the sake of your ancestor" (*'la khaṭer jeddek*). In the past, visitors were the key to seeking the intervention of the Sherqawa in a wide range of matters, including the mundane. Their role at the present is greatly attenuated in this respect, although, as recently as an election in the early 1960's, a local candidate successfully consolidated his tribal support by persuading Sherqawa *zewwar*-s to work on his behalf.

The principal occasion for contact between the Sherqawa and their tribal clientele occurs during the fall festival (*musem*) of Sidi Mhammed Sherqi. Most groups renew their covenant with the Sherqawa during this period. As has been discussed, the timing of the festival varies with the specific ecological conditions of each client group. The predominantly transhumant Sma'la, for instance, prefer coming during a full moon in order to diminish the possibility of theft of the animals which they leave behind. Another factor which influences the pilgrimage of specific groups is the desire of Sherqawi visitors to avoid the copresence in Boujad of mutually antagonistic groups. Each group informs their visitor when they want to make the pilgrimage. The visitors of principal groups then informally consult among themselves and set dates. This activity is virtually the only one in which visitors coordinate their activities.

The festival lasts an entire month but "peaks" in the ten-day period during which tribal sections from the Sma'la are in Boujad. These and a few sections of the Bni Zemmur are the last to come on horseback and set up tents for the duration of their visit. The Sma'la tents form a crescent along Boujad's eastern side. Throughout the period of the Sma'la presence, "powder plays" (*tehṛăk*-s) occur daily between horsemen of rival local communities and tribal sections. As stated in Chapter 4, the patterns of participation in these, the arrangement of tents, and the patterns of contributions for collective offerings to Sherqawi marabouts and visitors all reflect the effective social units at that time. For groups that arrive by truck or bus, only the pattern of offerings to the Sherqawa indicates social alignments. Alignments of these groups are considerably more blurred than is the case with groups that arrive on horseback and muleback, because the occasions on which they are called upon to express group identity are fewer. Without horses, they cannot compete in "powder plays." Their stay in Boujad tends to be shorter; and their lodgings are scattered throughout the town. Under these conditions open breaks with other groups or within groups are less likely to be expressed. In fact, such groups often make joint contributions to the Sherqawa for reasons of economy and thus have even greater reason to attenuate any differences that exist among themselves.

Explicitly economic activities do not presently form a significant part of the festival, although they did in the past. The urban bourgeoisie, lacking substantial economic benefit from the festival, has become consequently more open in condemnation of it. Today, pilgrims buy in Boujad only those few supplies needed for their actual stay. Nevertheless, the government has in recent years associated an agricultural and livestock exposition to the festival in order to disseminate modern techniques to tribesmen. After a lapse of at least a decade, local government officials are also trying to use the festival to have tribesmen reaffirm their loyalty to the Makhzen. Such activity is hardly novel. Prior to the protectorate, sultans used a number of means to indicate their approval or disapproval of particular marabouts. Similarly, the French occasionally banned *musem*-s or restricted attendance in order to exert pressure upon particular tribal groups. The independent Moroccan government has also employed similar tactics in recent years.

The annual pilgrimage to Boujad is generally the one occasion which partially removes tribesmen from their ordinary cycle of agricultural and herding activities and weekly markets. Ritual activities accompanying the formal Islamic feasts and life-cycle occasions, such as births, circumcisions, weddings, and funerals, accomplish this to some extent but still are held in the social context of totally familiar social life. In contrast, the pilgrimage to Boujad is partially removed from these circumstances. Some contrasts with the pilgrimage to Mecca (*hajj*) help to discern what is characteristic about the pilgrimage (*zyara*) to the Sherqawi shrine in Boujad.[21] The pilgrimage to Mecca is obligatory for those Muslims economically and physically able to undertake it but is an act performed by individuals. The pilgrimage to Mecca and its associated rituals remove most Muslims to the periphery of the web of normative, local social structure. In Mecca itself, pilgrims from different parts of the Muslim world tend to unite in a spirit of what Victor Turner has called *communitas*. An ethos of the equality of pilgrims toward one another permeates their activities.

Many of these features are largely absent from the pilgrimage to Boujad. There is no free commingling of pilgrims from different social groups, although, as in traditional markets, there is a suspension of overt hostilities. Each group present has a dyadic tie to the Sherqawa, but this bond does not necessarily create horizontal ties among the groups themselves. The timing of the *hajj* to Mecca is determined by the Muslim lunar calendar, while the *zyara* to Boujad is tied to the agricultural and herding cycle. As with the *hajj*, the decision to go to Boujad is made by individuals on an annual basis, although in the latter case there usually is considerable group pressure to participate. Finally, the inequalities implicit in everyday social relations are preserved during the festival in Boujad.

The central feature of the fall festival is the renewal of the covenant with Sidi Mhammed Sherqi. Its modalities vary considerably, for the renewal is not effected in the context of a formal, stylized liturgy.

All covenanting groups offer animals, generally sheep or bulls, which are either sacrificed or accepted by the Sherqawa in lieu of sacrifice and later sold on the open market. This latter practice is a rationalization of the covenant and an attempt by the Sherqawa to mitigate urban hostility, including that of many Sherqawa, to maraboutic activities. Some tribesmen insist upon sacrifice, however, and for them there is a Sherqawi butcher at the main shrine who makes the sacrifice and then sells the meat to pilgrims at current market prices. The profits of this are then divided among the Sherqawa.

Collections for these sacrifices are made within each local community and tribal section by one of their number, generally the same person who acts as associate for the Sherqawi visitor. The share of contributing households is roughly scaled to their ability to pay. Considerable cajoling and public ridicule of recalcitrant donors often accompany these exactions up to moments before the sacrifice.

Most groups offer only sheep at the main shrine, but the tribal sections of the Sma'la evince a considerably more intense relationship toward the Sherqawa. They offer sheep at each of the principal Sherqawi shrines in Boujad and, in addition, a bull at the main shrine of Sidi Mhammed Sherqi. Until 1968, the latter was offered in what is known as a *t'argiba* sacrifice. This is a means used by tribes and tribal sections to secure and reaffirm major covenants or to impose a major supernatural compulsion (*'ar*). In the preprotectorate and early protectorate periods the *t'argiba* was often used to secure amnesty (*aman*) after rebellion from the Makhzen. Later it was used in the same fashion with the French. It last was used on the Tadla Plain in this way by the Sma'la in August 1955, to bring a halt to the aerial bombardment and reprisals of the Foreign Legion for the earlier tribal attack on Wad Zem that same month.[22]

The *t'argiba* sacrifice at the main shrine generally took the following pattern. The tribal sections of the Sma'la gathered at their tents on the outskirts of Boujad. Their Sherqawi visitors there said an invocation over the bull. Several barefooted tribesmen then led the bull, running, through the streets of Boujad to the shrine of Sidi Mhammed Sherqi. Other tribesmen of the covenanting group accompanied the bull on horseback or barefoot, all shouting their allegiance to Sidi Mhammed Sherqi. Some members of the procession beat drums, others went into trance (*jedba*), particularly as the group approached the shrine. Other pilgrims and a few townsmen often joined the procession as it ran through town. Most townsmen, however, stayed at a distance because the Sma'la had a reputation for being unrestrained during this procession, particularly if they saw the color red.[23] Finally, the bull was sacrificed in the interior court-yard of the shrine, in front of the room containing the marabout's sepulcher. As the throat of the sacrifice was hacked open, some of those in trance struggled forward to drink the victim's blood as it gushed out. Others, who were not in trance, smeared blood over their clothes or collected it in small vials. These were made into amulets to wear around their own necks and to give to their women and children. Tribesmen in trance were then led to the wooden grillwork (*garbus*) which surrounds the marabout's sepulcher, where they remained until they returned to their normal state. Sma'la say that when their faith (*niya*) was strong, those in trance saw water gush forth from under the marabout's tomb, and they then drank it.

Those who fall into trance are an exception to my claim above that the pilgrimage to Boujad largely constitutes a continuation of the ordinary social order. Such individuals claim no memory of events while in trance and thus are withdrawn from ordinary conventions. The consumption of fresh blood, for instance, is formally interdicted (*haram*) in Islam. Tribesmen are aware of this. It must be em-phasized, however, that such behavior has been confined to a few of the Sma'la. No other tribal groups act in this manner, nor did they do so in the past. Although none of the participants offers any ex-planation of this ritual, its form suggests that the covenant with the marabout is symbolized by blood sacrifice, which by its nature is an irrevocable act. The sacrifice is reciprocated by the marabout's endowing the land with fertility, symbolized by the water said to gush forth from under his tomb. The total lack of exegesis and of complementary rituals which form neat, closed patterns makes the interpretation of this ritual tentative. But perhaps its looseness of form is itself significant, since this looseness is replicated by the nature of groups in the social order.

The covenant of the Sma'la was last reaffirmed in the above man-ner in 1968. One reason for discontinuance of the ritual was pressure from townsmen, including many Sherqawa, who are hostile to this ritual and the view of Islam implicitly represented by it. Although even the governor of the province in which Boujad is located has at-tended the festival in recent years and made major donations to the shrine, his attendance is simply due to the importance of the festival in the eyes of the tribesmen. Another reason for the ritual's disap-

pearance is that the Sherqawa, in the distribution of the revenues of
the shrines (see next chapter), prefer that the animals be converted
into cash for distribution among themselves. Sherqawa persuaded the
tribesmen that the offer of a sacrifice was the same as its performance,
and this argument was accepted.[24] Thus the Sherqawa perhaps unwittingly spurred the rationalization of the covenant with their
clients. Tribesmen still run with the bull to the main shrine, and
some Sma'la continue to enter into trance as an expression, they say,
of their intense devotion to the Sherqawi *shaykh*. The tendency for
offerings in cash to replace offerings and sacrifices in nature has, I
suggest, the unintended consequence for the Sherqawa of emphasizing
the instrumental aspect of their relation with tribesmen. It also in-
duces a heightened awareness in their clients as to just what they
are getting in return. Offerings in cash are more directly comparable
to marketplace transactions than the traditional offerings in kind.

Tribal groups other than the Sma'la (and for that matter the
Sma'la at all Sherqawi shrines except the main one) are markedly
nonecstatic in renewing their covenant with the Sherqawa. There
usually is a procession from wherever the group is staying to the
main shrine, but it is at walking speed, wearing shoes, unaccompanied
by drumbeats, chants, or other ecstatic behavior. The sacrifice of the
sheep, when it occurs, is regarded nonchalantly. Attention of tribesmen is not particularly focused upon the act; so it is difficult for
outside observers to detect it taking place at all.

Although tribesmen maintain that covenants have been made on
behalf of their respective groups ever since the Sherqawa first came
to the upper Tadla Plain, they are conscious of the latitude of the
form in which their offerings are made and of the shifting composition of the groups involved. For instance, in recent years the Hwazem
tribal section of the Sma'la offered grains and sheep to their Sherqawi
visitors, in addition to sheep at each of the principal Sherqawi shrines
and a bull at that of Sidi Mhammed Sherqi. The Trosh and Wlad
Fennan tribal sections made similar offerings to their visitors but
none at the Sherqawi shrines in Boujad. After several years during
which the harvest of the Hwazem was markedly superior to that of
the other two tribal sections, tribesmen of the latter groups decided
that their relative misfortune was due to the displeasure of Sidi
Mhammed Sherqi. Consequently, since 1970, Trosh and Wlad Fennan have jointly offered a bull (not actually sacrificed) at his shrine.
In earlier years these two sections never made joint offerings. The

joint offering was made explicitly to reduce the expense, although tribesmen of both sections say that this economy does not reduce their expression of faith (*niya*) in the marabout. Similar reconsiderations of offerings occur among individuals. A tribesman of the Ṭrosh section of Smaʿla, a truck driver, recently stopped contributing to the sacrifice. Shortly afterward, he had an accident for which he was held responsible. His misfortune was attributed to the anger of the *shaykh*. He has since renewed his contributions.

Sacrifices and other offerings at the main shrine are generally made at the level of tribal sections rather than local communities. Tribesmen pragmatically say this is in order to make more substantial offerings which will be acceptable to the marabouts. In contrast, each local community acts alone in slaughtering a sheep for a communal meal with their Sherqawi visitor during the festival. This meal generally takes place in the guest tent of the local community. In the past it often occurred at the house of the Sherqawi in town—at least when the visitor was wealthy enough to have a large one—but adamant pressure from the neighbors of visitors has discouraged what they consider "non-Islamic" rituals in their quarter. A few of the most prestigious tribesmen are invited to the house of their visitor at some time during the course of the festival, but never as a group.

The symbolism of the communal meal at the guest tent is quite explicit. In offering part of the meat of the sacrifice to their visitor, tribesmen say to him: "This sheep is for your ancestor. Eat! [*Had el-hawli dyal jeddek, kulu!*]." His partaking of the meal reaffirms and strengthens the bond between the tribesmen and the marabout. At the end of the meal, a collection of money is made on behalf of the visitor. After it is handed to him, he responds with an invocation addressed to God and his ancestor Sidi Mḥammed Sherqi. Typical invocations mention the long association between the marabout and the local community in question, often referring in abbreviated form to the various myths known by the tribesmen. The visitor asks on behalf of his clients for good weather, the fertility of their crops and animals, and the resolution of any special problems which the group has experienced or anticipates. Problems facing individuals in the local community are also mentioned, such as a serious illness or the lack of male offspring. If a tribesman thinks that the visitor is skipping over any request too lightly or has forgotten something, he will simply interrupt and ask that the matter be dealt with. As with sacrifices, comportment at invocations is casual: ubiquitous transistor radios play in the background, conversations proceed only slightly subdued, and women and adolescents pay little attention, if any, to the proceedings. Despite the supernatural powers attributed to marabouts, the attitude toward them is generally not one of awe. The tone of invocations is that of reasonable men seeking to coax another into good conduct. The fact that at times tribesmen employ light sarcasm and taunting, not of Sidi Mḥammed Sherqi but of his descendants, implies the pre-existence of close ties between the parties.

Marabouts and Obligations

Underlying all ties with marabouts is the concept of obligation (ḥăqq). Requests to marabouts must be accompanied by offerings, sacrifices, or the promise (waʿda) of them.[25] Unlike the relations of Spanish villagers to saints, which run along a spectrum from relations of instrumentality to affective relations (Christian 1972), Moroccan relations with marabouts all tend to be construed in terms of obligation. One Sherqawi said, "You [must] bring something to 'open' a matter with God [Nta te-tjib shi-haja bash yefteḥ Allah l-amr biha]." The same principle applies equally to gifts intended to induce persons to grant requests made of them. A tacit corollary of this instrumental exchange is that the only effective marabouts are those who are able to receive offerings or who have descendants and other persons "close" to them capable of doing so on their behalf. The caretaker of one of the shrines in Boujad stated the point as follows: "If you give something [to a marabout], there must be someone to pick it up. If not, there's no point in giving anything." This applies equally to collective offerings and individual supplications. Of course, descendants of marabouts are present only at the larger and more popular shrines to take offerings and to aid supplicants in making their invocations.

As with other transactions of obligation, there is no formal economic reckoning of the exchange between marabouts and their clients. Nevertheless, a mutual sorting-out takes place. The faith (niya) of clients is thought to be shown in the value of their offerings. This must be commensurate with their own prestige, that of the marabout or visitor, and the nature of the request being made. An offering considered meager in relation to the rank (daraja) of the client or that of a marabout or visitor is construed as a lack of faith. Visitors do not hesitate to inform their clients when they are not satisfied with meager offerings. Moreover, correspondence from the nineteenth century indicates that such bartering for invocations is not a recent development. If offerings are meager, a marabout or prestigious visitor is thought to refrain from acting effectively on behalf of his clients, even if an invocation is actually made. In particular, the prestige of living marabouts suffers if they are accessible to clients able to offer only a chicken or a few eggs. Boujad's living marabout receives pilgrims during the fall festival and also writes amulets and says invocations on behalf of individuals throughout the year. Writing an amulet for a diminutive offering would serve to diminish his "word," since he customarily performs such services in exchange for significant cash contributions, the gift of animals, or, as once occurred in 1969, the title to a used car.

This marabout has the same problem as his predecessors of preserving his *baraka* through a comportment which maintains a social distance from all but the most prestigious of his clientele. In the last century Sidi ben Dawd daily rode on his mule around Boujad, listening to requests from townsmen, and regularly visited his tribal clients. But the actual settlement of disputes and other political negotiations, in which there always was the risk of failure or indecision, was tacitly delegated to Sidi 'Umar, his son. Significantly, Sidi 'Umar did not succeed his father upon his death but continued as the political counselor for the next marabout. The present marabout who actively encourages belief in his maraboutic powers can be seen publicly around Boujad, but he has virtually no clients in the town itself. No one pays him particular attention. However, on market days and during the annual festival he confines himself to his house, access to which is controlled by retainers, generally poor relatives. These stand at the door of his house and decide which pilgrims to admit. A direct refusal to a supplicant unable to afford the going price of his invocations would be considered improper. Occasional intervention on behalf of the destitute is considered an act of charity, but too frequent action on their behalf would dilute the economic and status base necessary to maintain his maraboutic reputation for *baraka*. Persons seeking an invocation with little to offer often try to secure recommendations, sometimes in writing, from the marabout's more affluent clients to avoid being turned away.[26]

The ideology of clients' remaining "connected" with marabouts emphasizes stability. Nevertheless, now, as in the nineteenth century, alliances between marabouts and their clients are contracted and broken. Tribal groups can become disillusioned with the ability of their marabout or visitor to sustain them with *baraka*. The visitor himself may drop some groups in favor of those capable of demonstrating their faith with more substantial offerings. As the scope of *baraka* attributed to marabouts has contracted in recent years and its intensity diminished, many such connections are broken at the death of the visitors, who, as I have indicated, often no longer have other Sherqawa willing to replace them.

Such shifts in alignments are not done whimsically but once decided upon are fairly easy to accomplish, both for the Sherqawa and for their clientele. Sherqawa do not comment among themselves upon who, if anyone, has *baraka* or the ability to communicate it. Only God, they say, has that knowledge. *Baraka* among the Sherqawa thus resembles the ethos of competitive settlement among merchants, who wait for God to bring them business rather than openly solicit it, so as to avoid overt friction among themselves. This ideological tenet is also secure from direct attack from Islamic reformists, as no formal assertion is made of the "closeness" of the Sherqawa to God. During fieldwork, I initially thought that certain Sherqawa were being evasive when, in response to my asking whether a particular marabout, living or dead, had *baraka,* they replied that the Bni So-and-So made such a claim. Their commentary was quite accurate. The "proof" of *baraka* is the existence of clients who act as if a particular marabout has it. This comes very close to a pure example of Weber's concept of charisma (Weber 1968:401).

This populistic determination of *baraka* is particularly apparent in the careers of living marabouts but holds equally for the careers of visitors and enshrined marabouts. Shrines, at least such major ones as that of Sidi Mhammed Sherqi, have a manifold symbolic appeal which partially insulates them from immediate political and economic vicissitudes. They also have an economic base not immediately dependent upon the offerings of pilgrims. The Sherqawa who manage the affairs of the main shrine have not distributed the accumulated offerings to the "children of the *shaykh*" in recent years. Instead, they have redirected this income into enlarging the shrine and building a hostel for pilgrims. Similar decisions have been made by the claimed descendants of enshrined marabouts elsewhere on the Tadla Plain. The effect is to upgrade the prestige of the shrine and to conceal the overall attrition of revenue.

As for living marabouts, at the turn of the century all client tribal groups were tied with either the lord of the 'Arbawi Sherqawa or

the rival lord of the Zawya Sherqawa. As the ability of living marabouts to exercise their influence waned, so did their ties with client
groups. Many groups have ceased maintaining ties with living marabouts, but continue them with visitors and make the annual pilgrimage. Groups that continue to renew their covenant with living
marabouts (or in the case of the 'Arbawi Sherqawa, with a close
relative of a person with such a reputation) generally have maintained allegiance with the same Sherqawi faction since prior to the
protectorate. The longevity of these ties is largely due to the new
social conditions introduced by the protectorate. The possibility of
new marabouts emerging among the Sherqawa and asserting their
identity was crippled by the French action in "freezing" the two rival
lords and their successors into positions of prominence and fixing the
lines of political identity for potential clients.

The situation of the one remaining Sherqawi marabout who actively seeks to maintain his reputation is especially precarious, since
he depends directly upon revenue from pilgrims. Even as some groups
sever ties with him and those who remain "connected" cut the size
of their offerings, he is pressed to live up to his reputation for unrestrained generosity (*karama*) in entertaining them. During the
fall festival, groups of several hundred pilgrims arrive in relays at
his house. Each group stays for anywhere from one to three days and
brings with it the animals and grain needed for its sustenance. To
retain pilgrims, this marabout has in recent years added music and
female dancers (*shikha*-s) for their entertainment, but their number
is still declining steadily. A pending inheritance dispute may also
bring about the division of the large house which is a manifestation
of his *baraka* and in which he entertains guests. If the dispute goes
against him, then he will lose most of the manifest symbols of his
baraka. Unlike that of his predecessors, his own reputation for
baraka is largely demystified. Even through the 1930's. tribesmen
popularly attributed to Sherqawa marabouts the capacity to change
themselves into lions. among other miraculous deeds. The uncle of
the present Zawya marabout (2-14) was reputed to have this capacity.
The current marabout is not. Demystification means that living
marabouts are now much more vulnerable to their immediate successes and failures.

The French tried to sustain the prestige of the Sherqawi marabouts
by providing them with official sinecures, but their hold over other
Sherqawa nonetheless became much less firm. This hold became

even weaker with independence. Where once the Sherqawa were firmly identified with maraboutism, many Sherqawa now strive to separate the two identities as far as possible. I describe the cultural basis of Sherqawi identity and the process by which it became dissociated from maraboutism in the next chapter.

Table 5.
Principal Collective Visits to Living Sherqawi Marabouts,
September 1969

Lord of 'Arbawi Sherqawa	Lord of Zawya Sherqawa
Ait 'Attab	Bni 'Amir
Shawya	1. Several local communities of
1. Wlad Bu Ziri	Bni Brahim
2. Jrari	2. Wlad Ziyyan
3. 'Qawqa	3. Krifat
4. Wlad Sidi ben Dawd	4. Wlad 'Ali
Werdigha	5. Wlad 'Ali Dhirat (recently
1. Urada	split from Wlad 'Ali)
2. Thamna	6. Wlad Bu Herru
Bni Musa	7. Wlad 'Ali Mulay l-Wad
Several sections (*traf*-s)	8. Merbe'
Bni Meskin	9. Brawna
600 pilgrims, sections unknown	10. Wlad Sasi
Berbers from Walmas region	11. Bradiyya
Bni Zemmur	12. Wlad Messun
1. Hamrayn	13. Khalfiyya
2. Rwashed	Bni Musa
	1. Mesghuna
	2. Ait l-Wali

7
Sherqawi Identity

A Cultural Definition

A Sherqawi is defined by Moroccans as a patrilineal descendant of Sidi Mhammed Sherqi. Persons who claim descent from a common ancestor are normatively thought to constitute a descent group. When the claimed ancestor is a marabout, such persons are considered to be members of a maraboutic descent group. Sociologically viewed, however, they can best be described as what Harold W. Scheffler has called a "descent category." In other words, the idiom of patrilineal descent "itself gives form only to *categories* of persons" of common patrilineal descent, and "these categories remain nondiscrete and only vaguely bounded" (Scheffler 1965:62). Membership in such a category does not imply an obligation to act in the common interest of that category. Rather, it is the presence of what are perceived as common interests, among which is the possibility of achieving or maintaining higher status, which encourages the formation of *groups* based on the claim to Sherqawi descent. Scheffler's distinction between descent categories and descent groups is analytically quite useful. Some persons who are in the Sherqawi descent category are denied membership in Sherqawi descent groups. This largely comes about when the intensity and quality of their interaction with other persons recognized as Sherqawa falls below a certain level. Moreover, place of residence and propinquity to other Sherqawa, formally having nothing to do with the ideology of descent, are in practice crucial factors in shaping Sherqawi identity.

Predictably, those groups within the Sherqawa with significant interests to defend have their boundaries more sharply defined than the others. Recognition of Sherqawi identity follows the same principle of "closeness" that was introduced in Chapter 4. Thus the key question throughout this chapter is why and how identity as Sherqawa and as marabouts or their descendants is manipulated.

There are two separate aspects to Sherqawi identity. One is the formal genealogical ideology, which serves as a framework to conceptualize and legitimize a wide range of social relationships. The other is the question of how identity as a Sherqawi is pragmatically achieved and maintained. Signs of such identity include membership in a local group composed largely, but not exclusively, of persons appearing in a Sherqawi genealogy and residence in a Sherqawi quarter. They also include rights of inheritance as a Sherqawi through Islamic law, the conventions governing the distribution of offerings made at the various Sherqawi shrines, hypergamous marriage with commoners (i.e., the taking in marriage of commoner women but the giving of none in return), and explicit or tacit acceptance as a Sherqawi by recognized Sherqawa of high prestige.

As Scheffler has noted, the concept of descent group is itself inherently ambiguous: "A descent group is any *group* in relation to which a descent concept may be said to serve as one or more of the following: (1) a principle of recruitment (i.e., a criterion for membership); (2) a conceptualization of the unity of the group; (3) a statement of the actual or 'proper' composition of the group; and (4) a statement of the nature of the group's relations with other such groups within the same set of groups (or society)" (1965:42). The Sherqawi claim of shared patrilineal descent from a common ancestor shifts, often imperceptibly, between these various meanings. Sherqawiness, so to speak, is a condensed symbolization of several bases of social honor. The same is true of other assertions of "closeness" throughout Moroccan society. What distinguishes the Sherqawa in this respect is the intensity with which such identity is maintained and manipulated.

Ideologically, Sherqawi descent is characterized by claims to certain genealogical and mystical attributes. First, all Sherqawa are *foqra* (sg., *fqir*), patrilineal descendants of 'Umar ben l-Khaṭṭab.[1] In some respects, *foqra* are treated like patrilineal descendants of the Prophet Muḥammed (*shorfa*; sg., *shrif*). Like *shorfa*, the Sherqawa practice hypergamous marriage with commoners (*'awam*; sg., *'ammi*), that is, all those persons unable to claim descent from the Prophet or 'Umar. Sherqawa and *shorfa* are, moreover, equal for the purpose of intermarriage. Thus, Sidi Mḥammed Sherqi is said to have taken a wife from the Sa'adi dynasty of *shorfa* (1555–1659). A more contemporary example of Sherqawi equality with *shorfa* is the current marriage of a prominent Sherqawi to the sister of the present king and royal consent to prefix Mulay to their son's name, a prerogative normally reserved for *shorfa*.

As for mystical descent, Sidi Mḥammed Sherqi is thought to possess mystical knowledge transmitted to him through a name-chain (*silsila*) of marabouts which ultimately reaches back to the Prophet. This knowledge has in turn been communicated by Sidi Mḥammed Sherqi to other marabouts, primarily his own descendants but also some non-Sherqawa. As indicated in Chapter 1, the notions of the transmission of mystical knowledge and of patrilineal descent have popularly fused in Morocco, although, when the subject is explicitly discussed, educated Sherqawa distinguish between the two concepts. After all, it is known that *baraka* is very unequally distributed among the descendants of marabouts. In principle, God determines the Sherqawi who has the most *baraka* at any given time, who then becomes lord (*sid, mqaddem*) of the *zawya*. But intense fights for succession in the past indicate that the signs of possession of such *baraka* have been highly contested by those who felt they could successfully stake a claim. Descent from or "closeness" to these maraboutic lords conveys substantial prestige to the rest of the Sherqawa. Some *baraka* is hereditary; "closeness" by descent from or kinship ties to a marabout in itself carries a presumed privileged access to their maraboutic relations. Even for those who presently deny that marabouts have the powers popularly attributed to them, Sherqawi prominence can be legitimated on other grounds: ancestors who have been distinguished both as religious scholars and as guarantors of social order in earlier, turbulent times, and the leading role of some Sherqawa in the contemporary Moroccan polity. But the possibility of separating genealogical from mystical descent is more apparent to the Sherqawa themselves than to their clients (or other commoners), who assume that all Sherqawa share in some degree the mystical powers of their ancestors.

The Sherqawa consider themselves at present to be divided into eight descent groups, each of which is associated with a residential quarter in Boujad. I specify "at present" because there are clear indications that the number of effective descent groups has historically shifted. Genealogies, after all, refer to the social situation of contemporary groups and persons, not to the dead. Six of these descent groups claim descent from six sons of Sidi Mḥammed Sherqi—Sidi ʿAbd l-Qader, Sid l-Mursli, Sid l-Ghazwani, Sid l-Meknasi, Sidi ʿAbd es-Slam, and Sidi ʿAllal. The remaining two groups claim descent from maraboutic lords of the nineteenth century. (All Sherqawi lords claim descent from another of Sidi Mḥammed Sherqi's sons, Sidi ʿAbd l-Khaleq [2-3]).

All prominent Sherqawa of the last two centuries have been from these latter two groups. Because they have had at their command the greatest material wealth and prestige, their members have had a competitive edge over other Sherqawa in controlling the resources of the religious lodge, access to both traditional and modern education, links with influential Moroccans elsewhere, appointment to government posts, and other strategic advantages. These are value-added, in the sense that prerogatives enjoyed in the past make it more likely that the same persons or those sponsored by them—generally members of their household, kinsmen, or clients—will enjoy similar advantages at later times.

The ideological core of Sherqawi identity and its internal differentiation is contained in genealogies and chains of "mystical" descent. These are regarded by the Sherqawa and others as symbolic encapsulations of Sherqawi histories. I use the plural because there are multiple ways in which the genealogies are constructed, understood, and related to each other. Each history is construed in terms of the social reality as seen by certain elements of society, even though the underlying pattern governing the generation of these histories is constant. At the same time, these conceptions of the past shape that reality both by internally relating the Sherqawa to each other and by linking them with the rest of society. In contrast to the genealogies of commoners (*ʿawam*), the span of Sherqawi genealogies, that is, the number of contemporaries included in them, and their generational depth are significantly larger.

These qualities in themselves do not distinguish maraboutic from nonmaraboutic genealogies. Similar qualities are represented in the genealogies of "those who are distinguished" (*nas khaṣṣa*) on the basis of claims to prestige other than descent from Muḥammed and 'Umar: families that claim a long tradition of Makhzen service, urban merchant families, families with a tradition of religious scholarship, and the like. As I indicated in my example of the formation of the Qsayra quarter (Ch. 4), social honor is legitimated whenever possible by the claim to a distinguished genealogy. For a commoner to assert similar genealogical knowledge would be considered presumptuous and improper. In contrast, the core genealogy of the Sherqawa is in the public domain. Not everyone, even among the Sherqawa, knows all of its key components, but everyone is aware of the centuries of maraboutic prestige of the Sherqawa, their numerous shrines in Boujad and throughout the Tadla Plain, and the reputations of some prominent contemporary Sherqawa (most of which are no longer based upon maraboutic activities). Claimed relations of kinship among the Sherqawa are also frequently much more complex than those that exist among commoners. For instance, the core of the 'Arbawi descent group claim kin relations through one of the fourteen sons and five daughters of Sid l-Ḥajj l-'Arbi (2-9). This lord had one legal wife and at least eight concubines. Many of these descendants, in turn, had large households, multiple marriages, and—for those who reached maturity in the years immediately preceding the protectorate—significant numbers of concubines. The Zawya Sherqawa show a similar complexity of internal relations. These descendants share complex rights to undivided inheritances through Islamic law, rights to the revenues of shrines, access as kinsmen to prominent Sherqawa, and such complex bonds of "closeness" based upon kin ties and other factors that multiple interlocking links can be made with other Sherqawa.

Few commoners elaborate their identity as a descent group in a similar fashion. Even among the Sherqawa, the importance attached to genealogical knowledge and to descent ideology varies considerably. The thinnest genealogical knowledge tends to be possessed by members of the six nonlordly descent groups. Each of these is associated with a shrine and a quarter in Boujad, although there are no formal activities associated with their particular shrines. The boundaries of inclusion in these groups are much more permeable than those of the remaining two "main-line" descent groups, 'Arbawi and Zawya. Long-term residents of the quarters associated with the non–main-line descent groups frequently claim Sherqawi descent and have this claim unchallenged in many contexts, even though they may not be able to claim a share (*ḥăqq*) of the offerings of the principal shrine.

In principle, the Sherqawa maintain registers of descendants of Sidi Mḥammed Sherqi, just as registers of descendants of the Prophet are supposed to be kept. Nevertheless, such formal determination of descent-group membership is germane only for the distribution of offerings made at the main Sherqawi shrines. These registers are largely inaccessible, and many Sherqawa correctly maintain that they are incomplete and out-of-date. Much more important is being "known" (*me'ruf*) as a Sherqawi in face-to-face, ongoing social relationships. In these terms, members of the non–main-line groups have only a truncated body of genealogical lore to establish their legitimacy. They know by name none of their intervening ancestors between the present and the sons of Sidi Mḥammed Sherqi from whom they claim descent. Moreover, the span of known contemporary relationships is generally much narrower than that known by members of the main-line groups. Nor do these individuals have anything to gain in material interests by expanding the span of their relationships or by drawing attention to their genealogical claims.

In contrast, members of the main-line 'Arbawi and Zawya descent groups show a much greater awareness of the boundaries of their groups and can generally trace in detail their genealogical links to one of the nineteenth-century Sherqawi lords. Consequently they sharply delineate between members of their descent groups and mere inhabitants of their quarters who may claim "closeness" with them. These two groups have substantial common interests and have in general managed to defend them. Many of the estates of their prominent nineteenth-century Sherqawi ancestors have remained undivided, entitling many of them to substantial revenues through Islamic inheritance in addition to those from shares in the offerings at the main shrine, available in principle to all Sherqawa. In themselves, these two forms of rights are insufficient to provide members of the main-line groups with a livelihood, although they constitute an important addition to the income of many households. More so than members of other groups, main-line Sherqawa maintain houses in their respective quarters to substantiate their identity, rather than locate themselves wherever there is satisfactory housing, as members of other descent groups tend increasingly to do.

Even in these two descent groups, most Sherqawa do not know in detail the wealth of genealogical resources available to them, although all parts of the genealogy described below are known by them to exist and can be activated when there are reasons to stress or to forge specific links. Significantly, it is the most influential Sherqawa who possess the most elaborate knowledge of these genealogies and capacity to use them to further their interests. This social distribution of knowledge has already been described in the context of rural Morocco (Ch. 4). For all but certain highly educated Sherqawa, these genealogies are accepted in their entirety as being historically valid. They unquestionably are, in the sense that for many they constitute history as locally understood. Other Sherqawa discriminate between those sections of the genealogy which are corroborated by written historical accounts and are relatively fixed—such as the succession of Sherqawi lords (Fig. 2)[2]—and other elements of the genealogy, such as the links between Sidi 'Umar in the seventh century and Sidi Mhammed Sherqi in the sixteenth or the links of descent from one of the non–main-line sons of Sidi Mhammed Sherqi. The act of writing and formally recording parts of the genealogy renders them immutable, while the other, unwritten claims are tacitly recognized by the Sherqawi elite as mutable.

The various sections of the genealogy presented below do not quite add up to a composite whole, since each of its components tends to be used as the ideology for certain types of social relations. Even over the last forty years, there have been considerable shifts in how they have been elaborated. For this reason I think it important to specify as carefully as possible the social contexts in which they are elaborated.

"Closeness" with 'Umar: The Proto-Sherqawa

The claimed patrilineal link between Sidi Mhammed Sherqi and 'Umar ben l-Khattab is not known in any detail to the great majority of the Sherqawa and their clients. Nor is there any concern to know it, since there is no active contest of the claim and no current use to which this part of the genealogy is put. The fact that Sherqawa have for generations intermarried with descendants of the Prophet on the basis of such descent is considered sufficient evidence of such a link. Claims to descent from 'Umar have been subject to skepticism by Moroccan religious scholars for centuries, an indication that the current skepticism of educated Moroccans about such claims is not novel.

In one elite account of the links of Sidi Mhammed Sherqi with

'Umar (Fig. 10) there are twenty-two intervening ancestors. Alternate generation naming is a very common feature of Moroccan genealogies; so the repetition of names in this genealogy is to be expected. However, no biographical information is attached to any of the first fourteen descendants of 'Umar, those who presumably remained in Arabia.

There are several uses which the Sherqawa make—or, more accurately, made—of the remainder of the genealogy, depicting Sidi Mhammed Sherqi's ancestors who lived in Morocco. One is purportedly to document their association with Morocco's reigning dynasties. The other is to relate the Sherqawa to some of their tribal clients. Thus, Sidi 'Abdallah (10-1) is said to have left the port of Yanbu' in Arabia at an unspecified time for the Tafilalt region of southern Morocco. This region is important as the birthplace of the two major Moroccan dynasties that claim descent from the Prophet Muhammed, the Sa'adi and the 'Alawi. Since more concrete examples of such ties can be found at later periods and in the present, these earlier assertions of association with the *shorfa* dynasties are generally offered in a tentative fashion and are not pressed if skepticism is raised about them.

There is a third use for this part of the Sherqawi genealogy. As recently as forty years ago, a claim of descent from a proto-Sherqawi was a means of asserting a tie of "closeness" between Sherqawi marabouts and their clients without giving the clients the status of maraboutic descent. Unfortunately, the lack of more detailed contextual information of how these claims to "closeness" were asserted makes it difficult to assess their significance with any precision. In the period of my fieldwork, several Sherqawa and some of the tribal elite still claimed a *fqir* status for their tribes without being able to specify the basis of this claim. In the 1930's, in contrast, Claude Ecorcheville elicited an elaborate schema of such links from Sherqawi notables (Fig. 11). Since the number of Sherqawi clients has contracted in recent years and maraboutic ties have been significantly downgraded and divested of political implications, there is currently less interest attached to elaborating such links. In Ecorcheville's tribal version, Sidi Mhammed Sherqi's ancestors are part of the twelfth-century Bni Jabir of western Morocco.[3] I have heard no one carry this claim to its logical conclusion and assert that all the tribes of western Morocco descended from 'Umar are *foqra* like the Sherqawa. In particular, neither the Sherqawa nor the tribal elite suggest that the assertion

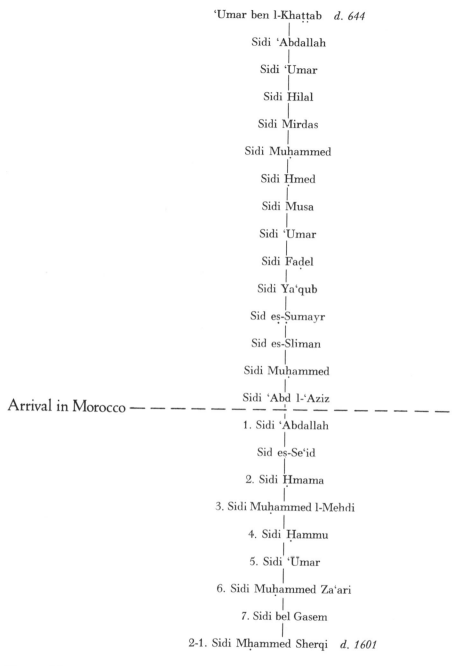

'Umar ben l-Khaṭṭab   *d. 644*

Sidi 'Abdallah

Sidi 'Umar

Sidi Hilal

Sidi Mirdas

Sidi Muhammed

Sidi Hmed

Sidi Musa

Sidi 'Umar

Sidi Fadel

Sidi Ya'qub

Sid es-Sumayr

Sid es-Sliman

Sidi Muhammed

Arrival in Morocco — — — — — — — Sidi 'Abd l-'Aziz — — — — — — — — —

1. Sidi 'Abdallah

Sid es-Se'id

2. Sidi Hmama

3. Sidi Muhammed l-Mehdi

4. Sidi Hammu

5. Sidi 'Umar

6. Sidi Muhammed Za'ari

7. Sidi bel Gasem

2-1. Sidi Mhammed Sherqi   *d. 1601*

Figure 10.
Descent from 'Umar. (Based on Ecorcheville 1938.)

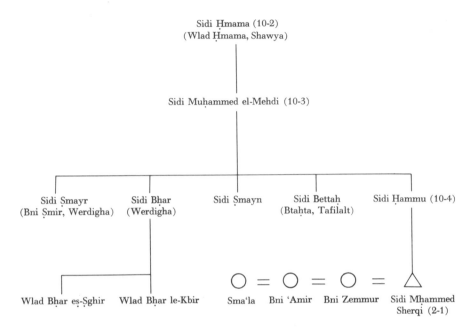

Figure 11.
Ancestors of Sidi Mhammed Sherqi. (Based on Ecorcheville 1938.)

of descent from 'Umar enabled such tribes to take women homog-
amously from Sherqawi *foqra* or from *shorfa*. This conceptual
ambiguity in the use of the term *foqra* does not constitute any
perplexity for informants. Clearly, the claim of *fqir* status has two
components, patrilineal descent from 'Umar and, as shall be described,
mystical ties with Muhammed.

It is a mistake, I think, to assume that these genealogies are intended to be rigorously scrutinized. Each serves as a conceptual grid,
parts of which can be utilized to construct or legitimate contem-
porarily significant social relationships. What is important is that
there are available certain nodes on the genealogies through which
certain relationships can be asserted. These are not random, of course,
yet evidence a considerable flexibility. Many of the Sherqawa
represented in the various genealogies have shrines or tombs on the
upper Tadla Plain, although the exact identity of such marabouts is
often ambiguous. For instance, informants are uncertain as to which
represent ancestors or brothers of Sidi Mhammed Sherqi. These am-

biguities mean that Sherqawa and tribesmen can convincingly manipulate the genealogies to provide meaningful representations of contemporary social realities. The physical presence of shrines of certain Sherqawa (or proto-Sherqawa) who figure in these genealogies, even if only vaguely perceived by many tribesmen, anchors the Sherqawa securely in the geographical and social morphology of the region under their influence.

Thus, in Figures 10 and 11, Sidi Ḥmama (10-2) is claimed as the ancestor of the tribe in Shawya (located near the town of Ben Ḥmed) which bears his name. Sidi Muḥammed el-Mehdi (10-3), whose tomb is in the midst of a public garden constructed by the French at Wad Zem, is not currently connected with any tribal group. In the 1930's, however, individuals claiming descent from him attempted to initiate collective pilgrimages from the surrounding tribes (Ecorcheville 1938). Had this attempt been successful, then it is likely that elaborate genealogical schema would have been produced and accepted to link this marabout to his clients. The proof of "early" relations is the pattern of existing or potential social relations.

The biographical glosses associated with the sons of Sidi Muḥammed el-Medhi confirm this suggestion. Sidi Bettaḥ is said to have remained in Tafilalt, while Sidi Ṣmayn was "childless." In collecting contemporary kinship data, childlessness is attributed equally to persons without descendants and those whose descendants are unknown. In the latter case the term also implies that no one presently claims relationships through a particular person. Sidi Ṣmayr and Sidi Bḥar are eponymous ancestors for tribal groups that are Sherqawi clients located about forty kilometers to the northwest of Boujad. Finally, Sidi Ḥammu (10-4) and his grandson, Sidi Muḥammed Za'ari (10-6), have tombs in Boujad's rural hinterland. The former is on the Wad Bu Gerrum (Tashelḥit dialect, "Stream of the Marabouts"); the latter on Wad Tashraft (Tashelḥit, "Stream of the *Shorfa*"). No known tombs represent the remaining persons who figure in this part of the Sherqawi genealogy.

Claims of descent from one of the eight brothers of Sidi Mḥammed Sherqi are used much in the same way as claims of descent from one of the proto-Sherqawa. These eight are Sidi 'Ali Filali, Sidi 'Abd er-Răhman, Sidi l-Werdi, Sidi 'Abd en-Nebi, Sid et-Tunsi, Sid es-Se'id, Sidi 'Abd l-'Aziz, and Sidi 'Ali (or Muḥammed) Ṣmuni. One of these, Sidi 'Abd en-Nebi, has a shrine adjacent to that of Sidi Mḥammed Sherqi. Another two, Sidi 'Abd l-'Aziz and Sidi 'Abd er-Răhman, have shrines near Wad Zem. One, Sid es-Se'id, has a shrine in Tetouan. Three of these brothers (Sidi 'Abd l-'Aziz, Sidi 'Ali Smuni, and Sidi 'Abd en-Nebi, are claimed as eponymous ancestors of tribes in the Shawya that are clients of the Sherqawa. Not all informants agree on the number of brothers attributed to Sidi Mhammed Sherqi. Some are considered by different informants to be merely "close" to him, his brothers, or possibly his ancestors. Informants often do not consider the exact relationship to be as important as the fact that a relationship exists. Like descent from an ancestor of Sidi Mhammed Sherqi, the genealogical grid provided by the *shaykh*'s brothers has the potential for establishing new links between marabouts and clients. Thus in the 1930's, when there was still considerable maraboutic activity, some tribesmen from Wlad Se'id (Shawya) claimed descent from Sidi 'Abd l-'Aziz and unsuccessfully tried to establish his tomb near Wad Zem as a pilgrimage center (Ecorcheville 1938:36).[4] In the past, such descent was also frequently claimed by groups of inhabitants of Sherqawi estates (*'azib*-s) (Eickelman 1972–1973:52–53). There is no indication, however, of whether such a status provided individuals with prerogatives beyond those enjoyed by the other inhabitants of the estates.

Claimed descent from a brother of Sidi Mhammed Sherqi can also be used as a means of legitimating social honor. Currently a family of non-Sherqawi merchants who have supplied prominent local leaders of the nationalist movement claim descent from Sidi 'Ali Smuni. This reputed brother of the *shaykh* has no shrine in Boujad. although a quarter (6-20) founded in the 1930's bears his name in addition to the now more common name Khaluqiyin. His claimed descendants maintain that Sidi 'Ali, in contrast to Sidi Mhammed Sherqi, was like themselves a "progressive," thus making descent from him more significant (although they admit, less known) than descent from Sidi Mhammed Sherqi. For the benefit of outsiders, such as myself, they reasoned that, since they were descendants of 'Umar and of a brother of Sidi Mhammed Sherqi, they also were Sherqawa. Sherqawa point out that the family in question is of fairly recent tribal origin and that in any case no one else claims such descent. This latter argument is reminiscent of that used by al-Qadiri in the seventeenth century to question the Sherqawi claim of descent from 'Umar. Seen sociologically, the claim of such descent has the advantage of avoiding a direct threat to the material rights of direct descendants of the *shaykh*.

The Mystical Heritage

Until the 1930's, particularly in rural Morocco, a traditionally educated person was assumed to know something of the religious sciences (*'ulum*; sg., *'ilm*) and of the connections which historically existed among marabouts with mystical knowledge (*al-asrar*; lit., "the secrets"). Such knowledge legitimated their claims to high status in the eyes of others. At present, only the elderly know such ties with any detail. Since the ascendancy of the reformist and nationalist movements in the 1930's, specific awareness of this body of knowledge has ceased to be part of the intellectual baggage of the younger elite.

The particular name-chains (*silsila*-s) through which mystical knowledge is acquired once were of vital political significance, as in the sixteenth-century struggles between marabouts supporting the Ottomans in Algeria (see Ch. 1). Knowledge of such chains continued to be significant through the 1930's, at least as a means of social legitimation of mystical insight.

Most Sherqawa and tribesmen know these chains of legitimation only through the myths and legends associated with the maraboutic tombs and shrines that dot the landscape. For instance, Sidi Mhammed Sherqi is linked in popular myths with the marabout Sidi Hmed bel Gasem, whose shrine and descendants are in Bni Mellal. In the popular conception of "closeness," this physical propinquity assumes more weight than the written record, known only to a few, which states that the two marabouts studied together (Qadiri 1913: 129). But this interlocking of written sources, known to exist even by tribesmen, with more popular accounts of these marabouts serves to reinforce the popular acceptance of the latter.

These mystical ties, like all others in society, are represented as dyadic relationships. Some of Sidi Mhammed Sherqi's mystic links with the Prophet are through his father, Sidi bel Gasem (10-7). His shrine is not far from Qasba Tadla, on the southern bank of the Umm er-Rbi' River. On the opposite bank is the shrine of Sidi Mhammed Sherqi's mother, Lalla Rǎhma.[5] Sidi bel Gasem is said to have studied religious sciences and mysticism with 'Abd l-'Aziz et-Tebba (d. 1508), one of the fountainheads of the pro-Moroccan mystic tradition mentioned in Chapters 1 and 2.

Most of the major marabouts of western Morocco are popularly considered to follow the teachings of Shaykh et-Tebba. Their shrines form a line along the piedmont between the Atlas Mountains and the

western plains. Besides Sidi Mhammed Sherqi, these disciples include
Sidi 'Abdallah ben Dawd esh-Shawi, whose shrine is at Ksiba (originally said to be from Wlad Bu Ziri in Shawya); Sidi 'Ali u Brahim
and his disciples, whose shrines and clientele are in the Bzu region,
near Sraghna; and Sidi Rehhal, who founded a religious lodge east
of Marrakesh which bears his name. All of these marabouts are
mentioned in traditional historical accounts and figure in popular
myths and legends as mutually confirming and acquiring each
other's *baraka*. One myth, for instance, describes Lalla Rahma as
childless until, unaided by her husband, she took a bull as an offering
to 'Ali u Brahim. Subsequently she gave birth to Sidi Mhammed
Sherqi. Later, when she again encountered 'Ali u Brahim, the infant
Sidi Mhammed Sherqi sucked nine of the ten toes of Sidi 'Ali while
he was asleep and thus acquired much of his *baraka*.

One distinct facet of the heroic age of Sidi Mhammed Sherqi as
popularly represented is the tendency of mystic insight to flow freely
among those who sought it, regardless of their other bonds. Later,
such insight is seen to be preferentially (but never exclusively)
transmitted along the lines of patrilineal descent. The term *secret of
the ancestors* (*sirr l-aslaf*) applies mostly to the transmission of
baraka after this heroic age, not before. (Traditional educated opinion
does not make the synthesis of transmission of knowledge through
mystical ties and through genealogical descent.) Sidi Mhammed
l-Ma'ti (2-4), the third lordly successor of the founding marabout, is
buried just outside Marrakesh in the same shrine as one of his Sufi
masters, Brahim Tamili (Ecorcheville 1938: 38). Such physical
propinquity is often taken as evidence of the transmission of *baraka*
between two marabouts.

Descendants of Sidi Mhammed Sherqi

The Sherqawa proper are those who claim direct descent from Sidi
Mhammed Sherqi. Because such claims involve substantial material
rights and social honor, they are more sharply defined and contested
than those previously discussed. Still there is considerable variation
among the Sherqawa proper as to how their identity is conceived.
Even among the Sherqawa there is a shifting of claimed ancestors
similar to the pattern described earlier for the residents of the
Qsayra quarter. This is particularly apparent in the changing relationship between descent groups and enshrined marabouts. As men-

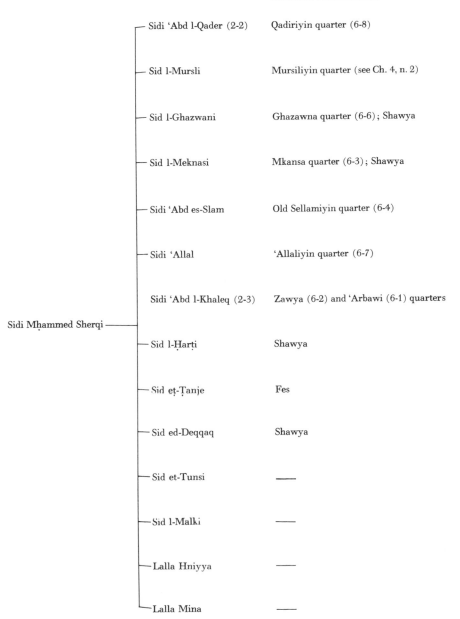

Principal Locations of
Claimed Descendants

Sidi 'Abd l-Qader (2-2)   Qadiriyin quarter (6-8)

Sid l-Mursli   Mursiliyin quarter (see Ch. 4, n. 2)

Sid l-Ghazwani   Ghazawna quarter (6-6); Shawya

Sid l-Meknasi   Mkansa quarter (6-3); Shawya

Sidi 'Abd es-Slam   Old Sellamiyin quarter (6-4)

Sidi 'Allal   'Allaliyin quarter (6-7)

Sidi 'Abd l-Khaleq (2-3)   Zawya (6-2) and 'Arbawi (6-1) quarters

Sidi Mhammed Sherqi

Sid l-Harti   Shawya

Sid et-Tanje   Fes

Sid ed-Deqqaq   Shawya

Sid et-Tunsi   ———

Sid l-Malki   ———

Lalla Hniyya   ———

Lalla Mina   ———

Figure 12.
Sons and daughters of Sidi Mhammed Sherqi.

tioned above, there are presently eight Sherqawi descent groups in
Boujad, but a larger number of Sherqawi ancestors are available to
serve as points of differentiation. Several other descent groups are
vaguely recognized or thought to exist elsewhere. Thus, there were no
recognized descendants of Sid et-Tanje, a son of Boujad's founding
marabout who has a tomb in Boujad, until a group of roughly one
hundred persons living in Fes claimed a proportionate share of offerings to the Sherqawa in the late 1920's. According to one Sherqawi
notary, this claim was supported by the sultan, perhaps to irritate
certain Sherqawa.[6] The annual share of these claimants was in principle forwarded to Fes by the *qaid* of Boujad until independence in
1956. With independence it became impolitic to press such claims,
which seem to have disappeared with the transfer of power. Older
Sherqawa are aware of the earlier existence of this group; younger
Sherqawa are not. Similarly, the Sherqawa in Boujad recognized the
existence of descendants of Sid ed-Deqqaq and Sid l-Harti in the
Shawya (Ecorcheville 1938) and of Sid l-Malki among the Bni Hasan
in the Gharb (Gouvion and Gouvion 1939). Of these three marabouts,
only Sid l-Harti has a tomb in Boujad, although all three are mentioned in myths. Currently, even older Sherqawa are unaware of
any descendants of these three marabouts. No major community of
Sherqawa is currently known to exist outside of Boujad, although
there were many such groups in the late nineteenth century.

Each major descent group within the Sherqawa has shrines of its
key ancestors associated with it, although the correlation is not exact.
Two of the *shaykh*'s twelve sons, Sid l-Mursli and Sidi 'Abd l-Qader,
have shrines in the same compound which houses that of their
father. Five others, Sidi 'Abd es-Slam, Sid l-Ghazwani, Sid l-Meknasi,
Sid l-Harti, and Sid et-Tanje, are grouped on a promontory just outside Boujad.[7] Only the 'Arbawi and Zawya quarters currently have
shrines within them.

The principal 'Arbawi shrines are those of leading Sherqawi lords:
Sidi Mhammed l-Ma'ti (2-4), Sidi Saleh (2-5), Sid l-Ma'ti (2-6), and
Sid l-'Arbi (2-7). All of these are elaborate, ornate structures dating
from the preprotectorate era. Two of them also have adjoining
mosques. These shrines receive steady flows of donations, although
not so large as those offered at the shrine of Sidi Mhammed Sherqi.
Several also receive the collective visits of tribal groups during the
fall festival, although covenants with the Sherqawa are renewed
only at the main shrine.

The most significant of these shrines is that of Sid l-Ma'ti (d. 1766)
(2-6). This marabout is the only Sherqawi to have founded a religious
brotherhood (*tariqa*) that acquired as adherents a number of townsmen. Members of the brotherhood and subsidiary lodges are found in
Bni Mellal, Qasba Tadla, Wad Zem, Fqih ben Saleh, Rabat, and
Casablanca. One also was located at Khnifra, in the Middle Atlas
Mountains, according to François Berger (1929:47).[8] However, no
Sherqawa are presently aware of the existence of this lodge or of
when it disappeared. In the past, tribesmen also swore alliances
between groups over Sid l-Ma'ti's sepulcher (see Ch. 4). As with the
other shrines in the 'Arbawi quarter, no sacrifices are permitted, although each shrine has a box (*senduq*) in which offerings are placed.
These go entirely for the upkeep of the shrines and are not distributed
to descendants.

The shrines located in the Zawya quarter all date from the protectorate: those of Sid l-Hajj Muhammed (2-10), Sid l-Hajj 'Abd
l-Qader (2-14), and Sidi ben Dawd (2-15). In contrast with those of
the 'Arbawi quarter, these are all modest structures which are locked
most of the time and receive only rare visits from pilgrims.

Although common descent from these marabouts gives their
descendants certain rights and prerogatives, it would be wrong to conclude that even with respect to their shared rights they act collectively. The critical factor is how individual members of these
descent groups view such rights in relation to their overall interests.

Sherqawa claim there are two activities that represent their collective identity: (*a*) formal visits paid by representatives of each
descent group to Boujad's prayer-leader (*imam*), presently a non-
Sherqawi, on major feast days and (*b*) shares (*hăqq*-s) in the offerings made at the shrine of Sidi Mhammed Sherqi.

Each Sherqawi descent group has a flag, which is usually draped
over the tomb of the group's ancestor or kept in custody by a group
member. On feast days each group has a representative who carries
the flag of their common ancestor to the house of the *imam*. There
they breakfast prior to the public prayer and then accompany the
imam to the prayer-ground or mosque. Similar emblems are kept
by each of the "respectable" religious brotherhoods present in Boujad,
the Kittaniya, Tijaniya, Qadiriya, and Nasiriya. Their representatives
also accompany the *imam*; so participation in this ceremony does
not in itself distinguish the Sherqawa from other groups, although
only the Sherqawa participated in it prior to the protectorate.

In the past, however, this ceremony was more distinctive, for the lord of the Sherqawa was also the *imam*. This meant that he was the symbolic leader both of the Sherqawa and of the Muslim community as locally represented. In principle, there is only one prayer-leader in each town for the major Islamic feasts. He offers a sacrifice of a sheep at the mosque or prayer-ground (*msalla*) before the assembled community. After the communal sacrifice, others are made in individual households. Since the Sherqawa had in effect two lords (*sid*-s) after the split of the *zawya* in 1901, both served as *imam*-s on feast days and sacrificed on behalf of the assembled community for at least part of the period of the protectorate—at least until the late 1930's. The "masters of the flags" (*mwalin l-'allama*) of the Sherqawi descent groups and religious brotherhoods paid visits to both. Eventually reformist pressure and a changing ideological climate among Boujad's bourgeoisie brought a halt to this de facto dual *imam*-ship. Informants are now reluctant to speak of this practice because it is in such open contradiction to current understandings of Islamic conduct.

At first sight, the present system by which the shares (*ḥăqq*-s) of the revenues of the main shrine are allocated appears to offer the sharpest delineation of Sherqawa from non-Sherqawa. Each patrilineal descendant of the *shaykh*, male or female, is supposed to receive an equal share. This system of distribution is in contrast to the rules of Islamic inheritance, which provide differential shares for men and women for varying degrees of relation. There is a register of all those entitled to a share of the shrine offerings. In 1969, it listed 5,582 shareholders, clearly not all of the living descendants of the founding marabout, especially given the multiple wives and concubines of his key descendants. In formal terms, each of the eight major Sherqawi descent groups has a spokesman (*mqaddem*). He looks after the shares of those in his groups, keeps track of who is entitled to them, and participates in the administration of the shrine.[9] These spokesmen form a council (*jma'a*), which is supposed to decide on the distribution of the offerings after deducting expenses for the maintenance of the shrine and salaries for certain of its employees, not all of whom are Sherqawa. One of the major decisions of this council in recent years has been to construct a hostel for pilgrims adjoining the shrine. They also offered a lavish reception for the king when he visited Boujad in the mid-1960's. In practice, this council is joined by prominent Sherqawa, who often have a decisive influence on the proceedings and who occasionally overshadow its formal

members. Under the protectorate, the council was effectively controlled by the Sherqawi *qaid*, but it presently acts with more
autonomy.

The utility of rights to the offerings as a means of identifying
Sherqawa dissolves upon closer examination. The present formal
system of allocations was the result of administrative intervention
early in the protectorate. Prior to 1912, no formal council managed
these offerings. Their distribution was made daily on an informal
basis to descendants of the marabout and anyone else who happened
to be present. Since such offerings were considered alms, wealthier
Sherqawa made no claim upon them. In practice, only the nonlordly
descent groups laid claim to them. Decisions relative to the upkeep of
the shrine were made by the lords. Since they received substantial
offerings directly from their regular clients and other pilgrims, the
cost of maintaining the shrine constituted no major burden upon
them.

Shortly after the French set up an administrative post in Boujad
in 1913, this arrangement broke down. One of the first acts of the
French was to allot tax and *corvée* obligations by quarters. For these
purposes, spokesmen for the two rival main-line descent groups, each
with their separate quarter, claimed to the French that they really
were one quarter.

The other six Sherqawi descent groups, which more than today
clustered in separate quarters, protested this decision. They were
led by a Sherqawi of the Mkansa descent group/quarter, who later
became one of the first government *shaykh*-s for Boujad, in part because he came to the attention of the French during this dispute. The
leaders of the two lordly descent groups—the *qaid*, Sid l-Ḥajj ʻAbd
l-Qader (2-14), and the *qadi*, Sidi ʻAbdallah ben l-ʻArbi (2-13)—
made a counterproposal. They would acquiesce to the demand that
their quarters be considered separate for the purposes of *corvée* and
taxation, on condition that henceforth each member of their descent
groups would receive his proportionate share of the offerings at the
main shrine. This significantly reduced the allocations to members
of the other descent groups.

The dispute was quickly carried to Rabat, where two crucial
decisions were made. First, it was decided that offerings to a maraboutic shrine were not governed by Islamic law and instead should
be divided in equal shares among all living patrilineal descendants of
the marabout. Second, to determine who these were and to distribute

the offerings, a spokesman (*mqaddem*) was designated for each descent group. Offerings were to be distributed annually after deducting the upkeep of the shrine.[10]

An unintended consequence of this formalization of descent-group rights and obligations has been to render apparent to the Sherqawa discrepancies between their formal ideology, according to which they include all living descendants of the marabout, and the reality, which is that they are limited to a considerably smaller number who actually claim this descent, primarily members of local descent groups in Boujad itself. Moreover, no Sherqawa entitled to share in the distribution of the offerings are under the illusion that the formal spokesmen act in their collective interest. "In the end," one of them said to me, "each of us is his own spokesman" (*koll wahed mqaddem 'la raṣu*). Consequently the formal overseers are complemented by "shadows" who meet with them whenever matters of shrine upkeep or revenues are discussed. Among these "shadows" are several notaries as well as other Sherqawa who claim to represent by proxy a certain number of shares. Many solicit the shares of Sherqawa who, because of antimaraboutic scruples or personal wealth, allow less affluent kinsmen to collect in their name.

In sum, the right to a share of the offerings at the principal shrine, like all other prerogatives claimed by the Sherqawa, exists in so far as it is defined and defended in social action. Rights held in common do not necessarily imply corporate activities any more than holding a formal office in itself legitimates authority in a given sphere of activity. Legitimacy is not sharply defined in traditional Moroccan society. Thus, in some circumstances the exercise of one's formal right to a share of the offerings at Sidi Mhammed Sherqi's shrine, or even the implicit assignation of it by proxy to another Sherqawi, can result in a diminution of social honor. Now as in the past, the distinction is blurred between rights or privileges abstractly held and their actual exercise.

Marriage Patterns

Another marker of Sherqawi identity is the maintenance of a pattern of hypergamous marriage with commoners and homogamy between themselves and descendants of the Prophet.[11] Boujadi-s and other Moroccans say that descendants of the Prophet (*shorfa*) and of 'Umar (*foqra*) constitute one "field" (*badiya*) for marriage. Commoners constitute another. This conception is accepted by all elements of society. One commoner (a tailor) said: "How can I marry a descendant of Sidi Mḥammed Sherqi or the Prophet? If I get mad at my wife, I want to beat her. Can I beat a descendant of the Prophet or Sidi Mḥammed Sherqi? Do I want their curse upon me?"

It is also popularly believed that the children of such marriages (i.e., of male commoners with female descendants of the Prophet or 'Umar) die soon after birth. Regardless of their other qualities, descendants of the Prophet and 'Umar possess a substance which makes them stand apart from those who do not possess it.

When expressing their ideas about marriage, neither Sherqawa nor commoners emphasize the hypergamous pattern described above. Instead, they explain their preference for marriage to those who are "close to us" (*qrib lina*). "Closeness," as I have emphasized throughout this study, has multiple dimensions, only one of which involves kinship. Frequently, Sherqawa claim that they are distinguished from commoners by their preference for marriage among themselves, but this is not borne out in practice (see Table 6). For instance, Sherqawi genealogies indicate that the most prominent household units have the highest rate of marriage to non-Sherqawa. This is not surprising, since marriage is one means of cementing political relations between individuals and groups. As Table 6 indicates, the rates of marriage to claimed kinsmen are roughly equal for both Sherqawa (48 percent) and rural commoners (50 percent).[12] This table should not be assumed to be an indication of the "actual" relations existing between marriage partners. As I have indicated in earlier contexts, criteria for kinship vary greatly.

The first column of Table 6 indicates the proportion of *bent 'amm* marriages—marriages between a man and his father's brother's daughter (or other woman so designated)—for each group specified. This type of marriage is often claimed to be a preferential one in Arab society, although informants cite as many proverbs and justifications against it as for it. My table represents informants' claims for such marriages, whether or not they could demonstrate with precision that the marriage was between paternal cousins. The actual relation of the wife to the husband often is that of father's father's brother's daughter, a matrilateral link, or one in which the genealogical tie is tenuous or undemonstrable.

How asserted genealogical links are manipulated depends on the total context of social relations between contracting parties, not just a

Table 6.
Marriage patterns of Sherqawa and commoners

	Bent 'Amm Marriages (N) (%)		Marriages to Other Claimed Kinsmen (N) (%)		Marriages to Non-Kin (N) (%)	
Sherqawa (N = 303)	92	30	55	18	156	51
Town-born commoners (N = 124)	17	14	a	a	a	a
Rural commoners (N = 234)	51	22	65	28	118	50

Note: Because of rounding off of decimals, percentages do not always total 100%.
ª A break-down for town-born commoners is not available. There were 107 town-born commoners who had non–*bent 'amm* marriages (86% of all town-born commoners).

narrow range of kinship considerations. One advantage of claiming a *bent 'amm* relation is that the groom's household can offer a smaller bridewealth than otherwise would be possible. The offering of a smaller bridewealth due to claims of a *bent 'amm* relation is particularly widespread among tribesmen and among rural immigrants to Boujad, among whom written marriage contracts are less often concluded because of the notarial fee levied on written agreements registered with the Islamic court and the reluctance of tribesmen to reveal their financial resources to notaries, whom they mistrust, often with justification.[13] The "closeness" of a *bent 'amm* relation generally is claimed between neighbors in the same or adjacent *dǎwwar*-s. In town, such "closeness" often emerges from (or fuses with) relations of residential propinquity, a shared craft or trade by the two heads of households, or similar ties.

The second column of Table 6 indicates marriages designated by informants as between relatives, but for which the genealogical link was not always clearly specified. Among the Sherqawa of Boujad, this generally meant marriage to a Sherqawi outside one's own immediate quarter or descent group, as when an 'Arbawi Sherqawi married a person who resided in Ghazawna quarter (6-6) and claimed descent from Sid l-Ghazwani. Since the 'Arbawi is the more prestigious

descent group of the two, the span and (to a certain extent) the depth
of exact genealogical knowledge of a person from that descent group
are usually much greater than those of one from Ghazawna. The
latter's identity as a Sherqawi depends more upon being "known"
as one to other Sherqawa than upon exact genealogical reckoning.
Neither Sherqawi would be able to demonstrate specific genealogical
links with the other. Thus, even among the Sherqawa of Boujad, there
is room for ambiguity in identifying who are descendants of the
founding marabout.

Hence the only significant difference which remains between
commoners and Sherqawa is that of hypergamous marriage. Of the
303 Sherqawi marriages analyzed, there were only 25 exceptions to
the pattern of Sherqawi women not marrying commoners. Twenty-
one of these cases were of women no longer living in Boujad who did
not maintain close ties with kinsmen in the town. Outside of Boujad,
they had more latitude of personal identity. Significantly, many of
these cases involved second marriages, the first having been with
Sherqawa. Of the remaining 4 cases in Boujad itself, the activities
of two of the husbands made them more or less the equals of
Sherqawa. One was a Qur'anic teacher; the other had for many
years collected offerings at the main Sherqawi shrine. The other 2
marriages both involved women of the non–main-line descent groups.

The Dynamics of Social Identity

The analysis of Sherqawi identity is important not only for an understanding of maraboutism but also for what it reveals of the dynamics
of Moroccan social structure. The problem of discerning the con-
stituent units of North African society has already been discussed
in earlier chapters. Maraboutic descent groups show the same flexible
patterns of boundary and identity as do urban quarters and rural
social organization, the two examples that were earlier discussed at
length. It is not the actual personal or group identities existing at any
given moment that are the key to understanding Moroccan social
structure, but the forces at work in any given situation. These include
both a shared consciousness of the nature of social reality and the
actual shape which social action takes. Under the impact of new
conditions, the concepts through which Moroccans understand the
social order, like those of other societies, themselves undergo transformations. Ordinarily, Moroccans are not aware of these trans-

formations in how they perceive social action. Here the "native" conception of the social order and the anthropologist's analysis of it necessarily diverge.

Sherqawi identity is a concrete manifestation of Moroccan symbolizations of the kinds of connections that can exist between persons and the ways in which these connections can be manipulated. It would be misleading to imply that Sherqawi identity is open to anyone who simply strives to acquire it. A combination of attributes, including residence, descent, marriage patterns, political and economic alliances, and other aspects of comportment make one "known" as a Sherqawi. Most Sherqawa are known to each other through face-to-face relationships, so that acquiring prominence on the basis of an assumed Sherqawi identity (i.e., one that has not previously been maintained) is quite difficult. But asserting a marginal identity as a Sherqawi, even in a "company town," such as Boujad, is not uncommon. Some persons are motivated to do so for the social honor that such a claim implies, at least to other non-Sherqawa. Others pose as Sherqawi "visitors" during the fall festival for financial gain. Only in certain contexts do at least certain Sherqawa make public issue of the boundaries of their identity.

Since Sherqawi identity is merely a specialized case of the more general issue of the nature of social identity in Morocco, I think it useful to present graphically my conception of how the cultural basis of Moroccan identity contrasts with alternative sociological notions. Figure 13 is a standard, downward-branching model of social relations and hence requires only a brief explanation. The irregular but firmly-bounded shapes at the bottom of the diagram represent actually existing groups. According to this model of society, these groups see their relations almost entirely through the various levels of patrilineal ancestors represented by the lines above the local groups.

Figure 14 is, I think, a closer approximation of how the Sherqawa conceive of their own social identity.[14] The key points in the diagram are the four lower triangles, representing living or deceased men of prominence to whom clusters of persons claim ties through patrilineal descent, matrilateral or affinal ties, friendship, clientship, and residential propinquity. It is from claimed ties with such prominent persons that Moroccans usually begin to depict the individuals to whom they are "close" (H. Geertz 1974:45–47). The boundaries of these clusters are not sharply defined, signifying the ability of at least some persons to shift the components of their identity. The four lines of ascending

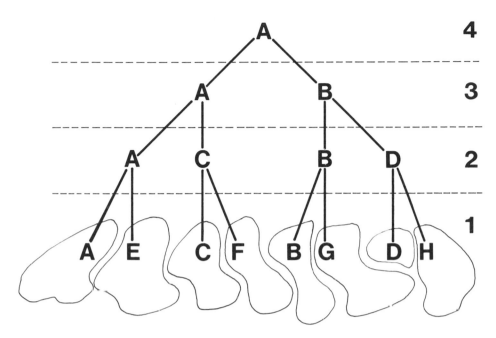

Figure 13.
A segmentary model of social relations.

triangles indicate immediately preceding generations. These lines,
A–D, are not connected on the diagram. To indicate the "closeness"
of present-day clusters, Moroccans consider such ancestors to be
brothers or construct some other plausible ties between them. When
combined in use with the name-chains that I have discussed in this
chapter, I think this model reasonably portrays how relations are
conceived among the various Sherqawi descent groups (or, sociologically speaking, descent categories) in Boujad. The same basic
model presented in Figure 14 can also be used to portray ideas of
"closeness" in other Moroccan contexts (see H. Geertz 1974).

As I indicated in my discussion of "closeness" in rural and urban
settings in Chapter 4, the key factor from a Moroccan point of view
is to consider the gains of elaborating certain sets of ties instead of
others. How these appraisals shift over time can be seen by returning
to a specific consideration of the Sherqawa.

The latitude that Sherqawa have in asserting their own identity
has enlarged as their firm identification with maraboutism has begun
to crack. That separation has recently been willed by at least some

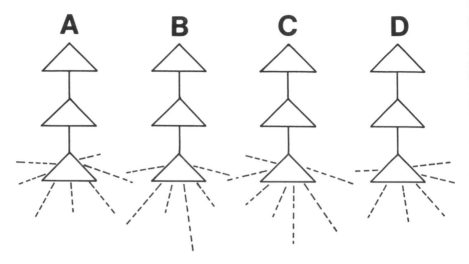

Figure 14.
A Moroccan conception of "closeness."

of them. A century ago, the Sherqawa actively maintained their identity as a maraboutic descent group. Much more than today, the life-chances of individual Sherqawa and their clients depended on claims of "closeness" to a living Sherqawi lord. Both clients and other Sherqawa contracted ties of obligation (*ḥǎqq*) to marabouts and valued these ties much more than at present. Being a marabout was a desirable quality. Whatever their differences and rivalries, Sherqawa able to do so sought to achieve maraboutic reputations. Clients of marabouts valued association with such persons. Under present conditions, the political and economic significance of mara- bouts is decidedly more limited; active attempts to maintain a maraboutic reputation carry a highly negative value among educated Moroccans. The remaining clients of marabouts, still a majority of rural Moroccans, have downgraded their ties with them. Ties of obligation with marabouts, like all other social ties, are continuously revalorized in the light of current social realities.

"Sherqawiness," what the Sherqawa assert their identity to be, has consequently undergone modifications. Sherqawi identity is still primarily associated with persons of prominence in the two main-line descent groups. Many Sherqawa now play down their identity with maraboutic ideology or assert that maraboutism constitutes only a residual component of their identity, maintained only by those ignorant of the "true" Islam. Popularly, especially among tribesmen, the identity of the Sherqawa with maraboutism still holds, so that material prosperity and largesse to pilgrims are direct measures of God's grace. As one tribesman said, "You get greasy doughnuts from the Ghazawna [Sherqawa] but cous-cous from the 'Arbawa. Of course the 'Arbawa have more *baraka*!" In towns, the maraboutic basis for Sherqawi prominence no longer holds, although no sharp break has occurred with the past. The "religious" component of Sherqawi prestige is simply being redefined. For example, a wealthy merchant of the Ghazawna Sherqawa, now in his fifties, is one of the few Sherqawa to live outside of the *medina* in Boujad. He is opposed to maraboutism and has relinquished his right to a share in the offerings at the main shrine. To indicate his "progressive" orientation, he invites the men of his quarter to gather at his house each Friday afternoon, after mosque, to read with him the Qur'an and pious recitations (*hizb*-s) written by his ancestor, Sid l-Ma'ti (2-6). He emphasizes in his conduct what he considers to be the "proper" Sherqawi tradition, that of serving for centuries as exemplars of Muslim conduct and guardians of a scripturalist Islam. Despite this reformist orientation, many neighbors interpret his conduct in terms of his maraboutic antecedents. For this reason, not for the recitation of pious texts for their own sake, they regard the Friday meetings with him as particularly beneficial. Many other Sherqawa have made similar reinterpretations of their tradition. Even those who continue to engage actively in maraboutic activities often refer to them apologetically, at least to ethnographers, as a "trade" just like any other.

The contracting social bases of marabouts have had an impact on the ideology of maraboutism. Even the clients of marabouts are no longer able to take belief in them largely for granted. They are aware much more sharply than in the past that there are other conceptions of Islam in which there is no room for marabouts. This fragmentation of religious ideology and its confinement to a clearly defined sphere are by no means unique to Morocco. The fact that such a shift has occurred is less interesting sociologically than an analysis of how it took place. My concluding chapter is intended less as a microhistory of this transformation than as an attempt to discern temporal patterns in social and cultural change. The last three chapters have emphasized the symbolism of the social order as perceived by Moroccans. To a certain extent, Moroccan conceptions of the social order and the anthropologist's analysis of it necessarily overlap. This convergence, however, can never be complete. The symbolic categories employed by Moroccans define the nature of the social order and serve as guides to the exigencies of social comportment. As I have indicated, Moroccans are not ordinarily conscious of the temporal shifts in these categories or in the elements of social reality which they define. Nor are Moroccans ordinarily concerned with comparing their own symbolic categories with those which exist in other societies or in comparing their understanding of Islam with that of Muslims elsewhere. The anthropologist is interested in such comparative, analytical activities, or at least in describing conceptions of the social order and comportment in it in such a way that such comparison is implicit.

8

From Center to Periphery:
The Fragmentation of Maraboutism

At the risk of shocking sociologists, I should be inclined to
say that it is their job to render social or historical content
more intelligible than it was in the experience of those
who lived it. All sociology is reconstruction that aspires
to confer intelligibility on human existences which, like all
human existences, are confused and obscure. (Aron 1970:
245)

Social Change: Periodization and Lived Experience

Ideally, historical periods are characterized by differences in the
fundamental patterns of events which occur in them. Clearly, what
constitutes a period depends largely upon the subject of inquiry.
Periodization is necessarily an imposition of form upon the past, an
attempt to comprehend and interpret meaning. It is important to
keep this arbitrariness in mind, particularly in the study of processes
of change. For one thing, periodization tends to emphasize the "core"
characteristics of each period, so that successive ones are contrasted,
with minimal reference to the transitions between them. Rather than
emphasize the mechanisms of change, such an approach can lead to
an overly abstract exercise in comparative statics in which only the
fact that some form of change has taken place is salient. Another
danger is an excessive zeal in locating temporal boundaries. Thus,
the official French protectorate over Morocco began in 1912. Yet, as
I have indicated, at least in western Morocco this event was merely
a formalization of de facto control that had been exercised since 1907.
From a retrospective viewpoint, the beginning of formal French
control is unquestionably an important "marker" event and un-

doubtedly appeared so at the time to a few Moroccans directly connected with the central Makhzen. But in a hinterland region, such
as Boujad, no such marker event stood out, especially since it took
several months for the French to extend even the skeleton of administrative control to the upper Tadla Plain. Men perceived the emerging
pattern of events in different ways. Some persons more than others
had the talent to delineate these patterns and alter their conduct to
take advantage of them. Some were simply in the right place at the
right time. Others saw the wrong patterns and failed to adapt to
events. The shading of periods into one another and the shifts of
emphasis that occur within them are crucial to an understanding of
how persons in a given society themselves perceive their social order,
react to significant events, and ultimately, usually in a process im-
perceptible to themselves, alter or bring into question their cognitive
maps of the cosmos and the social order.

To see how these shifts occur, I want, first, to sketch the main
periods in the social history of Boujad and its hinterland over the last
century. The last century has without question been one of accelerated social change, in the sense of significant patterns of events
and opportunities succeeding one another more rapidly than at any
prior time. This makes the processes of social and cultural change
more visible than would otherwise be the case.

By employing a periodization keyed primarily to Boujad and its
hinterland, I am not implying that it is possible to present a social
history that is hermetically sealed off from "external" events, as was
presumed by colonial ethnographers of earlier epochs. Still, the social
history of Boujad was once much more contained than is presently
the case. This remained true until the early 1930's. Among other
reasons, the protectorate "froze" local notables into positions of
authority as a means of securing its own legitimacy. For Boujad, this
meant the Sherqawa. Morocco unquestionably had a national identity
that permeated all elements of society. Nonetheless, the French were
remarkably successful in maintaining and encouraging attention to
local issues in most of rural Morocco through the 1930's. Beginning
in that decade, though, Boujad's history ceases to be locally oriented.
The town is increasingly swept into the vortex of national and even
international events. Even for the last few decades, however, there is
an advantage in focusing on the effects of major political and economic shifts in a local setting. Moroccans, like members of any other

society, interpret events and maintain their understanding of the social order primarily through interaction with significant others with whom they have ongoing, face-to-face relationships. Events elsewhere—wars, political decisions, economic opportunities—are interpreted in terms of their local consequences. A local study, such as this one, thus can place many events in a perspective more indicative of how Moroccans themselves experienced certain events than can more generalized accounts that focus only upon the activities of Morocco's national elite.

The periodization that I suggest here is meant to throw into relief transformations in popular religious beliefs. For this purpose, there are three significant periods into which Boujad's social history for the last century can be divided. The first is that of maraboutic hegemony, which characterized the preprotectorate period and lasted into the early years of the protectorate. In it, living marabouts continued to exercise a wide range of political, economic, and social roles. Sherqawa avidly competed to become marabouts and thought of their social honor primarily in terms of their alliances with maraboutic kinsmen. Because of the far-reaching political and supernatural consequences of clientship to marabouts, tribesmen placed a high value upon ties with them. The central Makhzen and, later, protectorate authorities recognized the importance attached to such ties and acted accordingly.

The second major period, which I have termed the Pax Gallica, lasted roughly from the inception of the protectorate (for this region of Morocco) through the Second World War. Throughout this period the French policy of maintaining existing notables in positions of authority was generally successful. Sherqawi marabouts were frozen into positions of prestige as local officials, but they no longer exercised political and economic functions as a consequence of being marabouts. Men in their maturity could remember when living marabouts had exercised a much wider range of functions but were aware, as were the marabouts themselves, that they no longer could do so. Younger persons, both Sherqawa and their clients, no longer had the personal experience of seeing marabouts exercise such roles. They could only be *told* about what marabouts had done. Moreover, after the establishment of the Pax Gallica, non-Sherqawi artisans and merchants no longer were dependent upon the Sherqawa for their well-being. These formed the core of adherents to forms of religious expression not directly associated with the Sherqawa and also constituted, together with younger, educated Sherqawa, the membership of the nascent nationalist movement from the 1930's onward.

The final period is that of the Second World War and its aftermath, during which France's hold over Morocco and its other colonies became increasingly fragile. More significant than this were the concomitant social and economic dislocations and opportunities generated by the war and the postwar economic boom. Sharp-eyed men able to grasp the realities of the new climate made fortunes in commercial enterprises and real estate. This shift was felt even by tribesmen, who were increasingly attracted by or pushed toward the alternatives of emigration to the coastal cities and military service. All of these transformations weakened the traditional social order which the French aspired to preserve in order to maintain their hegemony. Notables exercising formal governmental functions were somewhat handicapped in fully exploiting these opportunities, at least on the western plains, but urban merchants without such direct ties to the government were not. Also in this period, Moroccans who had been educated by the French came to maturity and, together with an older generation of traditionally educated scripturalists, openly began demanding independence for Morocco. Despite their continuing importance to rural tribesmen, marabouts no longer were capable of any significant political or religious initiatives. Beginning in the 1930's, scripturalist nationalists began major attacks on maraboutism, attacking it much more, in fact, than they did the French. After the Second World War, maraboutism was no longer a significant issue. Nationalists had appropriated the powerful symbol of the monarchy, with its coalescence of Islamic and national identity, to legitimate their own movement.

Seen from a peripheral center, such as Boujad, independence in 1956 was less the start of a new era than the consolidation and legitimation of earlier de facto shifts of economic and political power. Local merchants quickly took over the enterprises of departing Europeans and Jews, and Moroccans assumed control of the country's administrative apparatus. From the vantage of a decade or so from now, the impact of the expansion of educational opportunities that accompanied independence will be more fully realized. Then, retrospectively, independence and the chain of events it set in motion may appear to be more of a sharp break with the past than now seems to be the case.

In each of the periods that I have described, certain categories of persons acquired prominence: marabouts; notables (including marabouts) recognized and sustained by the French; and an educated bourgeoisie adhering to a scripturalist nationalism. What was a meaningful assessment of the alignments of power and opportunity in one of these periods did not hold for the next, nor did a comportment successful in one period ensure a continuing prestige and adjustment to "the way things are" in the next.

Moroccans did not respond uniformly to the pattern of events characteristic of each of these periods; nor was there general agreement as to what constituted either dominant or emerging patterns. These events were differently evaluated, not only according to what Weber called the "class" situation of men and their location with respect to economic and political power, whether or not they were aware of it, but also with respect to how generations of men were temporally located in relation to one another. A generation of tribesmen with no personal experience of marabouts who exercised significant social and political roles responded to marabouts quite differently from tribesmen with such experience. However clear such shifts appear in retrospect, it is important to try to grasp these events as they were initially perceived by Moroccans who lived through them.

Karl Mannheim's 1928 essay, "The Problem of Generations"[1] (translated and reprinted 1952:276–320), remains one of the most comprehensive attempts to consider the effects of time on social institutions and cultural categories. I want to present some key aspects of his argument in order to use it to analyze the process by which maraboutism was relegated to a peripheral status in Morocco. Mannheim saw two earlier trends in efforts to view generations sociologically. One, which he associated primarily with Auguste Comte, was the "arithmetical mysticism" of positivists, who sought to develop "laws" of historical development based upon the biological life span of men and the fact that old and new generations continually overlap. Proponents of such "laws" asserted that, when properly developed, they would constitute universal, "natural" formulae of social and cultural change. A second tradition, associated primarily with Wilhelm Dilthey, saw generations primarily in relation to qualitative, "interior" senses of time not directly related (as with Comte) to quantitative considerations. Mannheim points out that this approach was less a fully articulated one than a reaction to the mathematical,

unilinear concepts of development espoused by Comte and his followers (Mannheim 1952:281). Dilthey and others argued that
generations develop not merely because of the chronological coexistence of persons, but also because they experience the same significant
events in markedly similar ways. Thus time is not a pointlike event
but one with multiple dimensions, always experienced by several
generations at different stages of development (Mannheim 1952:
283).

To introduce the concept of the generation, Mannheim places it in
the more general category of "social location," the most familiar
dimension being class. Individuals can be said to be located in a certain economic class or related in a certain way to the power structure
of a given society regardless of whether they are conscious of it. A
given class situation cuts individuals off from certain types of experience and exposes them to others. This holds equally, writes
Mannheim, for membership in a generation. Those persons belonging
to the same generation and similarly located in the social and historical process are thereby limited "to a specific range of potential
experience, predisposing them for a certain characteristic mode of
thought and experience, and a characteristic type of historically
relevant action" (1952:291).

Generation location "is determined by the way in which certain
patterns of experience and thought tend to be brought into existence
by the *natural data* of the transition from one generation to another"
(Mannheim 1952:292). This transition comes about through the
continuous emergence of new participants in the sociohistorical
process and the withdrawal of others, making for a continuous "fresh
contact" with cultural traditions. Each generation has its own
consciousness of these traditions. Their acquisition is composed of two
elements. The first is that which is consciously or, more often, un-
consciously appropriated from other persons. The second is tradition
acquired by direct personal experience. The conscious and uncon-
scious models on which men base their conception of the world and
evaluate their actions are condensed out of their appropriated and
personally acquired experience. The continual fresh contact with
these traditions means that the cultural heritage is continually reinterpreted so as to maintain its meaning within the emerging
realities of a given time and place. The changes brought about by
this process are not necessarily apparent to participants in it. This is
especially so for concepts basic to the social order, such as *God's will*

and *obligations*, and implicit patterns of religious belief, such as maraboutism.

As mentioned, time is not uniformly experienced by generations. Thus, one is "old" in so far as one "comes to live within a specific, individually acquired framework of usable past experience, so that every new experience has its form and its place largely marked out for it in advance" (Mannheim 1952:296). In youth, in contrast, such formative forces are just coming into being, so that basic attitudes are still being formed by the molding power of new situations. Significantly, these two groups influence each other, directly to some extent, but through intermediate generations as well. Contrary to the unilineal direction of change described by Comte, often the oldest generation is more capable than younger ones of flexibility in the face of new events and of realizing the potential of new perspectives engendered by the young.

Mannheim emphasizes that generation creates a similar "social location" (which he terms an "actual generation") only to the extent that individuals "participate in the characteristic social and intellectual currents of their society and period, and in so far as they have an active or passive experience of the interactions of forces which [make] up the new situation" (1952:304). To adapt his argument to Morocco, it cannot always be assumed that tribesmen and townsmen of the same age belong to the same "actual" generation. In collecting genealogical data, for instance, I used Morocco's independence in 1956 as a marker of calendrical time. For townspeople, this was a significant event, although it was often reinterpreted, especially by women, as "the commotion"—referring to the riots, demonstrations, house-burnings, and ensuing reprisals which had occurred in the late summer of the preceding year. For Sma'la tribesmen, involved in an uprising against the French in this period, independence was also a significant event. In contrast, independence as an event simply did not significantly impinge upon the personal experience of Bni Zemmur tribesmen, most of whom took no part in the events immediately preceding it. Hence for them, independence cannot be used as a temporal marker against which to plot other, more local experiences and events. The beginning of the protectorate constituted such a marker for them ("when the Christians came"), but its end did not.

Mannheim further divides actual generations into what he calls "generation-units." These are "groups within the same actual generation which work up the material of their common experiences in different specific ways" (1952:304). Membership in a generation-unit means acceptance of its characteristic values and, more importantly, "the ability to see things from its particular 'aspect,' to endow concepts with its particular shade of meaning." It also entails absorbing certain "formative and interpretive principles" that enable individuals "to deal with new impressions and events in a fashion broadly pre-determined by the group" (1952:306). Such generation-units are not limited to concrete groups, although concrete groups in face-to-face relationships often form their nucleus (1952:307). Just as an ideology can spread beyond the confines of the class to which it initially appealed, so can formative principles peculiar to certain generations (1952:308). This is not to say that every generation evolves "its own, distinctive pattern of interpreting and influencing the world" (1952:310). Experiences which act as crystallizing agents to form distinct generation-units do not always occur. Also inherent in Mannheim's approach is the idea that the "mentalities" unique to society at a given period do not entirely pervade it. Generation-units can put their intellectual stamp on coexisting groups without either destroying or absorbing them (1952:313). The clearest Moroccan example of this is the Islamic reformism of some of the urban bourgeoisie from the 1930's onward. In relation to the total population, the carriers of this ideology represented a tightly knit but restricted minority of the urban population, but they can be seen retrospectively as "characteristic" of their period and exerting an influence well beyond their numbers. Although reformist Muslims were deeply antagonistic to it, maraboutism continued to survive as a significant force among Morocco's rural majority, coexisting with reformist ideology.

The Pax Gallica and the Sherqawa

I think it worthwhile to present the events immediately following the formal installation of the protectorate in greater detail than subsequent events. It was in the confusion of the early years of the protectorate that the Sherqawa, like the Moroccans elsewhere in Morocco, were compelled to make decisions that were to affect their fortunes for several decades.

The signing of the protectorate treaty of 30 March 1912 brought no immediate formal shift in the status of the Sherqawi *zawya*. Less than two weeks after the signing of the treaty, violent anti-French riots broke out in Fes and elsewhere. Their military suppression was the immediate concern of the French, so that for a few months the upper Tadla Plain was left to itself. Immediately after the protectorate treaty was signed, Sultan Mulay Hafed abdicated and was succeeded by his brother Mulay Yusef. News of this shift spread quickly throughout Morocco. But with no immediate pressure from the French to legitimate the new sultan and an aversion to making precipitate declarations of loyalty, neither the Sherqawa nor any of the tribes of the upper Tadla offered an oath of fealty (*bay'a*) to the new sultan.

Only by late summer of 1912 were the mechanisms of Makhzen legitimacy engaged on the Tadla Plain, although in a somewhat confused fashion. In mid-August, Sultan Mulay Yusef sent a proclamation to the Zawya lord, Sid l-Hajj Muhammed (2-10), notifying the "notables and *qaid-s* of the Bni Zemmur" of his enthronement and requesting their oath of fealty (E, 17 August 1912 / 4 Ramadan 1330). Shortly afterward, Hajj Muhammed's sixteen-year-old son, 'Abd l-Qader (2-14), was sent to court bearing the oaths of the Tadla tribes and of the population of Boujad. Three weeks later, his visit was acknowledged in separate letters by the Grand Wezir, Muhammed l-Moqri, and by H. Lyautey, who by this time had become resident-general of Morocco (both letters in E). The central Makhzen and presumably the French clearly were confused by the situation on the Tadla Plain. A few weeks after the proclamation sent to Hajj Muhammed, an identical one was sent to the rival 'Arbawi lord, Sidi 'Abdallah ben l-'Arbi (2-13) (E, 5 September 1912 / 23 Ramadan 1330). The latter, of course, had been the "exclusive" lord of the Sherqawa in the eyes of the sultan's immediate predecessor, but such niceties of legitimacy seem to have been quickly forgotten at the time.

By the autumn of 1912, the French had established Boujad as their first military outpost on the upper Tadla Plain. There was limited initial resistance from some of the tribes of the region, notably the Sma'la, but in general military action was directed only to the south of the Umm er-Rbi' River. With the Sherqawi leaders and other notables, Lyautey was punctilious in his reassurances of all they had to gain by supporting France. Just as declarations of fealty were being extracted from the Tadla notables in late August, Lyautey wrote Hajj Muhammed to say that he was aware of the prestige of the Sherqawa and of their active role in aiding the French in the Shawya.

Lyautey defined his role to the marabout as one of collaborating with the Makhzen to bring order and peace to Morocco. Initially, Hajj Muhammed was frequently consulted on the selection of *qaid*-s, as he had been in the past, and was often used as an intermediary to arrange for the submission of dissident groups. In turn, the French frequently intervened to "chastise" tribal groups (e.g., Bni Khiran) who menaced Sherqawi holdings in their territories. (Sherqawi estates outside of the Shawya were allowed at first to maintain their traditional prerogatives.)

By November, the French began to organize the formal administration of the Tadla. General Franchet d'Esperey came to Boujad on 12 November for this purpose.[2] He attended receptions given by both Sherqawi lords. Sidi 'Abdallah ben l-'Arbi and Sid l-Hajj Muhammed. He claimed in the course of the day to have "reconciled" the two opposing factions so that henceforth only Hajj Muhammed was recognized as lord of the Sherqawa (Ecorcheville 1938:112–113; Cimetière 1913:289; interviews with informants). The next morning, as "proof" of their settlement, both marabouts accompanied the general to Wad Zem, where he established a new military post. In actuality, both Sherqawi leaders recognized the danger of openly opposing French intentions or of allowing the French to interpret their internal rivalries as weakness.

The practical modalities of this "reconciliation" are not spelled out in detail, but one component was a division of influence between the rival Sherqawi factions. Hajj Muhammed advised on the selection of *qaid*-s over tribes in a client relation to him as marabout, including the Wlad Yunes (a subdivision of the Bni Smir), Wlad Bhar es-Sghir, and Gnadiz. He was also appointed *qaid* of Boujad. His brother, Hajj Hmed, became *qaid* over Bni Zemmur. Hajj Hmed was adamantly anti-French, refused to receive French officers at his house, and ignored French "suggestions" concerning his activities. Moreover, the tribesmen were hostile to having a Sherqawi as *qaid*. After a few months the French removed him from office.

Sidi 'Abdallah ben l-'Arbi of the 'Arbawa was allowed to designate *qaid*-s for the Wlad Bhar le-Kbir, Mwalin Dendun, and Sma'la, all groups that recognized him as marabout. A few years later he also became *qadi* of Boujad. This was considered at the time by both the French and the Sherqawa to be a much less important post than *qaid*. Within two decades this evaluation was to be reversed.

These first administrative arrangements were unsatisfactory to

Lyautey. He removed many of the Tadla *qaid*-s from office in April 1913, including the Sherqawi Ḥajj Ḥmed. In relation to the difficulties with the latter, Lyautey reminded his subordinate, Col. Emile Mangin, then responsible for the Tadla Plain, not to make formal appointments (or more exactly, not to arrange for the sultan to make appointments from among three nominees selected by the French) until an appointee had indicated his capacity to govern during a trial period of several months. Lyautey also insisted that each *qaid* should be chosen from the tribe over which he was placed. Moreover, the rural *qaid*-s of the upper Tadla Plain were deliberately selected for their independence from the Sherqawa.[3] Those of the Boujad region, as throughout Morocco, rapidly acquired personal fortunes through the formal and informal advantages attached to their positions. Throughout the periodic administrative reorganizations of the protectorate, essentially the same *qaid*-s, their brothers, and their sons retained hold over their offices. Later in the protectorate, some of these *qaid*-s had consolidated their positions to the point that they supported open attacks on the influence of leading Sherqawa. The French were not adverse to encouraging such local rivalries.

As for Boujad and the Sherqawa, Lyautey knew that Ḥajj Muhammed was dying (he died on 17 May 1913) and emphasized to Mangin the political importance of choosing an appropriate successor to "the *baraka*." Lyautey delegated Lt. Col. Emile Simon of Military Intelligence to discuss the situation with Mulay Yusef (Lyautey 1953:73, 83, 88–92). At this point, of course, French understandings of *baraka* began to be as important as those of Moroccans in determining maraboutic succession, since the French were in a position to impose their understandings of Moroccan society upon the social order and thus mold Moroccan social reality to fit their conceptions of it.

Ḥajj Muhammed was replaced by his son ʿAbd l-Qader, regarded by both French and Boujadi-s as not particularly bright or skilled but, like his father, a "friend" of France.[4] As *qaid*, ʿAbd l-Qader (he became a *hajj* in 1917) appointed primarily his Zawya kinsmen to subordinate posts. The nature of his office was such that he had many more patronage positions to offer than his ʿArbawi rival, Qadi ʿAbdallah ben l-ʿArbi. Moreover, the posts over which the *qaid* had control rarely required literacy and so were open to a number of his supporters. Fewer subordinate positions were attached to the *qadi*'s court, and most of these required a high degree of literacy. Since only an estimated 1 or 2 percent of the population of the country was literate at the time, there was much less direct patronage that he could offer his relatives and clients. But Qadi 'Abdallah and several other 'Arbawi Sherqawa placed a high value upon traditional letters and, beginning in the mid-1920's, upon French education, as it became locally available for younger Moroccans. Some 'Arbawi Sherqawa sought out higher education elsewhere in Morocco. The Zawya Sherqawa primarily confined themselves to the immediate rewards of local posts. Until the last years of the protectorate, few of the Zawya Sherqawa were educated beyond primary school, which was locally available.

The French were aware of the continuing importance of maraboutic activities to the Sherqawa but began actively to return the *zawya* to its "original" and "proper" concern with "spiritual" matters. In effect, this meant a quite untraditional separation of the "religious" from the secular activities of the marabouts. "Religious" activities were for the first time sharply set off from "nonreligious" ones. Of course, the two leading Sherqawi marabouts, as the *qadi* and *qaid* of Boujad, exercised the functions of these offices. But these, at least in principle, were limited to territorially circumscribed and formally defined administrative and judicial functions. Even the tribal clientele of these two marabouts soon sharply distinguished their maraboutic from their political and judicial authority.

The split of religious from political authority became more pronounced for the first few years of the protectorate, at least at the local level. The sultan, of course, continued to embody both spiritual and secular authority. In the first years, the French still used the Sherqawa as intermediaries to unsubmitted groups, but their role as intermediaries had been significantly transformed. No longer could the Sherqawa negotiate compromises. They could only indicate what were the terms of submission acceptable to the French. The standard French tactic for dealing with "dissident" groups was to strangle them economically by denying them access to their agricultural lands and their customary markets. As a result of this tactic, most tribesmen of the upper Tadla Plain, often on the basis of individual local communities, submitted to the French in late 1912 and 1913. The only exception to this monotonous pattern was a coordinated attack in early June 1913 by the Berber leaders Mha u Hammu ez-Zayyani and Mha u Se'id on French positions in the Tadla. Mha u Hammu led an attack against the French post at Wad Zem, while Mha u

Se'id's tribesmen took up a position just south of Boujad. Colonel Mangin led the relief column for the French and was accompanied by the 'Arbawi lord, Sidi 'Abdallah, with whom most of the Sma'la were in a client relation. Always punctilious in acknowledging services rendered, Lyautey later wrote to thank Sidi 'Abdallah. One consequence of Mha u Hammu's raid was that the trade route between Boujad and Khnifra was cut, although in July of that year Mha u Hammu sent his son to Boujad to negotiate its reopening. This was the last major incident in which the Sherqawa served as intermediaries.

After the above incident, the Sherqawi marabouts were effectively excluded from the scope of action considered by the French to be political. Thus the contingent supernatural curse (*'ar kbir*) which marabouts had once been able to invoke to compel disputing tribes to cease hostilities could no longer be implemented, nor could the marabouts even collect offerings outside of Boujad without French consent; and, since both marabouts held official Makhzen posts, such permission was simply not granted. French policy was to discourage local officials from exercising influence beyond those territories for which they were specifically charged. There also was an intent, at least on the local level as opposed to the sultanate, to separate secular functions from those considered religious. Secular disputes were now the domain of the French, and they insisted on being informed of any outbreaks of violence. The French military negotiated settlements or imposed them by force. Tribesmen were aware that the French had pre-empted the Sherqawi marabouts (as well as marabouts elsewhere in rural Morocco) in the settlement of disputes. For a while, Sherqawi visitors were sought to mediate low-level quarrels, such as land disputes between tents or households. But, as antagonists realized that settlements could be appealed either to their *qaid*-s or to the French, even this contracted field of activity largely disappeared.

The Pax Gallica stimulated a political and economic differentiation that ostensibly maintained the "traditional" prestige of the Sherqawa but made it impossible for them to undertake the range of action upon which, in large part, they based their livelihood. Besides a developing oligarchy of autonomous rural *qaid*-s, a second important category of persons who became largely independent of the Sherqawa were Boujad's merchants and craftsmen. After the effective imposition of French control, Sherqawi marabouts were no longer required to facilitate the safe passage of commerce in rural Morocco. It is also significant that, after 1912, most leading Sherqawa held local Makhzen sinecures. As a consequence of French policy, they were banned from simultaneous active participation in commerce and, on the double count of being marabouts and members of the Makhzen administration, were no longer able to secure patents of protection from foreign governments. Such patents, which exempted their holders from direct Makhzen (and after 1912, French) control, were invaluable for securing vital commercial networks in the Moroccan interior. The French and the Makhzen could act against patent holders only by registering a complaint with the European power that had granted the patent. Altogether eight key merchants in Boujad—six non-Sherqawi Muslims and two Jews—acquired such patents as local agents for major foreign trading firms.[5] Thus the protectorate gave non-Sherqawa (and by the 1920's a few Sherqawa who had dissociated themselves from the activities of the *zawya*) a valuable competitive edge in commercial undertakings.

Changes in patterns of belief gradually followed the confinement of Sherqawi marabouts to narrower social roles and the growing economic and social differentiation of society. Prior to the protectorate, Sherqawi hegemony was such that any threat to Sherqawi interests on the upper Tadla Plain, and especially in Boujad, was not tolerated. Soon after the end of the European hostilities in 1918, one significant development throughout western Morocco was the rapid growth of urban religious brotherhoods (*tariqa*-s), especially the Kittaniya, Derqawa, Tijaniya, and Qadiriya. Each of these quickly established subsidiary lodges in Boujad and in the other, newer settlements that had appeared in the region. Outside of Boujad, the lodges connected with the eighteenth-century Sherqawi lord, Sid l-Ma'ti (2-6), also expanded rapidly, but in Boujad itself they acquired no significant membership. At first, however, most Boujadi-s maintained ties with the Sherqawa. As elderly townsmen explain, this was done out of a mixture of material interest and fear of the supernatural sanctions at the disposal of the Sherqawa. But the economic hegemony of the Sherqawa was curtailed with the protectorate; at the same time, the burgeoning of non-Sherqawi, urban-based brotherhoods provided alternative access to the supernatural.

The sudden growth of these urban brotherhoods can be seen as an expression of autonomy from Sherqawi marabouts. Adherents to these brotherhoods tended to make the same implicit assumptions about the desirability of using intermediaries to relate to the super-

natural as were made by clients of the Sherqawa, but access to the
supernatural was now more effectively differentiated. An increasing
number of persons, primarily townsmen and elements of the rural
elite, no longer felt themselves dependent on the Sherqawa or any
other marabouts to ensure their well-being. The growth of these
brotherhoods engendered no immediate ideological conflict with the
Sherqawa, although the leaders of some of them fostered attempts
to drive a wedge between the Sherqawa, who controlled the apparatus
of the local government, and the French. The local *mqaddem* of the
Tijaniya order repeatedly sent letters to the French accusing various
Sherqawa of improper official conduct, and some of the charges were
acted upon by the French. The French also suspected the leaders of
two other brotherhoods of making anonymous denunciations of the
Sherqawi *qaid, qaḍi*, and some of their kinsmen (B.31.BO. confidential, 23 November 1932; B.2261, 30 December 1934).

The principal adherents to these brotherhoods were non-Sherqawi
town dwellers, primarily merchants and craftsmen, who had not
belonged to such orders prior to the protectorate. The brotherhoods
appealed to a relatively homogeneous bourgeoisie. The core membership of each tended to consist of the members of certain crafts or
trades. None of the orders appears to have had any evangelical fervor
in recruiting membership. When the national leader of a brotherhood,
such as 'Abd l-Ḥayy Kittani of the Kittaniya order, came to Boujad,
crowds of thousands, including tribesmen, flocked to the town. But
few tribesmen subsequently joined his or any other order. It is
significant that by this time Sherqawi marabouts no longer attempted
to draw crowds in such a fashion.

Exact figures on local membership are not available in all instances,
but by the late 1920's the Qadiriya brotherhood, not considered to be
the largest in Boujad, had six hundred adherents in a population of
eight thousand (B.10/BC, 23 February 1928). From the 1930's until
just after the Second World War, their leader (*mqaddem*) was a
merchant who had begun his trading activities prior to the protectorate but who had made his fortune by seizing the opportunities
made by the French "pacification" of the region. Until the middle
of the 1920's, he offered sacrifices at the conclusion of each weekly
market at the shrine of Sidi Mḥammed Sherqi in Boujad. Other
merchants then began pressuring him to make contributions instead
to the Qadiriya lodge, which he soon joined, to local mosques, and to
other religious institutions not connected with Sherqawi marabouts.

The shifts in religious affiliations of the urban bourgeoisie affected only minimally the overall numerical support of the Sherqawa. Only a few tribesmen were attracted to these brotherhoods. These generally were clustered in certain local communities, and such adhesions were miniscule in relation to the overall rural population.[6] Still, the presence of an alternative to being a client of the Sherqawa meant that even tribesmen in Boujad's immediate hinterland no longer simply took for granted their ties with the Sherqawa. In the past, dissatisfaction with certain Sherqawa resulted in a shift of allegiance to other Sherqawi marabouts. Henceforth, a shift of allegiance away from the Sherqawa was a further, although rarely exercised, possibility. Yet the fact that such an alternative was consciously known to be available was in itself significant. In any case, by the 1920's, the Sherqawa were effectively stripped of their nonrural, nontribal clientele. Some townsmen made occasional offerings in times of personal crisis, but not the regular offerings characteristic of an earlier period. Moreover, those who made irregular personal offerings tended to be older rural immigrants who had all along maintained ties with Sherqawi marabouts. Younger rural immigrants tended more to drop these ties.

For the most part, tribesmen assiduously maintained ties with the Sherqawi marabouts[7] but were aware of their contracted utility. This was reflected in the offerings and sacrifices to the Sherqawa, which no longer flowed as freely as they once had. Diminished revenues meant that fewer Sherqawa were able to sustain themselves from the activities of the *zawya*. As offerings diminished, so did the services that marabouts performed for their clientele. At the same time, the formal and informal resources available to the two leading marabouts of the Sherqawa, the *qaid* and the *qadi*, effectively blocked the emergence of rivals.

The ideology and membership of urban religious brotherhoods, on the whole, constituted no overt ideological challenge to maraboutism. But the contracting of ties of obligation with *shaykh*-s of urban religious lodges was not simply a substitute for equivalent ties with the Sherqawa. The *shaykh*-s of urban lodges were more distant; their hegemony over the affairs of the Tadla Plain was not so multifaceted as that of the Sherqawa. However, a more pronounced revalorization of maraboutism emerged locally by the 1920's and by the mid-1930's had acquired considerable momentum. This challenge came primarily from the Salafiyya, or Islamic reform movement, proponents of which I have often labeled as "scripturalists" in this study. Like their counterparts who emerged in the eastern Arab world in the late nineteenth century, Salafi Muslims argued that the Qur'an and the traditions of the Prophet were the only true bases of Islam, thus sharply distinguishing what they considered "true" Islam from the popular Sufism of urban religious brotherhoods and of maraboutism. Most of these reformists were traditionally educated urban bourgeoisie and were primarily situated in Morocco's largest cities, notably Fes and Marrakesh. Although their numbers were quite limited, their influence was considerable in such centers of Islamic learning as the Qarawiyin Mosque-University in Fes (where the Moroccan nationalist Allal al-Fasi was then an instructor) and its counterpart institution in Marrakesh, the Madrasa ben Yusef. From these institutions, the reformers had a considerable impact upon the urban bourgeoisie throughout Morocco and upon significant numbers of the urban proletariat in the larger cities.

The first Boujadi-s to be attracted to the reformist movement were several merchants in their mid-twenties who had attended one or the other of these centers of traditional religious learning. Boujad also was the forced residence from 1924 to 1934 of the Tunisian 'Amer ben Nefti ben Hajj Mansur bel Ghayb, who had a wealthy in-law in Boujad, also a Tunisian, who was a grain merchant. Ben Nefti was locally active in propagating his ideas and, although Boujadi-s today claim that his ideas did not strike a responsive chord among them, was expelled by the French on the omnibus protectorate charges of "doubtful morals" and "nationalist tendencies." Several other Moroccans in forced residence during the late 1920's and early 1930's also seem to have contributed to making elements of Boujad's bourgeoisie aware of alternative ideologies. The main activities of this loosely knit body of individuals in Boujad was to set up a series of ephemeral, ad hoc committees that, like similar groups elsewhere outside of Morocco's larger cities, confined themselves to negotiating with the local protectorate administration on the development of schools and other issues. In Boujad there were less than a hundred such persons, but these were very influential with other merchants and craftsmen of their generation. Membership in these committees tended to overlap considerably. In addition to negotiating with the French administration locally, these same committees in Boujad eventually established a "free school" in 1947, independent of the educational apparatus provided by the French. Elsewhere in Morocco, such schools began to appear in the 1920's (Damis 1973). Other activities included the establishment of an orphanage. The links set up by activists on these committees in the 1930's eventually formed the local nucleus for the nascent nationalist movement.

In Boujad, this movement initially attracted younger bourgeois merchants and craftsmen, many of whom had never, or only marginally, been involved in the urban religious brotherhoods that attracted an earlier generation of urban bourgeoisie. Nor had most of them ever been clients of Sherqawi marabouts. As I have mentioned, the membership of urban religious brotherhoods in the rural centers of the western plains consisted primarily of non-Sherqawa who had reached maturity when the Sherqawa *as marabouts* were still politically and economically influential. Recruitment into the brotherhoods flourished from the beginning of the protectorate until the late 1920's and then abruptly declined.

Later generations of the urban bourgeoisie, those who in Boujad joined or sympathized with the protonationalist movement, matured in significantly altered social and economic circumstances. Most had no personal experience of preprotectorate maraboutic hegemony. In larger cities, such as Fes and Salé, there existed a young, more militant French-educated intelligentsia (see Brown 1973), but such individuals were almost totally absent in Boujad, where the nationalist movement remained dominated by men with a more traditional, scripturalist orientation. Especially after the Berber *daher* of 1930, there was a growing popular urban support for this protonationalist movement, primarily because of its emphasis on the purification of Islamic life and institutions and its resistance to what was popularly considered to be a French threat to Islam. As the movement became more politicized in the larger towns, there was a growing split between the politicized militants, concerned primarily with presenting demands to the protectorate administration, and the more traditional Muslim reformists, concerned more strictly with religious issues, such as maraboutism and, to a limited extent, the threat which the colonial regime posed to Islam. In Boujad, such a clear split never developed. In part this was due to the small number of such protonationalists and the limited range of action they could take. Negotiations undertaken with local French authorities were generally amicable;[8] attempts to discourage maraboutism almost never took the form of direct confrontation. After all, the merchants who formed the core of the protonationalist movement lived in daily contact with the Sherqawa. In the coastal cities, the nationalist concerns of the elite quickly spread to the growing urban proletariat, but in small interior towns, such as Boujad, they remained the concern of a limited cadre of educated bourgeoisie until the last years of the protectorate (Rezette 1955; Halstead 1967). Similarly, in larger urban settings it is necessary to provide finer distinctions among types of Islamic modernism and nationalism, such as are provided by Laroui (1974). In smaller centers, such as Boujad, such distinctions were jejune for all but a few educated persons until after the Second World War.[9]

Oblique attacks on the Sherqawa in the 1930's took the form of denunciations to the French *contrôleur civil*, especially of official abuses of power, and the quiet persuasion of fellow townsmen to allow their support of maraboutism to lapse. In these actions the reformists were largely successful. No public meetings were involved, but reformist merchants employed subtle pressures within their personal networks of acquaintances, kinsmen, and clients. Significantly, these same neoorthodox reformists did little to carry their convictions to tribesmen associated with them. Many rationalized this neglect by saying that sustained attempts to disseminate reformist doctrines would have incurred the wrath of rural *qaid*-s and that tribesmen, in any case, were too "ignorant" to understand the significance of reformist doctrines. These rationalizations mask the inability of the reform-minded bourgeoisie to propagate their ideology in other milieus and their lack of interest in doing so. The various protean organizations which made up the nationalist movement did not, on the whole, begin active recruitment until the late 1940's.

Until the Second World War, the protectorate was fairly successful in cutting rural Morocco into a grid of impermeable sealed compartments, each with "its own life" and local identities (Montagne 1941:19). In each compartment, the French nurtured a local elite whose interests were articulated with those of the French. In the first few decades of the protectorate this policy worked remarkably well. In the Rousseauistic phrase of one early administrator, the "natural leaders" (Berriau 1918:4–5), that is, the existing local elite, were given positions in the local Makhzen administration or were designated as "notables" by local officers of the French administration. For a time such designation carried with it considerable advantages, including access to French education for the children of these individuals and a certain favored treatment in dealing with the administration. During this period the competition for influence and prestige among members of the rural elite was primarily focused upon the administrative zones established by the French. Most quarrels found their way into the office of the local *contrôleur civil* or Native Affairs officer. Local French officers often became arbiters as well as monitors of these disputes. In contrast to later periods of the protectorate, they were actively invited to play such roles. The monthly political reports for the early 1930's almost exclusively concern such local conflicts. Nationalist activities among the elite begin being reported for Boujad only in the late 1940's.

A valuable index of the patterns of influence which built up during this period is the official protectorate newspaper in Arabic, *es-Sa'ada*, to which all Moroccans considered notables by the French received free subscriptions. This newspaper meticulously recorded weddings and similar celebrations for all of the rural elite. Thus the wedding of one influential Boujadi in the late 1920's was given front-page coverage in two successive issues, including a list of all notables who attended and the number of animals slaughtered for the feast. Such reporting is, of course, entirely absent from contemporary newspapers, which rarely go beyond a chronicle of movements of officials of the central government and sports events. This shift in emphasis accurately mirrors the shift in the loci of political power. The pattern of power prevailing during the protectorate contrasted sharply to that which existed prior to the protectorate, when Sherqawi lords intervened in a wide range of issues. In preprotectorate days local issues often were closely articulated with those of national importance. Likewise, the sultan and his entourage in those days closely followed the vicissitudes of tribal disputes and other matters which under the protectorate were considered to be of only local import. During the protectorate, there was formally no direct contact between local Moroccan officials and the central Makhzen. Such contacts as there were had to be made through the hierarchy of the protectorate administration.

Postwar Transformations and the Sherqawa

The position of local elites in Boujad was not entirely frozen, as was indicated by the patterns of growth of New Boujad from the 1930's onward. Significant cracks in the hermetically sealed blocks into which the French had divided rural Morocco began to appear with the rise of the nationalist movement. This movement rapidly gained momentum with the economic and political opportunities and dislo-

cations of the Second World War and the period immediately following. Fortunes were consolidated and broken, creating a significant
gap between those who held formal positions of prestige and authority
(local officials appointed by the French) and those who increasingly
held real economic and political power.

The postwar years also saw a sudden resurgence of the sultan (by
then popularly, if not officially, known under the more modern title
of king) as an authority independent of the protectorate administration. Muḥammed V used the Feast of the Throne (20 August) and
other occasions to establish direct, personal contact with his *qaid*-s,
pasha-s, and other, nonofficial Moroccans of prominence. At the same
time the palace took a somewhat more active part in the campaign
against maraboutism. For the first time since the misadventurous
antimaraboutic campaign of Sultan Mulay Sliman in the early nineteenth century, a reigning sultan was involved in a deliberate fight
against saints and religious brotherhoods. As a symbolic gesture, the
sultan ordered destroyed the shrines of marabouts in the vicinity of
Ifrane, his summer residence in the Middle Atlas Mountains (Montagne 1953:217). No similar action was attempted elsewhere in Morocco, and there is no indication that the sultan's move was meant
to precipitate any widespread attacks on physical representations of
maraboutism. The general attitude seems to have been one of encouraging a benign neglect of maraboutic ties, coupled with a rekin-
dled strength in the religious and political symbolism of the monarchy.

Networks of nationalists in all parts of the country grew rapidly
in the postwar period. At first, these were confined primarily to the
urban bourgeoisie, but they were greatly enlarged after the French
deposition and exile of Muḥammed V in 1953. Contrary to the claims
of Boujadi nationalist leaders and the French (e.g., Montagne 1953),
there is no indication that the "cells" of the nationalist movement
were organized into well-defined, centrally directed hierarchies. The
pattern that emerges both from interviews with local nationalists and
from French reports of the interrogation of suspected nationalists
suggests a more protean organization of personal ties.[10] Local leaders
had clusters of supporters, with more casual clients at their periphery.
In turn, local leaders had informal ties with leaders elsewhere in Morocco.[11] These were adept at using local antagonisms and quarrels
to gain further support for the nationalist movement. Among tribesmen, nationalists stirred up resentment against Francophile *qaid*-s

and promised the successful resolution of land quarrels and other disputes in exchange for political support (B, untitled document [a
draft?] summarizing interrogations from 2 March to 31 July 1953).[12]

In many ways the structure of these networks at the local level resembled that of ties to the Sherqawi *zawya*. The major difference was
that efficacious political and economic power no longer was in the
hands of the Sherqawi lodge or of those most associated with its activities. Marabouts continued to be regarded as significant by a majority of the population but were popularly recognized as peripheral
to new patterns of economic and political action. By the early 1950's
some Sherqawa, especially those of the Zawya faction, which held
the *qaid*-ship of Boujad and associated posts, found themselves locked
in increasingly untenable positions, despite efforts to avoid action regarded as inimical by either the French or the nationalists (B: confidential report on *qaid*, 21 January 1952). In the latter years of the
protectorate, this descent group lost heavily in prestige. Just prior to
the French deposition of Muhammed V in 1953, the aging marabout
Qaid Sidi ben Dawd (2-15), went to Rabat and asked the sultan what
stand he should take in the growing conflict between the French and
the nationalists. "Go on as you have," the sultan enigmatically replied. A close relative of the marabout present at the interview interpreted these remarks as justifying Sidi ben Dawd's continuing as *qaid*,
which he did until his death in 1956.[13] The sultan's words could also
be interpreted as implying that nothing which Sidi ben Dawd could
do either as *qaid* or as lord of the *zawya* would be of significance in
the light of the contemporary political situation.

Another indication of the decline of the Zawya Sherqawa is the
shifting pattern of marriage alliances of the leading households. Prior
to the protectorate, central Makhzen officials, *qaid*-s of the western
plains, wealthy merchants, and others sought such alliances. This pattern was sustained on a reduced scale in the first decades of the protectorate. By the 1940's, such ties were no longer sought.

Predictably, the fortunes of the 'Arbawi Sherqawa were just the
reverse. Their position was progressively enhanced in the later years
of the protectorate and after independence. *Qadi*-s, notaries, and other
personnel attached to Islamic courts were relatively independent of
direct French control. To be sure, the French had a decisive influence
over appointments and had effected subtle but decisive modifications
in the system of Islamic justice. But by and large the Islamic courts

were autonomous, so that with independence in 1956 very few of the
court personnel were removed from office. In the early part of the
protectorate, most of the leading 'Arbawi Sherqawa were associated
with the courts and, as I mentioned, placed a much higher value on
both traditional and French educations than did the Zawya Sherqawa.
By the 1930's and 1940's, various 'Arbawi Sherqawa were engaged
in a range of activities. Some remained with the Islamic courts. Others left the sinecure provided by the French and engaged in commerce. One 'Arbawi, for instance, began his career as a notary but
spent most of his time judiciously investing in agricultural estates in
regions that the French began opening up to irrigation in the 1930's.
After making a fortune in black-market operations during the Second
World War, he plowed his profits into urban real estate in Casablanca, which quickly skyrocketed in value. Other 'Arbawi Sherqawa
became active in nationalist politics and from the postwar years to
the present have been strong supporters of the revitalized monarchy.
Their traditional maraboutic prestige and its accompanying control of
wealth and property have been successfully parlayed into other forms
of activity that in the colonial and postcolonial setting have led to
greater power, wealth, and social honor. For the more successful
'Arbawa, maraboutism is a thing of the past, appropriate to an earlier
era but no longer cause for sustained Sherqawi prominence.

Conclusion

Patterns of social structure and the prevailing systems of meaning
through which religious beliefs are expressed are not always isomor-
phic. Peter Berger has remarked that, seen historically, the relationship is often one of irony (1969:107). An ideology introduced because
of a certain intrinsic logic for one social situation or status group often
assumes, when adopted or reformulated in a new setting, implications
far removed from those that were originally, consciously intended. A
particularly dramatic instance of such a transformation seems to have
occurred during the Maraboutic Crisis, as the carriers of popular
Sufism found themselves regarded in a very different light and performing for the first time a wide range of critical political, social, and
economic roles. The religious knowledge possessed by marabouts soon
became popularly regarded as "secrets" transmitted in the patterns of
"closeness" that I earlier described. North African maraboutism, like

popular Sufism elsewhere in the Muslim world, sustained an implicit hierarchy between those to whom this knowledge was attributed and the remainder of society.

Sources for this earlier period are sufficient to indicate the broad dimensions of these transformations but provide little concrete evidence of the processes by which the contours of popular belief were modified. These are in much bolder relief for the last century. In the late nineteenth century, as today, a marabout had the reputation of being a particularly efficacious intermediary with the supernatural. There was no clear boundary between "spiritual" and "mundane" powers, so that marabouts had a wide range of action. Since God's will was, and is, thought to be revealed through this-worldly patterns of action, success in their multiple endeavors sustained the reputations of Sherqawi marabouts and effectively handicapped the ascendancy of rivals. To secure the benefits of access to the supernatural, the clients of marabouts contracted ties of obligation to them that were sustained by the same underlying principles that governed all other ties in society and were evaluated just like these other ties.

The transformations in the ideology of maraboutism and of the social role of marabouts have been discussed at some length. What sort of orderly patterns can be found in these changes? Maraboutism, like any other belief, constantly affects and is affected by the political and economic realities in which men find themselves. It is important to keep in mind that belief systems are not free-floating Platonic entities. They are, as Peter Berger writes, "socially constructed and socially maintained. Their continuing reality . . . depends on *specific* social processes" (1969:45). Such ideologies as maraboutism are neither captives to local social structures nor by-products to be mechanistically deduced from them. For at least four centuries, maraboutism represented a meaningful formulation of Islam for tribal and urban Moroccans. It has remained a significant component of social reality for some. But the ideology of maraboutism has been far from static. As a primarily implicit, multivocal ideology, maraboutism owed its vitality to its flexibility in adapting to a number of varying situations. But the social conditions created by the protectorate, in Morocco at least, reduced the specific social processes which had maintained maraboutism throughout earlier centuries. This was especially the case in urban settings, where the transformations engendered by the protectorate were more pronounced than in rural areas and where alternative patterns of Islamic belief were ascendant and appeared to offer a superior formulation of "the way things are" in relations with the supernatural. Even among rural clientele, from the 1940's onward the spread of cash instead of animals and cereals as the principal medium in which offerings were made accelerated the conscious instrumental re-evaluation of the worth of these ties.

For most Moroccans, God continues to be the cause of everything and responsible for every turn of fate. But with the contracted sphere of influence of marabouts, there are now clear de facto boundaries on the intervention of the supernatural in the specific affairs of this world. With the disappearance of living marabouts, there is no concrete instrumental medium through which God's assistance can be invoked for specific situations.

The restriction of the roles that marabouts could play in Moroccan society was one component of a growing social differentiation made possible by the protectorate. There developed locally in the Boujad region a greater range of bases on which social honor could be established and power acquired. Nonmaraboutic elites developed that acquired considerable influence and prestige from commercial and political undertakings. These persons increasingly adopted and acted upon nonmaraboutic conceptions of Islam, locally an impracticable option in the preprotectorate era.

A Weberian sensitivity to the differentiation of interests and beliefs within a society is a more useful perspective in the study of the shifts in belief than are theoretical perspectives which emphasize (as do most Durkheimian studies of religious belief and practice) only those beliefs held in common by all elements of society. Thus, over the last century, the assumption that access to God is patterned on the relations which exist among men has appeared increasingly unrealistic to many Moroccans. Even many Sherqawa now play down the idea that their ancestors and certain of their living relations had a special relation with God. Instead, following the conventions of traditional Muslim historiography regarding marabouts, they maintain that the leading Sherqawa of the past were men like any others; the only difference was that they were distinguished for their piety, scholarship, and prestigious descent from 'Umar.

I have tried to show that this overall shift in meaning and social identity followed patterns discernible through time. An ahistorical study focusing upon contemporary patterns of belief without regard to their historical development would misrepresent the relationships of maraboutism with specific social categories. An equal distortion re-

sults from considering historical shifts only in superimposed synchronic slices. Although useful for some analytic purposes, periodization tends to blur the ongoing process of the reinterpretation of
cultural traditions, particularly the interaction of different generation-
units, to use Mannheim's term. Reinterpretations of Islam, or of other
religions, do not follow as knee-jerk utilitarian reactions to changed
economic and political situations, although such changes provide a
heightened awareness of ideological commitment and thus provide a
favorable climate for such re-evaluations.

The onset of the colonial period, particularly in urban settings,
gave rise to a loss of orientation among many Moroccans and an effer-
vescence of explicit ideological activity. Much of this took the form of
an increased receptivity to ideological currents in the Arab east, where
Muslims had an earlier and in some cases protracted experience with
the problems of foreign domination that now faced Morocco. The explicit ideological positions adopted by Moroccans were by no means
unique to them (Laroui 1967). Nor was the contracted base of maraboutism. Although still far from moribund, it lost much of its capacity to respond to new situations. In particular, maraboutism has not
inevitably been replaced by reformist ideology, as accounts of these
movements sometimes imply. Maraboutism continues to hold its
ground among the majority of the population. The power attributed
to individual marabouts has markedly declined, but maraboutism remains for many what Weber called the "religion of everyday life"
(1968:416). Marabouts relate to the concrete life situations of their
supporters in a way that the formal, egalitarian tenets of Islam cannot. Maraboutism implies a conception of the supernatural that is immediately present. It implicitly offers a degree of control over the unknown and the supernatural. Men contract and sustain dyadic bonds
with marabouts by the same conventions that govern all other social
interaction. The pervasiveness of this concept is apparent in the ties
that many men, including some who formally denounce maraboutism, continue to sustain with marabouts. It also is apparent in popular interpretations of the symbolism that surrounds the Moroccan
monarchy, in which the king is popularly seen as the vehicle for sustaining the country with *baraka*. In this light, the centralization of
authority and de-emphasis upon primordial and regional loyalties
that began during the protectorate and continued after independence
have their counterpart in the popular religious symbolism of the monarchy. Its homology with the assumptions that govern the social uni-

verse is also, as I have sought to emphasize, the fatal weakness of maraboutism as an ideology.

A relatively small group of educated, generally well-to-do Boujadi-s (like similar Moroccans elsewhere) are activated by and committed to the explicit ideology of Islamic reformism. They interpret this reformist ideology as demanding the rejection of marabouts and of maraboutic ideology. Many more now say they subscribe to reformist tenets but continue quietly to act as if they believe in the efficacy of marabouts. The transcendent image of the divinity provided by Islamic reformism is in itself too alien from their experience of the realities of this world and the common-sense assumptions that guide their actions in it to carry conviction. This is so despite the fact that both in towns and in the countryside there is a resurgence of participation in formal Islamic rituals and observances. Awareness of this "official" Islam is undoubtedly stronger today than in the past.

In any major religious tradition, beliefs are responsive to social actualities. The two alternative conceptions in Islam of relations between man and God that I have illustrated here have allowed Moroccans, at least until now, to contain the impact of social change within the boundaries of the Islamic tradition. Thus a continuity of religious identity is sustained in the midst of altered social situations. The hierarchical conception of man-God relations represented by maraboutism is now in eclipse, but there is no reason to suppose that it will necessarily remain so. Islamic reformism, now ascendant, is self-consciously less compromised by the social order. But Islam, like other major world religions, constantly must face anew cycles of compromise and noncompromise with the social order.

Appendix
The Wheel of Fortune:
The Last Maraboutic Intrigues

There are several compelling reasons to present in detail the struggle for the lordship of the Sherqawi *zawya* that began in the mid-1890's. It was the last such major struggle to occur in a "traditional" setting. With the protectorate, the groups supporting aspirant marabouts contracted rapidly in size. A detailed account also checks the tendency to describe individuals in nascent factions as consciously striving to establish autonomous groups. The account presented here suggests, rather, that the process is one of heightened identity, in which the possibility of establishing an independent group emerges only gradually among the participants in such struggles.[1]

A mere enumeration of the sons of the major Sherqawi marabout of the nineteenth century, Sidi ben Dawd (2-8), suggests the problems inherent in maraboutic succession. At his death in 1889, he had twenty-one living sons. Whether their mothers were legal wives or concubines, technically all were equals in Islamic law. But in Sidi ben Dawd's and other major households, this legal precept failed to form a model for actual practice. The long lordship of Sidi ben Dawd meant that he was in a position to choose his successor. He was the last Sherqawi marabout for whom this was unequivocally true. The confusion of events from his death to the beginning of the protectorate allowed none of his successors to establish a similar position.

In 1889, Sultan Mulay Ḥasan I confirmed Sid l-Ḥajj l-ʿArbi (2-9), the eldest of Sidi ben Dawd's sons, to succeed him. Sid l-ʿArbi, then sixty-seven, had earlier spent many years in the sultan's entourage. Sidi ʿUmar, his brother, continued to exert considerable influence as the "grey eminence" of the *zawya*. As mentioned earlier, ʿUmar's son, Driss (d. 1915), had settled in Casablanca, where he operated as factotum with the Makhzen and merchants, arranging for the passage of caravans through Boujad and the Tadla Plain, and frequently provided detailed advice to his father on the position to take in negotiations with the sultan.[2] After 1904 he had become in addition an employee of the French consulate. In this capacity he advised the Sherqawa, or those Sherqawa whose interests he represented, on how best to deal with the French. He performed much the same services for the French.

The Sherqawa wielded considerable influence in the 1890's. This is evidenced by Sid l-Ḥajj l-ʿArbi's assistance in getting the sultan's expedition (*meḥalla*) safely from Dar weld Ziduḥ to l-Bruj when Mulay Ḥasan I, accompanying the expedition, died in 1894. His death occurred in hostile territory. Had it been known to his entourage, they would have panicked and made likely a major crisis of succession, although the sultan had designated one of his sons, Mulay ʿAbd l-ʿAziz, as his successor. By keeping his death a secret for two days, until the return of the expedition to more secure territory, the sultan's chamberlain (*hajeb*) Ba Ḥmed was able to retain his power and secure the confirmation of Mulay ʿAbd l-ʿAziz (who reigned from 1894 to 1908), still a minor at the time. A proclamation reconfirming Sid l-Ḥajj l-ʿArbi as lord of the Sherqawa *zawya* was soon issued in the name of the new sultan (E, 26 August 1894 / 23 Ṣafar 1312), but Ba Ḥmed, the Grand Wezir, Mehdi l-Mnebhi, and others in the sultan's entourage had already begun seeking ways to undermine the strength of the Sherqawa (Ecorcheville 1938:89–90).[3]

From the beginning, Mulay ʿAbd l-ʿAziz's reign was marked by growing foreign threats and tribal uprisings. The Sherqawa were frequently called upon to negotiate with tribes on behalf of the Makhzen. Thus, when the Rhamna tribe rebelled upon the death of Mulay Ḥasan, they cut off Marrakesh from the rest of Morocco. Sid l-Ḥajj l-ʿArbi was sent to negotiate with them. A later royal decree (E, 27 July 1895 / 4 Ṣafar 1313) congratulates the lord upon his success and

agrees to the terms for an amnesty which he negotiated. These included a *t'argiba* sacrifice, the traditional sign of submission, and the
delivery to the Makhzen of the leader of the rebellion. In a face-saving
compromise, the sultan acknowledged that, since the rebel leader had
escaped, he was satisfied with the burning of the tents of the rebel
and his followers and confiscation of their property, reported by the
Sherqawi lord. Later, in 1898, the sultan camped near present Wad
Zem for four months in an expedition intended to bring dissident
tribal groups within the pale of the Makhzen.[4] Fifty-five heads were
collected during this raid for display at Marrakesh. Again the Sherqawi lord served as the sultan's principal emissary. Despite their association with Makhzen interests, the Sherqawa preserved a measure
of autonomy that some of the sultan's entourage found intolerable.
Qaid-s fleeing the wrath of the Makhzen often successfully sought
sanctuary in Boujad until favorable settlements could be negotiated.
During this period there were also increased signs of tension between
local *qaid*-s in Shawya and the Sherqawa.

From at least 1895 onward, the Makhzen directly subsidized a few
descendants of Sidi ben Dawd who were not formally recognized by
the Makhzen as being in control of the *zawya*. This act in itself signaled to ambitious Sherqawa the possibilities for intrigue among
themselves. Subsidies were paid on feast days to the leader of this
nascent faction, Sid l-Hajj Muhammed (2-10), through the overseer
(*amin*) of customs in Casablanca. Hajj Muhammed wrote the sultan
on each festive occasion, saying that he had invoked divine blessings
on his behalf. He also specified to the sultan what he needed as a
subsidy.

The core of the subsidized dissenters, who eventually became known
as the Zawya Sherqawa, appear to have only gradually asserted a separate identity and acquired the resources to make this possible. Three
months after the death of Sid l-Hajj l-'Arbi (2-9) (23 October 1898),
one of his sons, Sid l-Hajj l-Hasan (2-11) was given "the direction of
the *zawya*, to the exclusion of all other individuals, as was the case
with your deceased father" (E, Sultan 'Abd l-'Aziz to Hajj l-Hasan,
25 January 1899 / 13 Ramadan 1316). A second decree reaffirmed
his leadership two years later, although its very issuance was indicative of the growing challenges to the new lord's position.

The split of the Zawya Sherqawa from the 'Arbawa formally culminated in 1901. The sultan ordered Hajj Muhammed (2-10) of the
Zawya Sherqawa and his nephew, Sid l-Hajj l-Hasan (2-11) to his

court at Marrakesh. There he announced that the *zawya* and all of its holdings were to be divided equally between them. They were henceforth to be known as its "co-lords."

The difficulties in dividing the Sherqawi holdings have already been discussed in Chapter 2. In general, Ḥajj l-Ḥasan got control of the estates (*'azib*-s) to the south of Boujad and in regions peripheral to Makhzen control. Ḥajj Muḥammed of the opposing Zawya group got the estates of Shawya and Tadla, regions at that time under relatively firm Makhzen control. To facilitate Ḥajj Muḥammed's gaining control of his half of the lodge, Sid l-Ḥajj l-Ḥasan was detained for several months in Marrakesh. There he is reported to have said that the sultan should not be suspicious of his actions because he did not intend to remain lord of a *zawya* controlled by the Grand Wezir and the *qaid*-s of Shawya (Ecorcheville 1938:95).

The sultan's division of these estates only roughly coincided with the loyalties of tribal groups toward the two rival lords (see Table 7). Ḥajj l-Ḥasan still was the more prestigious of the two, despite the intention of the Makhzen to equalize their followings. When Ḥajj l-Ḥasan finally was allowed to leave the sultan's entourage (he did so from Rabat), he returned by way of the territories of several tribes

Table 7.
Tribal clients on the Tadla Plain, ca. 1905

'Arbawa	Zawya
Smaʻla	Ghraba
Bni Zemmur (Ait Ṣaleḥ)	Bni Zemmur (except Ait Ṣaleḥ)
Bni Khiran (except Bni Manṣur)	Bni Khiran (Bni Manṣur)
Bni Musa	Gettaya
Wlad Brahim (about half)	Wlad Brahim (about half)
Bni Khlef (sections)	Bni Khlef (sections)
Wlad 'Abdun (sections)	Wlad 'Abdun (sections)
Bni Ṣmir (sections)	Bni Ṣmir (sections)
Wlad Bu 'Ali	Wlad Yeʻish
Bni Maʻdan	Wlad 'Azzuz
Bni 'Amir	Mfassis
	Mwalin bel Ghorraf
	Gfaf (sections)

Source: Ecorcheville 1938:96.

which, at least a few years later, were clients of the rival Zawya lord: Zyadiya, Mdakra, Mzab, and Werdigha.

Neither Sherqawi lord took tribal alignments for granted. They were to fluctuate markedly, especially during the struggle for the sultanate which broke out in 1907. The agents of both lords actively canvassed tribesmen and Makhzen officials in the Shawya for their support. These intrigues often flared into violence. In a decree dated 25 January 1903 / 25 Shawwal 1320 (E), Mulay 'Abd l-'Aziz ordered the *qaid*-s of Werdigha, Bni Zemmur, Ait Rbu' (near Qasba Tadla), Bni 'Amir, and Bni Khiran to "respect" Sherqawa of the 'Arbawi descent group.

In general, Mulay 'Abd l-'Aziz endeavored to strengthen the position of Ḥajj Muḥammed and his descent group, which never appears to have gained the stature of the 'Arbawi group. To dampen potential rivalries within his descent group, Ḥajj Muḥammed secured a decree designating the elder of his two sons (2-14) as his deputy (E, 27 June 1903 / 1 Rbi'a II 1321). Since both sons were children, he relied primarily upon his brothers as emissaries to the Makhzen.

Correspondence for this period indicates that Ḥajj Muḥammed was treated virtually as a servant of the Makhzen. As the French later became aware, much of his influence was based on his ability to secure Makhzen appointments for clients in exchange for whatever price the market would bear. For this privilege, the Makhzen held him responsible for nominating persons who could satisfactorily assert Makhzen interests. Essentially this meant the collection of taxes and settlement of all disputes inimical to Makhzen control. Ḥajj Muḥammed was held responsible for the conduct of the *qaid*-s whom he nominated. Thus, when the Bni Musa refused to obey their *qaid*, appointed on the recommendation of Ḥajj Muḥammed, the sultan wrote him: "You have informed us . . . that the Bni Musa ask to have as their *qaid* the son of their old *qaid* in place of the present *qaid*, Ma'ti ben Ziduḥ. Ma'ti ben Ziduḥ came with a letter from you and was named their *qaid* by your recommendation, while the son of the old *qaid* was named as his deputy" (E, 22 October 1904 / 12 Sha'ban 1322).

Despite its support of the Zawya Sherqawa, the Makhzen was aware of the strength of the 'Arbawi rivals and did not unnecessarily alienate them. When Sid l-Ḥajj l-Ḥasan of this faction died in 1903, the sultan named as his successor co-lord and as overseer of pious endowments his brother, Sidi Muḥammed ben Sid l-'Arbi ("Weld Zohra") (2-12),[5] bypassing his nineteen sons. When Weld Zohra complained about unfairness over the division of water rights of a subsidiary *zawya* which he jointly held with his rival, Hajj Muhammed (2-10), at the edge of the Berber highland near Bni Mellal, the sultan gave a courteous response and delegated the Berber *qaid* of the region, Mha u Se'id, to look into the matter (E, 29 September 1905 / 29 Rejeb 1323). In general, neither faction appears to have gained a definite advantage over the other. This stalemate presumably was what the Makhzen intended. Until 1907, the policy was relatively successful.

By 1907, Mulay 'Abd l-'Aziz had become, in the eyes of many Moroccans, the creature of European, and especially French, interests. In an attempt to meet the threat of European intervention, the sultan undertook a series of well-intentioned but ill-conceived fiscal reforms which further weakened his position. Tribesmen believed that the sultan was losing his *baraka* because of close contact with Europeans. In contrast, his brother Mulay Hafed owed his initial popularity to his being a symbol of resistance to European penetration. His supporters ranged from Fassi intellectuals, who saw an opportunity to undertake the same style of reforms as those desired by the "young Turks" for the Ottoman Empire, to tribesmen of such regions as the Shawya, who, for economic reasons (among which were new taxes considered to be non-Islamic), as well as religious and nationalistic ones, were increasingly disenchanted with the reign of Mulay 'Abd l-'Aziz.

Open conflict for the sultanate broke out when Mulay Hafed was proclaimed sultan by the *'ulama* of Marrakesh on 16 August 1907. The French used the occasion as a pretext to land troops in Casablanca later that month. Ostensibly this landing was to protect their interests in Casablanca and Shawya, but it was also intended to support Mulay 'Abd l-'Aziz. Nevertheless, Mulay Hafed steadily gained support, first from the tribes of the Marrakesh region and by December from the *'ulama* of Fes, led by Mulay le-Kbir le-Kittani of the powerful Kittaniya religious order. The Fassi support was conditional upon the insurgent sultan's enacting certain reforms and undertaking to eliminate European influence over Morocco. Soon two leading Middle Atlas Berbers, Mha u Hammu ez-Zayyani and Mha u Se'id, also joined the insurgent movement.

In the growing conflict it was difficult to maintain equivocal positions. From the point of view of the 'Arbawi Sherqawa, in any case, nothing was to be gained by equivocation. For almost a decade the 'Arbawa had been systematically undermined by Mulay 'Abd l-'Aziz

and his entourage. Shortly after Mulay Ḥafeḍ was declared sultan in
Marrakesh, the lord of the 'Arbawa, Weld Zoḥra, pledged allegiance
to him. When in December 1907 a delegation of Fassi-s went to Marrakesh to see Mulay Ḥafeḍ, they traveled with a Berber escort across
the Middle Atlas Mountains; then across the Tadla and Ṣraghna
plains they were personally escorted by the 'Arbawi lord for part of
the way (Ecorcheville 1938:100).[6]

The Zawya Sherqawa were decidedly at a disadvantage because of
their close ties with Mulay 'Abd l-'Aziz. Nevertheless, Sid l-Ḥajj Muḥammed (2-10) wrote to Mulay Ḥafeḍ, imputing to him long-standing
ties with the Sherqawa. Mulay Ḥafeḍ replied to this attempt at
alliance-hedging, thanking the Zawya lord for his sentiments but not
revealing his intentions toward him (E, 26 December 1907 / 21
Qa'ada 1325).

'Arbawi support for Mulay Ḥafeḍ was rewarded in 1908. Mulay
Ḥafeḍ issued a decree naming Muḥammed "Weld Zoḥra" as the
"sole" lord of the *zawya* and authorizing him to secure all prior royal
decrees concerning Sherqawi matters from his relatives (E, 6 April
1908 / 4 Rbi'a I 1326). The wording of the decree suggests its entrepreneurial nature, since Mulay Ḥafeḍ and his advisors do not seem to
have had a clear idea of just what were the Sherqawi prerogatives.
Shortly afterward Mulay Ḥafeḍ ordered Ḥajj Muḥammed (2-10),
along with the "*qaid*-s, notables, and council" of the Bni Musa and
Bni 'Amir, to his court (E, two identical proclamations sent to the
two tribes, dated 23 April 1908 / 21 Rbi'a I 1326). Both tribes were
already supporters of Mulay Ḥafeḍ. Predictably, although the sultan
assured Ḥajj Muḥammed that he had "absolutely nothing to fear,"
the latter never left Boujad.

Mulay 'Abd l-'Aziz rapidly lost support on the Tadla Plain. In
April 1908 he asked the Bni Khiran to furnish him with horsemen for
an expedition. A few days later he made a similar request to the Werdigha that indicated the weakness of his position: "We are aware that
you followed Mulay Ḥafeḍ against your will. You did not have the
necessary strength to resist him. For this reason we accord you complete pardon" (E, 1 May 1908 / 29 Rbi'a I 1326). There no longer
were the customary menaces of retribution.

From their arrival in Casablanca, the French military carefully
monitored the local political situation of the Shawya and, ostensibly
only to protect the Shawya, the neighboring regions. Since Driss ben
'Umar of the Zawya Sherqawa worked for them, the French tended

for years to underestimate the importance of the rival 'Arbawi faction. Moreover, the French presumed a notion of maraboutic legitimacy in which only one person could be recognized as lord of the *zawya* at any given moment, so that rivals were dismissed by them as "malcontents." Even after the French established a forward intelligence post at Ben Ḥmed in the Shawya in late April 1908, to provide them with better intelligence on the Tadla Plain, they did not alter their assessment.

Mulay Ḥafeḍ passed through the Tadla Plain in May 1908 to consolidate support there.[7] Throughout this visit he was accompanied by Ḥajj Qaddur, a brother of the lord of the 'Arbawa. By the early summer, most of the tribesmen of Werdigha and Bni Khiran had shifted their support to Mulay Ḥafeḍ. Moreover, Weld Zohra of the 'Arbawa gained the reputation of being Mulay Ḥafeḍ's political agent for the Tadla Plain. Anyone who wanted access to Mulay Ḥafeḍ (or his powerful ally, Qaid l-'Ayyadi of Rhamna) first had to speak with the lord of the 'Arbawa.

Two parallel administrative structures developed in this period, each supported by one of the Sherqawi lords and his clients. Ḥajj Muhammed of the Zawya Sherqawa counted on the support of tribal *qaid*-s who owed their posts to him. The lord of the 'Arbawa arranged for rival *qaid*-s to be appointed by Mulay Ḥafeḍ. Thus in Bni Brahim (Bni Musa), an unpopular *qaid* had been appointed on the advice of Ḥajj Muhammed. The 'Arbawi lord arranged for appointment of a rival Ḥafedist *qaid*, more acceptable to the tribesmen. Similar tactics were employed on a section-to-section basis.

Despite the weakened position of the supporters of Mulay 'Abd l-'Aziz and consequently of the Zawya Sherqawa, Ḥajj Muhammed was still considered by the French to be the "legitimate" Sherqawi marabout. When the French undertook a major reorganization of the *qaid* system in Shawya, they at least formally sought Ḥajj Muhammed's advice. The French were informed (by Driss?) that the Sherqawa were "traditionally" consulted in such appointments. The French were aware, however, that in consulting the Sherqawi lord, they served only to augment his prestige. On these grounds Lieutenant Colonel Fretay of Military Intelligence advised in late July against the appointment of Ḥajj Muhammed's nominee for *qaid* over the Mzab and 'Ashash tribes, especially since the appointment would not strengthen Mulay 'Abd l-'Aziz or the French (JP, 29 July 1908).

Fretay was also concerned with the "ambiguous" attitude of Ḥajj Muḥammed toward French interests.

In November 1908 Paul Marty, then an officer in Military Intelligence,[8] was sent to Boujad to report firsthand on the political situation. The timing of his visit and substance of his report suggest that his main purpose was to sound out the Sherqawa on the consequences of the imminent shift of French support to Mulay Ḥafed. Marty, although aware of dissent, remained convinced of Ḥajj Muḥammed's dominant position: "Everywhere the natives show signs of the highest veneration for him, listening to his advice and following his orders. Nevertheless, he has enemies. At the moment, the malcontents and ambitious of each tribe gather around his nephew, "Weld Zohra" Ismaʻil. The Smaʻla have always been troublesome to him" (Marty in JP, 1908). While in Boujad, Marty stayed at the house of Ḥajj Muḥammed. A day after his arrival, what he termed an "anti-French" demonstration occurred in front of Ḥajj Muḥammed's house, intended to show the "lack of authority" of the Zawya lord. Ḥajj Muḥammed's response was to order the notables of each quarter to call on Marty and express their lack of hostility toward France. Marty conceived of the Sherqawi position as follows: "[The ʻArbawi] faction [*parti*] relies on Berbers from outside [the region]: the Zayyani, Mha u Ḥammu and the Wirrani, Mha u Seʻid. Some statements of the Zayyani have particularly instilled a certain fear in [Ḥajj Muḥammed]. [Mha u Ḥammu] said that after the harvests he was going to destroy Boujad ... [Ḥajj Muḥammed] asks that the French come to his aid in such a case. . . . I made a dilatory reply and promised to relay his request" (Marty in JP, November 1908). Ḥajj Muḥammed seemed most concerned with securing from the French their guarantee that his interests would remain secure whatever the outcome of Makhzen politics:

> The Sid has marked sentiments for ʻAbd l-ʻAziz. He concluded by telling me that whichever Sultan France might recognize in Morocco, he avidly hopes that [a guarantee of his status] will be included in the conditions imposed on the new Sultan so that he will be maintained with all the advantages of his situation. . . . He is against all Makhzen intervention in the affairs of Boujad as well as in the estates [*fermes*] which he possesses in the exterior:

> Shawya, Dukkala, etc. This question is very important to
> him and I believe that he will soon come personally . . . to
> Casablanca [to discuss it]. (Marty in JP, November 1908)

Shortly after Marty's visit, the French issued a patent of protection
to Hajj Muhammed which exempted him from direct Makhzen administration.

Mulay 'Abd l-Aziz's position rapidly crumbled. Not long after
Marty's visit, Hajj Muhammed wrote General d'Amade, commander
of French forces in Casablanca, asking what position to take. The
general replied on 8 December, announcing that Mulay 'Abd l-Aziz
had abdicated and had been replaced by Mulay Hafed. He advised
the Sherqawi lord that his animals, clients, and other interests would
be protected. "Do not worry about news from the outside. If anyone tells you to rebel, do nothing." He was further assured that "mutual friends" had intervened to make the new sultan "forget" Hajj
Muhammed's support of 'Abd l-'Aziz (Ecorcheville 1938:105).

The sudden abdication of Mulay 'Abd l-'Aziz and reversal of the
French position did not bring an end to internal conflict. Moreover,
many Moroccan clients of the French were caught in an untenable
position. The Journal Politique of May 1909 acknowledges that when
the French were "led" to the support of Mulay Hafed, they advised
qaid-s and others "in contact with them" to shift their support to
Mulay Hafed. The French recognized, however, that there was little
they could do to ease the precarious situation of those who, at French
insistence, had earlier supported 'Abd l-'Aziz. Hajj Muhammed was
commended for his "Francophile sentiments" (writers of other reports
assessed his sentiments less favorably) but was recognized as one
such loser (JP, Sicard, May 1909).

Clashes between the supporters of the two sultans did not cease.
From the summer of 1909 onward, "anarchy" and "banditry," to
use the terms of the French reports, were on the rise. Significantly,
the reported upsurge of "anarchy" coincided with a growing desire
of the French military to intervene directly in the affairs of the Tadla
Plain. Throughout this period, Hajj Muhammed continued to be useful in quelling tribal disputes. At the end of 1909, Hajj Muhammed
combined a visit to the French outpost at Ben Hmed with a collection
of offerings from various Shawya tribes. In the course of these rounds,
he arranged for a truce (*sulh*) between the 'Azizist and Hafedist
factions of the important Bni Smir tribe by collecting fines from both

groups. Two weeks later, on 12 January 1910, he returned to the French outpost accompanied by his brother, Sidi Muḥammed Sulṭan, who was at that time *qaid* of Werdigha. Muḥammed Sulṭan requested the French to exempt both the Sherqawa and their clients from *corvée* labor. The French were aware that his intention, although clothed in the argument of "tradition," was to increase the strength of his own clientele by offering significant material advantages to his supporters. The French replied that they had done all they could to maintain or enhance the marabout's interests. Such demands, together with French awareness that the marabout was still influential but less than fully committed, or essential, to them, made at least one officer suggest that it would be in the French interest to confine marabouts to strictly "religious" affairs. The ensuing de facto separation of social roles initiated a chain of events which encouraged a similar differentiation in the realm of ideas, as I have argued. Ironically, the disturbances caused by the French occupation of the western plains and the struggle for the sultanate left virtually nothing of what the French considered the "spiritual" aspect of the *zawya*. The school (*madrasa*) of the *zawya* was irremediably crippled by the disturbances leading up to the protectorate. The Sherqawi marabouts, sensing no doubt the changed social circumstances, no longer showed any overt concern over its fate (Cimetière 1913).

By 1910 the French had consolidated their hold over the Shawya. The urban and rural elites of Morocco began clearly to realize that the French were significantly altering the rules of the game of political entrepreneurship in Morocco. Local centers of influence and prestige could still be maintained, but only through alliance with the French. An early French innovation was the requirement that marabouts, including the Sherqawa, obtain French authorization to make the rounds of tribesmen to collect their "rights," or offerings. Thus in 1910 Ḥajj Muḥammed was allowed to visit Wlad Se'id, Mzamza, Gdana, and Wlad Bu Ziri client tribes located in the French-controlled Shawya. The French were not entirely pleased with his ensuing conduct. The Journal Politique (January–February 1910) reports that he spread "alarmist rumors," among which were that the French had renounced the idea of further extension of their influence and that yet another change of regime was to be expected. However, the French were aware that Ḥajj Muḥammed was still influential among the tribes. In any case, he remained a significant conduit of intelligence regarding tribal politics on the Tadla Plain.

Another indication of changed circumstances was the constant stream of letters between Driss ben 'Umar and Ḥajj Muhammed, arranging frequent visits of the Zawya lord with the French "ambassador" (*bashador*), consul, and military officers. The principal concern of the Sherqawa in these visits was to maintain or extend their privileges in the Shawya. In a letter written early in April 1910,[9] Driss asked one of his brothers in Boujad to gather all royal decrees held by the descendants of Sidi ben Dawd (2-8)—in other words, those held by both the Zawya and the 'Arbawi Sherqawa. Driss mentions those individuals most likely to possess them, an indication of how little communication there was between the two factions, and promises their timely return. What was at issue, he wrote his brother, was the status of all Sherqawi '*azib*-s in the Shawya, but he asked that this be concealed from other Sherqawa. On 9 April, Ḥajj Muhammed was summoned to Ben Ḥmed to discuss the matter with the French. A second meeting took place a week later at Qaṣba l-Mzab. On both occasions the Sherqawi lord unsuccessfully attempted to convince the French of "traditional" Sherqawi prerogatives. Sherqawi '*azib*-s were stripped of their special status. Their inhabitants, Sherqawa and non-Sherqawa alike, became subject to taxes, *corvée* labor, and direct Makhzen administration. Late in 1910, another major administrative reorganization was made in the Shawya. In it, the French reduced substantially the number of *qaid*-s and *shaykh*-s and stipulated that henceforth such officials would be drawn exclusively from the groups over which they had authority. The Sherqawa were no longer to be consulted over the nomination of officials in Shawya, although their advice was still sought for the upper Tadla Plain as late as 1913. Alarmed by the exclusion of Sherqawa from Shawya affairs, Driss ben 'Umar wrote Ḥajj Muhammed (S, January 1911 / Muharrem 1329), suggesting that he oppose the French move. Driss also asked to be sent a list of Ḥajj Muhammed's nominees for the *qaid*-ships, together with their tribal origin and any information useful in maintaining Sherqawi influence. His efforts were unsuccessful.

Ostensible concern for the security of the Shawya led the French military to extend their activities to the Tadla Plain, although their instructions from Paris expressly forbade such action. The military's justification for the ensuing expeditions was that the marabout Ma l-'Aynin, who had effectively organized resistance against the French in Morocco's far south, had come to the Tadla Plain for the same purpose. His presence seems to have been conjured by the military, since intelligence reports for the period, usually precise in their documentation, provide no specific accounts of the marabout's activities. There were, however, other "agitators." The advantage to the French military of asserting Ma l-'Aynin's presence was that he was recognized as a formidable threat in ministerial and parliamentary circles in Paris, whereas the other "agitators" were not. Nonetheless, the raids organized by these "agitators" into regions nominally protected by the French suggested to many tribesmen that the French hold was tenuous. For this reason the military was anxious to stop them.

The French launched what was meant to have been, at least to the metropolitan authorities and the parliament, a secret punitive expedition. One column, composed largely of Senegalese troops under Commandant Aubert (the French often practiced the economy of using colonial troops to maintain their empire), left from Ben Ḥmed in the north and proceeded through Boujad, Qaṣba Tadla, and the "dissident" regions of Bni Musa and Bni 'Amir. A second column proceeded from the south of the Shawya. When Aubert reached Boujad, Ḥajj Muḥammed was asked to accompany the column in order to minimize resistance. Aubert clearly was under the assumption that a marabout had "authority" over his tribal clients. The Sherqawa had probably encouraged, or at least had not corrected, this assumption during their earlier attempts to maintain a voice in the political affairs of the Shawya. The assumption was now put to an empirical test.

Fearing stiff resistance to the French, Ḥajj Muḥammed pleaded illness and instead substituted a kinsman "with no prestige or authority" (JP, D.14, June 1910). When tribesmen in the Qaṣba Tadla region later offered only token resistance, Ḥajj Muḥammed quickly joined the column in an effort to take credit for this. But he refused to accompany the column to the Bni 'Amir. At this point, Ḥajj Muḥammed told Aubert that he had absolutely no prestige among that tribe and asked that the 'Arbawi lord, Muḥammed "Weld Zohra" (2-12), be asked instead. Aubert attributed Ḥajj Muḥammed's refusal not to the structural position of the marabout, which did not include the exercise of formal, political authority, but to a lack of character: "Without attaching more importance than deserved to the charges of his enemies, who portray him as playing a double game, one is led rapidly to the belief that this religious figure wavers above all through impotence and that his pusillanimity renders him in-

capable not only of leading a popular movement, but even of forseeing
it" (JP, D.14, June 1910). The French possessed earlier accounts that
the "malcontent" 'Arbawi lord had a sizable following, but only one
report (JP, D.20, Sicard, May 1909) correctly perceived that there
were actually two "legitimate" marabouts in the eyes of the Moroccans. Weld Zohra was summoned from Boujad and quickly joined
Aubert's column. There was an element of surprise in his acceptance,
for the French had been led to assume by the Zawya Sherqawa that
Weld Zohra was implacably anti-French. Aubert wrote that, as the
column progressed, Weld Zohra successfully "reduced fanaticism."
However, a fatally hostile assembly of tribesmen was waiting for
the column among the Wlad 'Ayyad of Bni Musa. Among the tribesmen there were reportedly some Ait 'Atta from the High Atlas
Mountains. The marabout tried to "reduce the fanaticism of the
crowd, some of whom accused the Sherqawa of having sold Shawya
to the French and of trying to do the same with Bni 'Amir and Bni
Musa!" A shot was fired, which killed the marabout.[10] Regard for
his maraboutic *baraka* was restored immediately upon his death.
Tribesmen fought over his remains in order to bury him, or part of
him, on their own lands, but the lord's retainers managed to regain
possession of the corpse and return it to Boujad. Weld Zohra was
posthumously awarded the French Legion of Honor for his services
(JP, Aubert, June 1910).

None of these events mitigated the hostility between the 'Arbawi
and Zawya Sherqawa. When he learned of Weld Zohra's death, Driss
ben 'Umar, in Casablanca, felt compelled to write to his uncle Hajj
Muhammed that it would be "reasonable" (*'aqil*) for him to present
condolences to prominent 'Arbawa. That such a letter was even sent
indicates the prevalent antagonism. Driss presumably was motivated
not only by propriety but also out of concern for the image of the
Zawya leaders in the eyes of the French.

Mulay Hafed waited for over ten months before appointing a successor to Weld Zohra. Finally, on 30 April 1911 / 1 Jumada I 1328,
he issued three proclamations naming Sidi 'Abdallah ben l-'Arbi
(2-13) as the "exclusive" lord of the Sherqawa and assigning all
Sherqawi estates to him (E). Despite Weld Zohra's sacrifice for
France and the Makhzen's appointment of an 'Arbawi as lord, the
French continued to assume that Hajj Muhammed was the only
"legitimate" Sherqawi lord. By now, however, the French were in a
position to impose their definition of realities upon Moroccans, and

their disregard for the action of the Makhzen was evidently not successfully contested.

Rather than mitigate hostile raids, the indecisive French action served only to exacerbate them. For one thing, marabouts and what the French called "war chiefs" were able to rally many tribesmen in a holy war (*jihad*) in the defense of Islam. The internal organization of these raiding parties has been discussed in Chapter 4. Unfortunately, the French reports give only terse, inconclusive comments on their ideological component. Another motivation to join anti-French raids was the fear of falling under Makhzen authority. The French were aware that anti-French resistance in Dukkala, for instance, was tenacious because of the heavy-handed rapacity of Qaid l-'Ayyadi of the Rhamna, one of the "grand *qaid-s*" on whom the French were soon to rely for control of the south (JP, Col. Braulière, September 1910). They were also aware, however, that the leaders of some raids seemed motivated only to demonstrate their importance to the French. Thus, a marabout from the *zawya* of Taneghmelt (Ntifa), Sidi Ḥmed ben 'Abbas, acquired a significant following on the southern Tadla and began raiding tribes that had submitted to the French. Through the intermediary of a *qaid* in Ṣraghna "friendly" to the French, he suggested that his neutrality could be purchased (JP, December 1910).

These raids continued throughout the summer and fall of 1910 and the following year. The Sherqawa used them as an opportunity to demonstrate to the French their ability to monitor and settle the tribal disputes of the Tadla Plain. At French request, the lord of the Zawya Sherqawa regularly undertook the settlement of disputes (e.g., S, Driss ben 'Umar to Hajj Muḥammed, 8 July 1910 / 29 Jumada II 1328). The 'Arbawi Sherqawa also tried to gain French attention in this manner. Thus in November 1910 Sidi Sherqi ben l-'Arbi Sherqawi, later to become overseer of pious endowments for the Tadla and Bni 'Amir plains under the protectorate, wrote General Monier and described the great expense he had incurred in arranging for the disbanding of the raiding party of Shaykh Mha l-'Aṭṭawi.[11] The French recompensed him, although they were skeptical of his influence in halting Shaykh Mha's activities. Sidi Sherqi was unsuccessful in attracting a following in the winter of 1911. At least some of the French were aware of the cyclical patterns of raids, which diminished rapidly with fall planting and did not resume again until after the harvests. In the fall of 1910 the French received

numerous tribal delegations seeking protection from these raiders
(and presumably also from the French). Some French interpreted
these delegations as a sign of their growing influence, although others
were aware of the vulnerability of tribesmen to French threats during
fall planting.

In general, the French were unimpressed with the ephemeral
truces arranged by marabouts. For instance, Hajj Muhammed was
often unsuccessful in arranging lasting settlements. He also reported
to the French that a deputation of tribesmen from Werdigha, Bni
Khiran, Sma'la, and Bni Zemmur had asked him what attitude to
take with Shaykh Mha and another anti-French "agitator." The
anonymous writer in the Journal Politique remarks that the marabout "prudently" advised them not to attack the French (JP, April–
May 1911). Earlier, the Journal complained of the "shady"
(*louche*) attitude of the marabouts of Boujad and of another *zawya*
in Dukkala, because maraboutic loyalties shifted with their perception
of the strength of the antagonists. The writer was particularly concerned with the Dukkali marabout, Sidi Ahmed Tunsi, who maintained a contingent of horsemen with orders to join the winning side
of any dispute in order to carry away a share of the booty (JP,
December 1910).

After the summer of 1911, the French report only minor conflicts
on the Tadla Plain. The reporting for this period, however, is also
rather thin, reflecting the transfer of French attention to the Fes
region where, by the end of the year, five thousand troops were
camped outside the walls of the palace. Having eliminated the last
international obstacles to their protectorate in November, the French
began in earnest to prepare for colonial rule. Henceforth, the
Sherqawa were to play only a minor role in their calculations.

Notes

Introduction

1. Parsons's judgment is curious, since he characterizes his own work as no more than a paradigm (1964:485). It would appear that Weber asserts no more for his own work (1964:109).
2. Dead, that is, from an observer's point of view. For those who believe in marabouts, "dead" ones are alive and well in their shrines, ready to influence the turn of events in this world.
3. Here I should point out that I use the term *maraboutism* in a broader sense than is usually found in the French litera- ture. Many French writers, including Berque (1957:14), distinguish between *maraboutisme, confrérisme,* and other forms of religious organization. Yet these all share the underlying notion of a hierarchical relation between man and God. Although useful in some respects, Berque's categorization is misleading for such maraboutic groups as the Sherqawa, which exhibit characteristics of various forms of organization that Berque sees as necessarily com- peting. To my knowledge, only Ali Merad uses *mara-*

boutisme in the broader sense that I do. One other caution is here in order. I have decided to reserve for a later study, which will deal with traditional Moroccan intellectuals, the exploration of varieties of what I here call "formal" Islam, such as modernism, reformism, neofundamentalism, and so on. From the vantage point of Boujad and other parts of rural Morocco, the distinction between these various intellectual currents tends to blur.

1. Morocco, Islam, and the Maraboutic Crisis

1. After the protectorate was established in Morocco, it would appear that the French regarded only the nonindigenous elements of society as inherently "progressive." For a detailed account of the formation of colonial stereotypes toward Moroccans, see Burke 1973:175–199.
2. Such assumptions became powerful ideological weapons in the hands of political advisors to the French Residence. For instance, they were used to justify the separation of native from European populations in the cities on the basis of a Muslim "preference" to be so isolated. They also justified such French policies as the famous Berber Proclamation (*daher*) of 1930, which removed Berber-speaking regions of Morocco from the jurisdiction of Islamic law. The goal was to foster a separate Berber (i.e., non-Arab and to a certain extent non-Muslim) identity. Jacques Berque has sarcastically referred to these policies as an attempt to create a Berber ethnographic reserve or "national park" (1967).
3. The translation is by the author, as are subsequent translations unless otherwise indicated.
4. Bel originally intended to complement his study with two other volumes. One was to have dealt primarily with maraboutism and religious brotherhoods. The other was to have dealt with "pagan survivals" in Islam. Neither was ever published, although his approach to both themes is readily apparent in his first, published volume.
5. The term *tariqa* also signifies a religious order to which affiliation is in principle individual and voluntary.
6. Along with other writers, Bel assumes that there is a conscious

deception involved on the part of many who claim to be
marabouts. Foreign travelers and diplomats in the late
eighteenth and early nineteenth centuries provided some
supporting evidence for this notion. Ali Bey (Domingo
Badia y Leblich) met a marabout, "a better sort of man,"
who admitted that he was a cheat. "He repeated often his
favourite saying, that fools are made for the amusement
of men of ability." The attitude of religious scholars toward
marabouts which Ali Bey reports is remarkably similar to
present-day attitudes: "The Fakih and the Taleb pass over
these tricks in silence, and leave the people in their folly,
though they themselves know very well what to think of
it, and conversed very frankly with me upon the subject"
(1816:48–49).

Chenier (1788:179–191) presents a similar view of
marabouts, although he differentiates types of marabouts
more clearly than Ali Bey. Chenier describes "sainthood"
as a lucrative profession or trade, passed from father to
son or sometimes from master to servant. He also claims
that among his friends was a well-known saint who admitted to him that he was an impostor.

7. The formal conception of educated Moroccans (and that of the
current Moroccan constitution) is that the king is only the
"commander of the faithful" (*amir l-mu'minin*). Nevertheless, for all practical purposes the doctrines of the
sultanate (temporal authority) and the caliphate (spiritual
authority) are popularly fused. Elsewhere in the Muslim
world the distinction between these two conceptions is often
highly significant.

8. This was the stillborn "Projet de constitution marocaine" drafted
by a "young Turk" coterie which surrounded Sultan Mulay
'Abd l-Hafed (reigned 1908–1912). This was one of the
last-minute efforts to reform Morocco to enable it to cope
with the growing European influence over its affairs.
Article 7 of this document reads: "Tout sujet du Royaume
doit obéissance à l'Imam chérifien et respect à sa personne
parce qu'il est l'héritier de la Baraka [All subjects of
the kingdom owe obedience to the Shrifian Imam and
respect to his person because he is the inheritor of the
Baraka]" (cited in Robert 1963:311).

9. Most of the royal decrees mentioned are from translations into French made under the direction of Claude Ecorcheville while he was *contrôleur civil* of Boujad in 1938. These are indicated by *E* in the text. (On the accuracy of these translations, see my note in the bibliography.) Material taken directly from the unpublished correspondence of Sherqawi families in Boujad is indicated by *S*. Dates are given in both Muslim and Christian Eras.

2. Marabouts and Local Histories: The Sherqawa

1. One exception is Da'ud's encyclopedic local history of Tetouan, which is still in progress (1959–). Although not explicitly a social history, it includes numerous references to marabouts and suggests the wealth of documentation available, at least in some regions, for local history. Mukhtar es-Susi has written a similar local history for the Sus.
2. The account of ed-Dila which follows is based primarily on Drague (1951:137–139), although Hajji (1964) has also been consulted.
3. Similar ties were earlier maintained with the declining Sa'adi dynasty. Sultan Mulay Zidan (reigned 1613–1627) is reputed to have built the shrine of Sidi Mhammed Sherqi's mother, Lalla Răhma. It is located along the Umm er-Rbi' River, to the east of Qasba Tadla. The sultan probably constructed the shrine as an attempt to gain favor both with the Sherqawa and with their tribal clients.
4. Al-Ifrani obliquely refers to a "great misfortune" which befell him. Evidently he fell out of favor at the court of Mulay Isma'il and sought refuge at Boujad for several years (Lévi-Provençal 1922:115, 119–120).
5. Myths and oral traditions concerning him that are current on the Tadla Plain will be presented and analyzed in chapters 6 and 7.
6. Examination of the tension between the sultanate and marabouts for a later period, the eighteenth century, is provided by Morsy's excellent essay on the Ahansal (1972). The presence of a European witness provided the key text for her examination of the otherwise reticent "official" historiographies and elements of local legends.

7. The maraboutic successors to Sidi Mḥammed Sherqi are called "lords" (*sid*-s). Names in the text which also appear in accompanying figures are given numbers to facilitate identification. The number before the hyphen refers to the figure in which an individual first appears. The same number is also used in later figures.

8. Mḥammed ben Naṣer also had ties with the *zawya* at ed-Dila. Likewise Sidi Mḥammed l-Maʿti was lord of the Sherqawi *zawya* during ed-Dila's apogee, but the texts again give no clue as to the substance of these ties. Drague is incorrect in describing the Sherqawi lodge as "subsidiary" to the Naṣiriya order, although his informants at Tamgrut in the 1930's may have made such a claim. Drague may also have simply repeated the error of Cimetière's earlier account (1913:287). The affiliation of individual Sherqawa had no effect on their descendants, according to contemporary Sherqawa.

9. This individual is a grandson of Sidi Mḥammed Sherqi. Ḥmadsha legends make Sidi ʿAli a disciple of Sidi Mḥammed Sherqi, a chronological impossibility (Crapanzano 1973:30–37).

10. I am grateful to Muḥammed Sherqawi for this information, which he bases upon manuscript sources which I have not yet been able to verify personally. I have, however, seen a deed (*resm*) authenticating the sultan's ownership of a house in Boujad.

11. For a detailed description of such arrangements in the Moroccan southeast, see Dunn 1971.

12. A more extensive analysis of these holdings and subsidiary *zawya*-s, with the documentation available for each of them, has been presented in Eickelman 1972–1973. To the list given there should be added Sidi Mekki Sherqawi, patron marabout of the town of Azemmur. A group of his claimed descendants lived about twenty kilometers from the town. Until the 1920's, a living descendant of Sidi Mekki lived in the town itself and accepted offerings (Le Coeur 1969:120).

13. The Makhzen itself seemed unclear as to the status of these estates. In 1901 Sultan Mulay ʿAbd l-ʿAziz ordered the properties of the Sherqawi *zawya* to be divided equally between two rival lords (E, 20 October 1901 / 7 Rejeb

1319). A marabout from the *zawya* at Wezzan was sent to supervise the division. According to Sherqawi informants, he discovered that, unlike the situation in Wezzan, where *'azib*-s were considered the collective property of the *zawya*, most of the Sherqawi *'azib*-s were owned by individuals and could be divided only by the laws of Islamic inheritance. Consequently he reported to the sultan that the Sherqawa were fighting for property which in any case could not be divided (Eickelman 1972–1973:45, Ecorcheville 1938:72). However, Jacques Berque has kindly informed me that there were also private *'azib*-s at Wezzan. This suggests that other factors came into play in the decision attributed to the Wezzani marabout.

14. In a posthumously published document, Foucauld quotes the following Sherqawi comment on relations with Mulay Hasan I: "We don't fear him and he doesn't fear us. He can't harm us and we can't harm him" (1939:135).

15. The *qadi* from 1894 until the early years of the protectorate was Mhammed ben Saleh, of the Qadiriyin descent group of the Sherqawa. Shortly after the death of Sultan Mulay Hasan I in 1894, one prominent Sherqawi sent Mhammed ben Saleh a note concerning an inheritance dispute in which he was an interested party. It stated his intent to pursue the dispute as soon as the authority (*sulta*) of the Makhzen was restored (E, Mhammed ben Saleh to 'Umar ben Sidi ben Dawd, 17 March 1894 / 10 Ramadan 1311).

16. If slaves were maltreated, they often ran away and sought refuge with marabouts or other intermediaries until given assurances by their masters that their condition would improve.

17. At the end of his stay in Boujad, Driss gave Foucauld a letter offering his services to the minister of France in Tangiers and asked whether he would be made a *qaid* upon the arrival of the French (Foucauld 1939:135). In 1907 Driss sought Foucauld's intervention to obtain his post with the French consulate in Casablanca (Gorrée 1939:62–72).

18. Evidence of 'Umar's role is primarily oral, although it is supported by the fact that correspondence relative to Mha, as well as copies of the correspondence which passed between the sultan and Mha, was found among 'Umar's

papers (S. 24 November 1882 / 13 Muḥarrem 1300; 20
July 1883 / 15 Ramadan 1300; 3 December 1883 / 2 Ṣafar
1301). These letters were addressed to Sidi ben Dawḍ.
19. The substance of the complaint was that 'Umar had appropriated
for himself revenues derived from allowing individuals to
be buried on the grounds of a Sherqawi *zawya* in Meknes.
20. This distinction eluded Drague (1951), among others.

3. Boujad: The Town and Its Region

1. The inhabitants of the region consider the Tadla Plain as stretching
roughly from Bni Mellal to Khuribga. This is the usage
which I follow. Recent geographical studies (Martin et al.
1967; Noin 1970) delimit the part of this plain surrounding Khuribga as the Phosphates Plateau. This delimitation
is based on the criteria of geomorphology and modern
economic activities but is peripheral to accepted popular
usage.
2. Jacques Berque, originally a *contrôleur civil* during the protectorate,
has suggested a connection between the appropriations
which did take place in this region in the late 1920's and
the Wad Zem massacre of 23 August 1955 (1967:35).
On the morning of that day, the Sma'la cut the telephone
lines to the town and invaded it, killing eighty-seven
Frenchmen out of a population of eight hundred within
a few hours. In reprisal at least five hundred tribesmen
were killed by French ground and air forces in subsequent
days; houses were destroyed and animals slaughtered. The
uprising was considered the most significant rural resistance to the French in the waning years of the protectorate.
3. In 1963, 35 percent of Boujad's adult (over age 21) residents had
been born in the surrounding rural area. Eleven percent
came from other regions of Morocco. The remaining 54
percent had been born in Boujad itself. (These figures are
calculated from the municipal electoral lists, 1963). The
assumption of an increased rate of immigration is based
primarily upon the qualitative appraisal of Boujadi-s and
upon more general demographic studies (e.g., Noin 1970:
II). Statistics comparable to those of 1963 are not available
for earlier periods.

4. *Zyara* is also the term used for visits to Mecca outside of the pilgrimage season.

5. In the dialect of the Tadla Plain, *derb* is synonymous with *huma*, although the latter term is rarely employed. This usage can be confusing, since, in the dialect of Fes, *huma* means "quarter," while *derb* signifies an alleyway or impasse. Thus, in Fes, a *huma* contains a number of *derb*-s. I point out this variation in order to avoid possible misunderstanding.

6. For a detailed, broadly analogous description of the internal changes of a market in northern Morocco and its postprotectorate transformation, see Fogg 1938.

7. Seventy-five percent of the animals brought to the market are sheep. Goats comprise another 12 percent, cattle 7 percent, and other animals—camels, donkeys, and horses—the remaining 6 percent (Raynal and André 1955).

8. In the late 1960's the rural holdings were taken over by the Ministry of the Interior and in principle exchanged for equivalent urban holdings in the interests of agrarian reform.

9. Two of the non-Sherqawi shrines are dilapidated, virtually unvisited shrines in an old, abandoned cemetery to the north of Boujad. One shrine belongs to 'Ali ben S'id; the other is supposed to be the shrine of a marabout of the neighboring Sma'la tribe. Both these marabouts are regarded as having lost their religious powers because of the empirical fact that their shrines are untended. They are also falling into obscurity. The third non-Sherqawi shrine is that of Rabbi Lewi, located in the midst of the Jewish cemetery. Jews of Boujad origin who now live in Casablanca still return on occasion to visit it and see to its maintenance.

10. There were fewer visitors in the remaining two weeks of the festival period. A very rough estimate is an additional ten thousand.

11. The term "shadow *qaid*" I owe to Clifford Geertz. He uses it primarily to refer to the common administrative pattern in which the "stranger" who is *qaid* in one region informally consults a native of the region who is *qaid* elsewhere. The latter person is the "shadow *qaid*." I use the term more broadly because in my experience in western

Morocco, such "shadows" are commonly locals who hold no formal administrative posts.

12. Since 1970 Boujad has had no regular *qadi*. The Ministry of Justice decided there was not a sufficient case load to warrant a full-time religious judge. One is supplied from a neighboring town on each market day.

4. Social Structure

1. This formulation of social structure owes much to discussions with Lawrence Rosen, Clifford and Hildred Geertz, and Lloyd A. Fallers. For Rosen's development of the concept, see his account of Arab-Berber relations (1973) and Arab-Jewish relations (1972). In addition, many of us interested in Morocco have been aided greatly by Fallers's earlier work on Buganda (1959: esp. 23). For a discussion of similar problems in Iran, see Bill 1973.

2. An example of this dissociation in a Sherqawi quarter is the one which claimed as eponymic ancestor Sid l-Mursli, one of the sons of the founding marabout. It was located next to the shrine of Sidi Mhammed Sherqi. Presently it is remembered by only the oldest Boujadi-s, although descendants of this marabout are still in Boujad and entitled to a share in the offerings of the main shrine. The buildings which constituted the quarter still exist. Many elderly Sherqawa still live there. It is simply not regarded as a quarter anymore. Some of the households are now tacitly assimilated into neighboring Sherqawi quarters. Jewish residential areas followed a similar pattern. As I mentioned earlier, Boujad never had a *mellah* in the strict sense of the term, although the quarter in which the synagogue was located was called the *mellah*. When all but one Jewish household departed in 1963 and the synagogue was deconsecrated, its quarter quickly became known as part of Qadiriyin, the Sherqawi quarter which encompassed it. A more dramatic indication of these shifts is the difficulty which local officials have in using an administrative map of quarters prepared by the French in the 1930's, which is still supposed to be em-

ployed for governmental purposes. Many of the boundaries have shifted, and several names are unidentifiable.
Although they are supposed to use the labels provided by
the official map for such things as election registration,
officials admit that they are unable to do so and instead
use the nomenclature "which everyone knows."

3. In recounting this episode, informants regarded this turn of good
fortune as a sign of God's favor to Bu Bakr and attached no
adverse connotations to his behavior.

4. A brother of Ma'ti's (7-6), actively seeking a government post at
the time of field research, indicated how the same calculations of "closeness" operate in other contexts. He told me
that his *weld 'amm* (father's brother's son), a government
clerk in Rabat (7-2), was helping him in the matter. In
this case, the "actual" link (i.e., in terms of Islamic law)
was known. The person claimed as *weld 'amm* by Islamic
law was actually his sister's husband's mother's sister's son
(*weld khut umm rajel khuti*) or—since both one of his
brothers and his sister had married into the same household—his brother's wife's mother's sister's son. Again the
justification offered for using the term *weld 'amm* was the
quality of "closeness" claimed to exist between the two
persons.

5. Bni Zemmur is an administrative creation of the protectorate. The
colonial government, like the precolonial Makhzen, often
created "tribes" for administrative purposes. Tribesmen
recognize the term *Bni Zemmur* as a vague clustering of
their "actual" tribes but not as a unit of effective social action, except in so far as the government treats the "Bni
Zemmur" as a reality. Tribesmen regard their "actual"
tribes—i.e., those with which they identify in nongovern-
mental contexts—as Rwashed, Shegran, Bni Battu, Bni
Zrantel, and Wlad Yusef. These are officially considered
to be sections of the Bni Zemmur.

6. It has sometimes been asserted that all tribes in North Africa can be
described in terms of segmentation. Elsewhere, I plan to
deal at length with the issue of segmentation theory and
its relation to rural social structure in North Africa. Attempts to apply segmentation theory to North Africa are

interesting for some of the epistemological considerations
they raise but are peripheral to the main concern of this
book. Besides, many anthropologists and social historians
interested in North Africa since the mid-1960's are only
now preparing monograph-length studies. A discussion of
broader epistemological issues will become more meaningful when these are available so that they can be contrasted
with the earlier contributions of colonial ethnographers.
For the nonce, the most thorough, and devastating, critique
of the concept of segmentation as sociological theory can
be found in Peters's (1967) account of the Bedouin of Cyrenaica, earlier described as segmentary by Evans-Pritchard
(1949) (although with none of the thoroughness of his
studies of the Nuer). Summaries of recent empirical research indicating that the concept is no more accurate as a
sociological description of the tribal organization of preprotectorate Morocco can be found in the contributions of
Seddon and Vinogradov, explicitly, and Dunn, implicitly,
to Gellner and Micaud, eds., *Arabs and Berbers* (1973). An
earlier but highly thoughtful French discussion of the problems of social identity inherent in defining *tribe* can be
found in Berque (1953).

7. No ties are claimed with the component groups of the Bni Zemmur
of the Boujad region, although in practice the two groups
have had multiple ties through the Sherqawa, shared pasture lands, and factional alliances prior to the protectorate.
In calling these groups "tribes," I am following local usage.
Several French administrative reports term the Sma'la and
Bni Zemmur "confederations," although this usage is not
consistent.

8. Since independence the Moroccan government has officially abandoned the division of rural Morocco into tribes. These have
been replaced with rural "communes" (*jma'a*-s), each of
which generally carries the name of the tribe residing in it.
In principle, each commune has popularly elected officials
who form its council. This group, under the tutelage of its
qaid, administers a small budget for public works. The
principle behind the reform was to replace primordial loyalties, encouraged during most of the protectorate, with

broader, national ones. Despite sincere efforts on the part of many administrators, the impact of the communal system remains politically and socially marginal.

9. Townsmen frequently claim that tribesmen are ignorant of Islam and thus pay no heed to these formal religious activities. Such claims are hardly new. There is preprotectorate evidence for the existence of such rural mosques for the neighboring Shawya region, along with denials of their existence by townsmen (Mission Scientifique du Maroc 1915:I, 121).

10. Informants claim a similar flexibility prior to the protectorate despite the much greater occurrence of intergroup hostility. The preprotectorate manuscript correspondence which pertains to the nature of "traditional" tribal organization mentions only the relations of tribes and tribal sections. This is to be expected, since most of the correspondence concerns Makhzen intervention in tribal affairs (S, 'Ali Mesfyuwi to Sidi 'Umar Sherqawi, 17 December 1881 / 25 Muharrem 1299; S, Driss ben 'Umar to Sid l-'Arbi, February 1894 / Sha'ban 1311; E, Mulay 'Abd l-'Aziz to Sid l-Hajj l-Hasan, 25 January 1903 / 25 Shawwal 1320).

11. Milk brotherhood is created when two children are nursed by the same woman. In Islamic law, persons thus linked are treated as full siblings for purposes of marriage, although they gain no rights of inheritance. It should be noted that, although the terminology reported here is current throughout western Morocco and the Middle Atlas Mountains, variations exist elsewhere. I quote in full a personal communication from Ross Dunn (1974): "Alliance through the milk exchange was called *tafargant* among the Ait 'Atta (particularly referring to their alliance with the Bni Mhammed). It is clear that the 'Atta made a clear distinction between *tafargant* (which included a marriage taboo) and *tata*. That is, the 'Atta do *not* seem to have regarded *tafargant* as a type of *tata*, but as something quite distinct."

12. There are two ways to account for this apparent anomaly of the mixing of "levels" of tribal organization. One is to suggest that, in the sixty years which have elapsed since this alliance was contracted, one group or the other has been either "raised" or "lowered" from local community to tribal section or vice versa as the result of the internal realignment

of tribal organization. Alternatively, it is equally plausible that such an arrangement simply made sense in terms of tribal geopolitics and the demographic size of the two groups involved. Informants from the two groups saw no anomaly; only tribal strong-men who deal regularly with the administration speak of clearly demarcated "levels."

13. Informants were unable to tell me whether in these cases *taṭa* also involved marriage prohibitions between the contracting groups. See note 12 above.

14. His name suggests that his tribe of origin was the Ait 'Aṭṭa, a powerful Berber group situated in the High Atlas Mountains to the south of Bni Mellal. Neither David M. Hart (personal communication, ca. 1971) nor Ernest Gellner (personal communication, 1969), both of whom have written extensively on this tribe, can identify him.

15. The French, misunderstanding the Moroccan concept of *baraka*, or perhaps understanding it all too well, recognized and supported only one of the two rival Sherqawi lords of this period as a marabout.

5. Impermanence and Inequality: The Common-Sense Understanding of the Social Order

1. For an excellent discussion of the same concept in a biography of a Casablanca merchant, see Waterbury (1972: esp. 155–156).

2. For a fuller elaboration of this term in its classical context, dissimilar but not unrelated to contemporary Moroccan usages, see Izutsu 1964:203–219 and the discussion in the text of reason as a social concept.

3. A Muslim general, d. 681.

4. D. 792.

5. "L-bashar 'ăndhom l-'qal. Tă-ymiyzu bin l-ḥaja lli ddorhom we-l-ḥaja lli ma ddorhom-sh."

6. The implicit metaphor is that thoughts, like vegetables, must ripen and mature before being offered for consumption.

7. For all practical purposes in terms of Islam as popularly understood in Morocco, Christians, generally called the *rumi*-s (Romans), fall outside the sphere of ordinary social action. The problem of how Christians demonstrate reason is one

which does not immediately present itself to Boujadi-s, few of whom have had regular contact with foreigners.

8. Abstinence from drinking usually begins a month prior to Ramadan.

9. This account is consciously meant to trace the inculcation of these concepts in men only. The socialization of females is similar with respect to propriety but differs considerably in other aspects crucial to male-female roles. For one thing, daughters traditionally remained in the care of their mothers, while boys were expected to move beyond the women of the household circle at an early age. The spread of education for girls, especially in towns, undoubtedly will rapidly result in changing conceptions of propriety in relation to public space. Unfortunately this topic has only begun to be investigated, and the best discussion to date (H. Geertz 1974) is still in mimeographed form.

10. My informant's wife called regularly at the house of the official. These visits were never reciprocated, since the wife of the high-ranking man was never allowed to leave her house. The visiting pattern indicated the ranking of the households in relation to each other.

11. In classical Arabic, *hăqq* is frequently used in the sense of "truth" or "that which can be verified." It is used in this sense in records of court proceedings, which, of course, are conducted in classical Arabic. In colloquial use, *'ăndek l-hăqq* can in some contexts also be translated as "you're right."

12. Of a nearly complete sample of 838, only 61 (7.3 percent) of Boujad's merchants and craftsmen had acquired capital from other individuals for their enterprises in 1970. Of these 61, 37 (60.7 per cent) had borrowed from kinsmen. In a few such cases, the owner of the capital would effectively assert dominance over the activities of the borrower. A very few cases of real partnerships existed, almost always between kinsmen, in which both worked in the same shop. Such partnerships, even between brothers, tended to have very short lives. The only exceptions to this overall pattern are Boujad's itinerant rural cloth-sellers. As mentioned in Chapter 3, these individuals were originally Qur'anic teachers (*fqih*-s) who took over the business of Jewish merchants shortly after independence. These traders act collectively

in their purchases, share storage space in Boujad, and in other ways regularly act in one another's interests. Boujadi-s consider this cooperation exceptional and attribute it to the fact that, as former Qur'anic teachers, the cloth-sellers are really trying to live according to the principles of Islamic brotherhood.

13. Men claim no formal knowledge of these processions but, since they involve activities in public space, quietly plan to the last detail the hire of carts and musicians and the route the public display will take in order to avoid possible embarrassment to the household. Male servants often accompany such processions to maintain order. No women and children of higher prestige participate in the public processions. Hence such processions tend to consist primarily of clients and lower-ranking neighbors, at least in the case of more distinguished households.

14. For an extensive presentation of examples of situations involving the "greater" and "lesser" *'ar* and the means for their invocation. see Westermarck 1926: I, 518–564.

15. The word is derived from *'ar* on the *istif'al* pattern of formal Arabic. This pattern is used to make up words which include in their meanings the action of asking for or requesting.

16. The term *'shur* is also sometimes used for offerings to marabouts.

17. This term is also used to denote a refusal to accept the political authority of the Makhzen, as in tribal rebellions.

18. The judge later counseled the father to drop the case. He tried—in his words—to make him "see reason and avoid *'ar*."

6. The Ideology of Maraboutism

1. Only one tribal informant ever directly applied the analogy of man-man and man-God relations and spoke of "dealing" (*msarfa*) with God and his associates (*ashab*; sg., *saheb*). Since the Qur'an explicitly states that God has no associates, other informants, including those maintaining ties with marabouts, spoke of the above statement as coming from someone ignorant of Islam (*jahel*).

2. I plan to devote a later, separate study to the analysis of the content and rhetorical form of these myths. Although such covenants are to my knowledge represented only in the

form of myths in western Morocco, *written* covenants exist elsewhere. Berque (1955:278) reports one that dates from 1840 for a Berber-speaking group of the High Atlas Mountains.

3. For the Arabic version of this myth and bilingual presentations of two others, see Eickelman and Draioui 1973.

4. Meknasi is one of the eleven children attributed to Sidi Mhammed Sherqi.

5. Ascent to the top of Mount ʻArafa is forbidden to pious Muslims. See the article on "Mount ʻArafa" in Gibb and Kramers, eds. 1961.

6. The underlying concept here is that life is a gift of God which can be taken back at his will.

7. This quotation is in *sajʻ* verse, a sort of limerick rhyme often indicative of supernatural inspiration. See the article "Ḳurʼān" in Gibb and Kramers. eds. 1961 for a more complete description. Note the implicit contradiction in the words of the marabout. He claims that those like him can forbear but then expresses his grief over the loss of his son.

8. Literally, *l-amana dyal l-ḥăqq*, "the trust which belongs to God."

9. I.e., "If this is our reaction to the loss of this son, what will we do at the death of another?"

10. It is unclear whether Sidi Mhammed Sherqi says this sentence as if his wife were not present or whether it is spoken by the narrator. I am assuming the latter to be the case.

11. A spring located in Boujad.

12. Semʻli is the singular of Smaʻla. Note that at this point the Bni Zemmur cease to be mentioned in the myth.

13. The implication is that the marabout was in a shrine.

14. *Tesqaw*: lit., "to irrigate" or "to nourish."

15. Khelfiya, Sidi Mhammed Sherqi's wife, is, like the marabout himself, considered to be a descendant of ʻUmar ben l-Khatṭab.

16. Human sacrifices are, of course, prohibited in Islam. Note that, for the second time in the myth, the marabout is compelled to take a particular action as a result of the interference of his wife. The first time was when her uncontrolled grief compelled him to settle elsewhere.

17. Sidi ʻAli died in either 1718/1719 or 1722/1723, over a century after the death of Sidi Mhammed Sherqi (Crapanzano 1973:23). Such historical precision is, of course, irrel-

evant to the social relations which are thought to have existed between the two.

18. In social actuality, the component groups of the Bni Zemmur maintain ties with the Sherqawa but are regarded as lacking faith (*niya*) by the Sherqawa and surrounding tribes. This lack of faith, indicated by merely nominal offerings to the Sherqawa, is said by many tribesmen to account for the poverty of the Bni Zemmur in relation to other groups.

19. A similar equivalency occurs in actual social relations. An isolated example occurred as recently as 1969. A tribal group in Dukkala wanted a Sherqawi whom they considered prominent to live among them. They built him a house and provided a tribeswoman as wife. The tribesmen themselves paid the entire bridewealth (*ṣdaq*) to the girl's father. The Sherqawi did not participate even symbolically in raising the bridewealth. This is the only such exchange that I know of to have occurred in recent years, but once they appear to have been more common. Le Coeur (1969:120), who studied the town of Azemmur between 1930 and 1933, reports that, until a few years before his arrival, there was a living marabout who claimed descent from Sidi Mekki Sherqawi, patron marabout of the town and its region. Offerings were regularly made to him, including young girls selected by lottery. Unfortunately Le Coeur gives no further details. Le Coeur was also told that this marabout passed his time smoking *kif* (hemp), drinking rum and tea, and openly avoiding prayers and the fast. Such activities evidently were taken as a sign of his special insights.

20. Some Sherqawa, usually from the same descent grouping, have competing claims to the right to "work" certain tribal groups. In this circumstance some agree to work in teams, others to divide the proceeds of such visits.

21. Some of these contrasts have been suggested by Turner (1973).

22. Significantly, each bull offered at that time represented a separate tribal section. As with sacrifices at the shrine of Sidi Mhammed Sherqi, the bulls were offered simultaneously, but not on behalf of any supersectional collectivity.

23. On the significance of this color and other points, neither the Sherqawa nor the Sma'la offer any explanation.

24. More distant groups from Shawya often simply offer cash.
25. Conditional offerings are called, literally, "that which the marabout picks up" (*l-merfuda dyal esh-shaykh*). These frequently are offered in the case of illness by individual clients. The father of a sick infant, for instance, will choose an animal of his herd, which ideally is the age of his child, and whisper in the animal's ear that it will belong to the marabout if the child recovers. The sacrifice is actually made only if there is a successful recovery.
26. The need to maintain *baraka* by controlling access to its possessors is a major reason why women are often discouraged by the Sherqawa from seeking access to marabouts and prominent visitors. One visitor explained to me that women can rarely make significant offerings of their own. They often offer small coins at the major shrine and occasionally will sleep overnight next to the sepulcher of Sidi Mḥammed Sherqi. Only men can make or offer to make sacrifices, so that husbands and wives generally go together to shrines for major invocations or to deliver sacrifices which have been promised to a marabout for services rendered. Many activities associated with women are strictly forbidden by custodians at the major shrines. At unattended shrines, women often smear henna on the portal or leave locks of their hair and small strips of cloth torn from their garments as reminders of the request they have made to the marabout. Such conduct is forbidden at major shrines, although it is often attempted.

7. Sherqawi Identity

1. *Fqir* has this sense primarily on the western plains of Morocco: Shawya, Tadla, and Dukkala (see Westermarck 1926:I, 35–36). David M. Hart (personal communication, ca. 1972) reports a similar use in the Rif. In addition to Sidi Mḥammed Sherqi, two other major marabouts on the western plains also base their legitimacy on 'Umari descent: Sidi Shegdal ben Ghilan (Bni Shegdal) and Sidi 'Ali u Brahim (Aid Bu Zid, Wad Nfis). In classical Arabic, *fqir* signifies a religious ascetic (Bel 1938:352), as mentioned in Chapter 1. In current speech the term is also a

polite way of referring to an impoverished individual. Among many young, urban Moroccans, the distinction between *foqra* and *shorfa* is currently often blurred or nonexistent.

2. Of course, even Figure 2 telescopes past events by omitting reference to any but recent contests for the lordship. Many Sherqawa, in reciting Sherqawi lords, omit one or the other of the variant lordship lines for this century.

3. A slightly different version of the ties of Sidi Mhammed Sherqi with some of the tribes of western Morocco is offered in al-Qadiri's seventeenth-century biography of the marabout (1913:127–129). He writes that the Sherqawi lord was originally from the Werdigha tribe (near present-day Khuribga), which in turn was from the Bni Jabir. Although many Sherqawa knew of the existence of this account, they saw no need to reconcile the two versions. After all, they reasoned, the ties of Sidi Mhammed Sherqi with these groups are "known," and they are all descendants of 'Umar.

4. Sultan Mulay 'Abd l-Aziz (reigned 1894–1908) was named after this marabout because he was born near the marabout's tomb while his father was on a military expedition.

5. These facing shrines are tended by a small group of descendants of Sidi bel Gasem (including one Sherqawi from Boujad), each of whom has specified days on which he collects offerings. There is also a small festival held each fall at the shrine of Sidi bel Gasem, attended primarily by Berber-speaking groups. Since knowledge of the clients of marabouts is highly concentric, few of the Boujad Sherqawa have any specific knowledge of the activities associated with this shrine.

Lalla Rǎhma is said to have been from the Drissi dynasty, the first descendants of the Prophet to rule in Morocco. In the 1930's, this claim was legitimated by an elaborate genealogy of twenty-four individuals, some of whom have tombs on the Tadla Plain (Ecorcheville 1938). No one to whom I spoke during my fieldwork could refer me to anyone able to recite this genealogy.

6. Partial evidence for this is a directive from the Grand Wezir to Qaid 'Abd l-Qader of Boujad (E, 7 February 1927 / 4

Sha'ban 1345) ordering the payment to be made. Other
directives from the Grand Wezir to the *qaid* from this period (E: 14 February 1927 / 11 Sha'ban 1345; 20 May
1927 / 18 Qa'ada 1345) indicate several other disputes
over revenues from Sherqawi shrines. There is no evidence
of any such official intervention in maraboutic affairs after
1929, a fact which indirectly confirms Marty's assertion
to that effect (1929:575–600).

7. There are also tombs for two daughters of Sidi Mḥammed Sherqi,
both of which are visited only by women. Neither tomb
has custodians. One is that of Lalla Mina, next to that of
Sidi Mḥammed Sherqi. She is said to have had the *baraka*
to weave a *jellaba* for him in a day, an activity that normally takes weeks or months. The other tomb, of fairly
recent origin, is that of Lalla Hniyya, supposedly efficacious at reconciling quarreling couples. Women leave
strips of their clothing stuck with henna to its door. So far
as I could gather, both tombs were maintained by the
municipal budget. The only explanation I received for this
was that both tombs were next to a main road, so that
it would be unseemly to allow them to fall into disrepair.

8. Boujadi-s and merchants from Demnat were affiliated with it (F.
Berger 1929:47). There were at least three other *zawya*-s
in Khnifra, each of which had as members merchants from
a particular city or region. Fassi-s affiliated with the
Tijaniya; Marrakshi-s with the Qadiriya, and so on. Each
"alien" community also had its own quarter and tended to
be occupationally specialized (F. Berger 1929:44–45).
Unfortunately, Berger does not indicate patterns of affiliation to these lodges, if any, for the Middle Atlas Berbers.

9. In 1969 the formal *mqaddem*-s included a *zewwar* who was also
a weaver, a retail grocer, a bicycle repairman, a government *shaykh* and prayer-leader in a mosque, the custodian
of a major Sherqawi shrine, a primary schoolteacher, and
a notary.

10. This account is primarily from a Sherqawi notary (*'adel*) actively
interested in the affairs of the shrine. The exact nature of
the administrative or judicial tribunal which handled this
dispute is unclear. Similar mechanisms for division exist
among groups of *shorfa*; so it is possible that the French

imposed the same pattern upon the Sherqawa by analogy.

Division of the offerings has not occurred in recent years because of charges of embezzlement raised in the late 1960's against several of the overseers. Some Sherqawa unsuccessfully attempted to bring the dispute before various local government agencies. These echoed an old protectorate stand that "religious" matters were not a governmental concern. Others claimed that the dispute was a "family" affair which had to be worked out among the Sherqawa themselves. Meanwhile the *mqaddem*-s keep the offerings for shrine expenses.

11. A tenet of Islamic law is that a woman can be married only to a man who is at least her "equal" (see Schacht 1966:162). What constitutes equality (*kafa'a*) in a legal context— wealth, social honor, education, descent from the Prophet or 'Umar—would make a fascinating study, especially if historical shifts in its definition were taken into account.

12. Unfortunately it is not possible to calculate the rate of such marriages for town-born commoners from my sample. My guess is that it would not differ greatly from the two known rates.

13. The notarial fee in 1970 was 1.5 percent of the bridewealth (*sdaq*). Rural bridewealth is called *'orram* (lit., "heap"). Rural marriages are almost always concluded before the number of witnesses required by Islamic law. If it is ever necessary to go before an Islamic law court, it is thus possible to prepare a formal contract at a later date, based on the declarations of these witnesses. (Courts do not recognize marriages for which there is no valid written contract. This is important in legal cases involving inheritance and support.)

14. In conceiving of Figure 14, I have benefited from discussions with Hildred Geertz and from her study on Moroccan kinship (1974).

8. From Center to Periphery: The Fragmentation of Maraboutism

1. Contemporary sociological usage prefers the more precise term *cohort* to *generation*. A *cohort* is defined as "an aggregate

of individual elements, each of which experienced a significant event in its life history during the same chronological interval" (Ryder 1968:546). In the discussion in the text, I follow Mannheim's older usage, which, in the context of his writing, is not open to the charge of ambiguity.

2. J. Cimetière, the first Native Affairs officer assigned to Boujad, incorrectly states that the visit occurred in October (1913: 289).

3. There was only one exception to this policy throughout the protectorate. In the early 1930's a brother of 'Abd l-Qader Sherqawi, then the *qaid* of Boujad, was appointed as *qaid* of Fqih ben Saleh. But this individual had totally dissociated himself from the affairs of the *zawya* and had served for some time as an officer in the French army.

4. This assessment of him was contained in the draft of a French intelligence report of the 1930's. The French administration required monthly intelligence reports from its local officers, a section of which were devoted to assessments of the various notables. In addition, special reports were prepared on an annual basis. I have seen some of those written in the 1930's and early 1950's, in the form of carbons and drafts which the French overlooked in removing their confidential records from Boujad. These were mixed with less sensitive documents in a storeroom of the *qaid*'s office in Boujad, to which I was given access by the local administration. Because of the disorder of the "archives" left behind by the French, they have evidently not been consulted since independence. Many of the documents, especially the drafts, lack the filing numbers that identify final copies. France has a fifty-year law concerning its archives but, for technical reasons, it is claimed, no post-1912 records concerning Morocco are available for scholarly research. The Boujad archives are identified in references as *B*.

5. For example, one merchant held an English patent as agent for an English-owned Shanghai firm with a branch in Tangiers which imported tea and sugar (B, Steeg to Commandant of Meknes region, 25/D, 23 March 1924). With the dispensation of the resident-general himself, a later patent

was granted to the brother of the local leader of a religious order that was highly antagonistic to the Sherqawa (B. 10/BC, 23 February 1928).

6. There were just under one thousand such rural adherents to non-Sherqawi brotherhoods in Boujad's tribal hinterland in 1952. The source for this estimate is the draft of a local intelligence report, which lists membership in the four major brotherhoods and breaks it down by local community. In no case are two brotherhoods found in the same local community, a fact that suggests the limitations upon personal maneuvers in the tribal setting. One order was limited in another way. The *mqaddem* for the Tijaniya brotherhood in Boujad told me that his order attracted only literate tribesmen, including some rural shopkeepers. The 1952 report partially confirms this, since only thirty-nine rural Tijani-s are claimed, never in the relatively larger concentrations indicated for the other religious orders.

   Although the general trends indicated by these figures are corrobated by interviews, they must be treated with extreme caution. These figures were gathered during an upsurge of anti-French feeling in tribal regions, one significant index of which was the inability of the French to collect rural taxes effectively. The French were extremely suspicious of organizations of any form in the tribal hinterland, so that the informants were undoubtedly under pressure to minimize the importance of the brotherhoods.

7. How tenaciously these ties were maintained can be seen in the fact that sixty-four tribesmen of the Boujad region fighting for the French in Indo-China in 1949 sent the marabout-*qaid* Sidi ben Dawd (2-15) a large sum of money to say invocations on their behalf (B.37/cl, 24 January 1949). Such offerings were also sent regularly from servicemen and workers in France, although not through official channels as were the offerings from Indo-China.

8. The cordiality of these encounters was stressed to me by both the Boujadi-s and the French involved in these negotiations. Local archives confirm that the *contrôleur* of Boujad supported various educational improvements suggested by local non-Sherqawi notables (B.1170 B / I, 6 June 1936; B.1181, 24 August 1938). To the credit of the local French officials,

this was often done over the opposition of local *qaid*-s who,
perhaps correctly, saw all expansion of educational facili-
ties as a potential threat to their positions.

9. For this reason, I am dealing with the topic of this small cadre of
intellectuals in a separate study, now in preparation.

10. Rezette characterizes the entire nationalist movement, even at
the level of its national leadership, in similar terms. He
calls this the "personalization" of power (1955:245–246,
282–285, 287).

11. One local nationalist suggested that the French unwittingly
contributed significantly to the nationalist movement by
repeatedly imprisoning its suspected members. His own
time in prison enabled him to meet at length and solidify
ties of confidence with nationalists elsewhere in Morocco.
What the experience of schooling had done for cementing
ties between many nationalist leaders in Morocco's larger
cities, prison accomplished for those of smaller towns.

12. To maintain the morale of servicemen in their overseas forces,
the French had for decades employed a similar strategy.
Special officers were assigned to France's native Moroccan
troops to aid in formulating and transmitting complaints
of the troops about land disputes and other matters in
Morocco. Such complaints seem to have been treated with
more consideration than many of those locally originated,
since written reports had to be prepared and retaliation
was impossible (e.g., B.1344, 27 October 1952; B, Capt.
Jeanlet, 2 December 1949; B.906, 11 July 1952). Overseas
servicemen also complained regularly to the special officers
about the excesses of *qaid*-s and certain Sherqawi notables.
Such accusations are notably absent in court proceedings
and other inquiries held in Boujad itself.

13. This *qaid* increasingly yielded to pressure from the nationalists.
Thus, after the bloody demonstrations in Boujad and Wad
Zem in 1955, Boujad's *contrôleur* sent the *qaid* a list of
fifteen "responsible" local nationalists, ordering their arrest. The *qaid*'s signature was needed for form's sake. Fearing reprisals, the *qaid* hurriedly consulted with one of the
men on the list, who told the *qaid* to write down all the
names of those killed during the day and to sign that list.
He did, so that the French issued arrest warrants for those

already dead. The local *contrôleur* was, of course, aware of the substitution, but in the waning days of the protectorate he was undoubtedly also aware of the futility and personal danger of challenging this maneuver.

Appendix. The Wheel of Fortune: The Last Maraboutic Intrigues

1. I have briefly indicated the sources for this account in the first section of Chapter 2. Arabic correspondence comes from the collections designated as *E* and *S*. There are several French accounts for this period. The earliest are contained in the archives designated as *JP*. The best of these accounts are J. Sicard's "Note sur la situation religieuse des tribus traversées par la mehalla du Caïd Layadi," JP, Série D, carton 20, May 1909, and Capt. Verlet-Hanus, "Notice comparative sur l'état politique des tribus traversées, rapport d'ensemble," JP, March–May 1909. The fullest account is Ecorcheville 1938:89–114. Ecorcheville has told me (interview, 1970) his method of preparing the account. As *contrôleur civil* of Boujad, he "invited" the two leading Sherqawi notables of the 1930's, Qaid Ḥajj 'Abd l-Qader and Qadi 'Abdallah, to provide him with any correspondence in their possession relating to the Sherqawa. These he supplemented with the files of his own archives. Ecorcheville's translator prepared translations from the Arabic of necessary documents. As he prepared his account, Ecorcheville frequently asked the two notables, particularly Qadi 'Abdallah, to clarify points of detail for him and to explain when necessary the relations among the protagonists. Since Qadi 'Abdallah had participated in some of these events and other Boujadi-s were also alive who had firsthand knowledge of them, I have used Ecorcheville's account extensively. During my initial fieldwork in Boujad I was unaware of Ecorcheville's study and constructed my own narrative of events based upon the Sherqawi correspondence (*S*) and the accounts of informants. The account in this appendix fully incorporates Ecorcheville's study.

2. For example, under the pseudonym Ḥajj al-Bashir ("the pilgrim

bearing good news"), Driss wrote his father in February 1894 / Sha'ban 1311: "If you should speak with His Majesty soon concerning the Werdigha [tribe], tell him the following: Bni Khiran is being led away from the Makhzen by the Werdigha. Second, have the sultan order the Sma'la to refrain from contact with Bni Khiran" (S). Much of the private correspondence which I have examined lacks signatures or in other ways seeks to obscure meanings, to prevent its use by hostile third parties. The identity of writers, however, is generally clear from their handwriting.

3. Ecorcheville's source was Sidi 'Abdallah ben l-'Arbi (2-13). As a youth he was with Mulay Hasan's expedition or royal progress when the sultan died in 1894.

4. *Qaid*-s were appointed, or reappointed, over most of the tribes of Tadla at this time.

5. His *laqab*, or nickname, means "son of Zohra," his mother. It is used because his personal name, Muhammed, could easily be confused with that of the leader of the rival faction.

It is difficult to assess the significance of his being named overseer of pious endowments. There are virtually no significant pious endowments in the immediate Boujad region, athough there are many to the south, in the region of Bni Mellal. It is unclear whether he was responsible for these, although the jurisdiction of the Sherqawi overseer of pious endowments appointed at French initiative after the protectorate included the entire region.

6. The delegation, which included Mha u Hammu, was met by Mulay Hafed at Meshra Shayr, on the Umm er-Rbi' River. They returned by way of the Sma'la. Their movements indicate a relatively widespread support for Mulay Hafed at that time on the upper Tadla Plain.

7. The following account is based primarily on an intelligence report by Captain Verlet-Hanus which appeared in the Journal Politique for May 1909.

8. He later was to become one of the principal architects of the Berber policy of the protectorate, which culminated with the Berber Proclamation of 1930 (Ageron 1972:144). An ardent Catholic, Marty allegedly passed out copies of the Bible in Arabic to Muslim visitors to his office.

9. The letter (in S) carries no date, but its context indicates when it was written.
10. A Berber from another region was reported to have fired the shot. The Sherqawa probably preferred such an account, although in the circumstances impossible to verify, since an attack by a Sherqawi client might be taken by the French as evidence of a complete loss of Sherqawi "authority."
11. The letter was anonymous, and the French account of the incident mentions no names (letter, S, November 1910 / Qa'ada 1328; French account is in JP). The identification of Sidi Sherqi rests on the fact that a copy of the request, in his distinctive calligraphy, was found in Boujad. The calligraphy was identified for me by a retired official of the Ministry of Justice.

Glossary

'alem (pl., *'ulama*): religious scholar.

annexe. SEE *melhaqa.*

'ar: conditional supernatural curse or compulsion.

'Arbawi Sherqawa: one of the two most prominent descent groups of the Sherqawa.

'ashur: tithe; in preprotectorate Morocco the term also signified a government tax or, with the consent of the sultan, a payment made to a designated marabout in lieu of a tax.

'azib: estate granted to marabouts by the preprotectorate Makhzen that was exempt from direct government taxes and controls.

baccalauréat: degree granted upon the successful completion of six years of secondary studies in France and Morocco.

baraka: supernatural blessing; abundance.

bay'a: oath or covenant of allegiance to a king or marabout.

Boujadi: person from Boujad.

cercle. SEE *da'ira.*

collège: school providing the first three years of the six-year cycle of secondary education in France and Morocco.

contrôleur civil: French official in charge of a *cercle* (*da'ira*); the lowest rank in the French Native Affairs administration in protectorate Morocco.

ḍaher: royal decree or proclamation.

da'ira (Fr. *cercle*): ordinarily the smallest unit in Moroccan administration, over which a *qaid* is placed.

ḍăwwar: rural local community (lit., "circle").

derb: an urban quarter, in western Morocco (in Fes the term merely signifies an alleyway or impasse).

fabor: gratuitous act thought to require no reciprocation.

Fassi: person from Fes.

foqra. SEE *fqir*.

fqih: a person who knows Islamic law; a Qur'anic teacher; a marabout, usually a minor one.

fqir (pl., *foqra*): a patrilineal descendant of 'Umar ben l-Khaṭṭab; a mystic; a poor person.

funduq: hostel for travelers or the urban poor containing small sleeping rooms and stables.

ḥajj: the pilgrimage to Mecca; also used as a title by those who have made the pilgrimage.

ḥăqq: obligation; share or right; truth.

ḥshuma: impropriety; impertinence; shame.

ḥshumiya (*theshshem*): propriety; deference.

'ilm (pl., *'ulum*): religious knowledge; religious scholarship.

imam: prayer-leader.

jinn: a form of supernatural being.

jma'a: council or gathering.

Ka'ba: the sacred house at Mecca around which the circumambulation is performed.

karama: miracle story; sign of God's bounty; generosity.

kelma: "word" or authority.

khayma: tent; residential unit.

madrasa: school; in this study, one of traditional Islamic higher learning.

Maghreb: North Africa; also the Arabic term for Morocco.

Makhzen: colloquial term for the Moroccan government; "the place where treasure is stored."

marabout: a person, living or dead, thought to have a special relation toward God which enables him to ask for God's grace on behalf of his clients and to communicate it to them.

Marrakshi: person from Marrakesh.

medina: city; in North Africa this term often specifically designates the traditional, precolonial part of a city.

mektub: "that which is written"; God's will.

melḥaqa (Fr. *annexe*): a subdivision of a *cercle* (*da'ira*) with a *qaid* appointed over it (an administrative anomaly in Morocco, of which Boujad is virtually the sole example).

mellaḥ: a quarter inhabited by Jews and containing a synagogue; also loosely designates any quarter with a heavy concentration of Jews.

mokhazni: soldier; guard attached to the office of a *qaid*.

mqaddem: spokesman; one who represents another (used in a variety of contexts).

mṣarfa: a general term for social exchange; dealing.

Mulay (title): honorific title prefixing the name of a patrilineal descendant of the Prophet Muḥammed.

musem: a periodic festival in honor of a marabout.

niya: faith or intent.

pasha: Moroccan official responsible for a town or city.

qaḍi: a religious judge.

qaid: tribal chief appointed over a tribe or small town during the protectorate; now a Ministry of the Interior official responsible for a rural or urban *da'ira*.

qa'ida: code for conduct; "the way things are done."

'qal: reason.

qodret Allah: God's will.

qrab. See *qrib*.

qrib (pl., *qrab*): a person with whom one has close agnatic ties; a person with whom one has sustained bonds of obligation developed out of friendship, clientship, alliance, residential propinquity, etc.

Residence: the office of the French Resident General in protectorate Morocco; the administrative center of the protectorate.

ryal: a unit of Moroccan currency. In 1970 a *ryal* was roughly the equivalent of one American cent.

ṣaheb (pl., *aṣhab, shab*): companion or associate; a person with whom regular transactions are made.

Salafi: a reformist Muslim.

ṣaleḥ: a pious or devout person; a saint; in some contexts, a marabout.

shaykh: religious teacher or head of a mystic order; government official.

Sherqawi (pl., Sherqawa): a person claiming descent from the marabout Sidi Mhammed Sherqi.

shorfa. SEE *shrif.*

shra‘: Islamic law.

shrif (pl., *shorfa*): patrilineal descendant of the Prophet Muhammed through his daughter, Fatima.

Sid, Sidi: honorific title of address used for marabouts and claimed descendants of ‘Umar ben l-Khattab.

Sufi, Sufism: Islamic mystic; Islamic mysticism.

t‘argiba: the sacrifice of a bull to conclude or renew an oath of allegiance or to seek a truce; involves the imposition of compulsion (*‘ar*).

tariqa: Sufi brotherhood or mystic "way."

tasawwuf: the practice of Sufism.

tata: contractual ritual alliances (preprotectorate).

theshshem. SEE *hshumiya.*

‘ulama. SEE *‘alem.*

‘ulum. SEE *‘ilm.*

wali: saint.

wejh: "face"; prestige.

zakat: alms tax.

zawya: religious lodge or residence of a prominent marabout.

Zawya Sherqawa: one of the two leading Sherqawi descent groups, formed in the late nineteenth century.

zewwar: "visitor," a maraboutic descendant who acts as intermediary between clients and his maraboutic ancestor.

zyara: local pilgrimage to a maraboutic shrine; an offering to a marabout.

Bibliography

Abun-Nasr, Jamil M. 1963. "The Salafiyya movement in Morocco:
   The religious bases of the Moroccan nationalist move-
   ment." *Saint Antony's Papers* 16:90–105.
————. 1965. *The Tijaniyya, a Sufi order in the modern world.* Lon-
   don: Oxford University Press.
Ageron, Charles-Robert. 1972. *Politiques coloniales au Maghreb.*
   Paris: Presses Universitaires de France.
Ali Bey [Domingo Badia y Leblich]. 1816. *The travels of Ali Bey.*
   Vol. 1. Philadelphia: M. Carey.
Annexe de Boujad. 1933–1956. Archives of the Contrôle Civil. Type-
   written and manuscript. (Abbreviated in text as *B.*)
Arnaud. Louis. 1952. *Au temps des mehallas ou le Maroc de 1860 à
   1912.* Casablanca: Editions Atlantides.
Aron, Raymond. 1970. *Main currents in sociological thought.* Vol. 2.
   Garden City: Doubleday Anchor Books.
Aubin, Eugène [Descos]. 1906. *Morocco of today.* London: J. M. Dent
   and Co.
B. SEE Annexe de Boujad.
Banfield, Edward C. 1967. *The moral basis of a backward society.*
   New York: Free Press.

Bel, Alfred. 1938. *La religion musulmane en Berbérie*. Paris: Librairie Orientaliste Paul Geuthner.

Bellah, Robert. 1970. *Beyond belief*. New York: Harper and Row.

Bendix, Reinhard. 1963. *Work and authority in industry: Ideologies of management in the course of industrialization*. New York and Evanston: Harper and Row.

Berger, François. 1929. *Moha ou Hammou le Zaïani*. Marrakesh: Editions de l'Atlas.

Berger, Peter L. 1969. *The sacred canopy: Elements of a sociological theory of religion*. Garden City: Doubleday Anchor Books.

Berque, Jacques. 1953. "Qu'est-ce qu'une 'tribu' nord-africaine?" In *Eventail de l'histoire vivante: Hommage à Lucien Febvre* 1:261–271. Paris: Librairie Armand Colin.

———. 1955. *Structures sociales du Haut-Atlas*. Paris: Presses Universitaires de France.

———. 1957. "Quelques problèmes de l'Islam maghrébin." *Archives de Sociologie des Religions* 2:3–20.

———. 1967. *French North Africa: The Maghreb between two world wars*. New York: Praeger.

———, and Julien Couleau. 1946. "Vers la modernization du fellah marocain." *Bulletin Economique et Social du Maroc* 7:18–25.

Berriau, Colonel. 1918. *L'officier de renseignements au Maroc*. Rabat: Imprimerie, Service de Renseignements.

Bill, James A. 1973. "The plasticity of informal politics: The case of Iran." *Middle East Journal* 27:131–151.

Bloch, Marc. 1964. *Feudal society*. Chicago: University of Chicago Press.

Bonjean, ———. 1928. "Le mouton dans la circonscription d'Oued Zem." *Revue de Géographie Marocaine* 7:52–90.

Bourdieu, Pierre. 1972. *Esquisse d'une théorie de la pratique, précédé de trois études d'ethnologie kabyle*. Geneva and Paris: Librairie Droz.

Brignon, Jean, Abdelaziz Amine, Brahim Boutaleb, Guy Martinet, and Bernard Rosenberger. 1968. *Histoire du Maroc*. Paris: Hatier.

Brown, Kenneth. 1973. "The impact of the *Dahir Berbère* in Salé." In *Arabs and Berbers*, edited by Ernest Gellner and Charles Micaud, pp. 201–216. London: Duckworth.

Bruno, H., and G. H. Bousquet. 1946. "Contribution à l'étude des

pactes de protection et d'alliance chez les Berbères du
Maroc central." *Hespéris* 33:353–370.

Brunot, Louis. 1923. Review of Lévy-Bruhl, *La mentalité primitive*.
Hespéris 3:536–538.

———. 1934. *Premiers conseils*. Rabat: Ecole du Livre.

Burke, Edmund. 1969. "Morocco and the Near East: Reflections on
some basic differences." *Archives Européennes de Sociologie* 10:70–94.

———. 1973. "The image of the Moroccan state in French ethnological literature: A new look at the origin of Lyautey's
Berber policy." In *Arabs and Berbers*, edited by Ernest
Gellner and Charles Micaud, pp. 175–199. London: Duckworth.

Cerych, Ladislav. 1964. *Européens et Marocains, 1930–1956*. Bruges:
De Tempel.

Chapelle, Lt. F. de la. 1931. "Le Sultan Moulay Isma'il et les Berbères
Sanhaja du Maroc central." *Archives Marocaines* 28:8–64.

Chenier, M. 1788. *The present state of the empire of Morocco*. Vol. 1.
London: G. G. J. and J. Robinson.

Christian, William A., Jr. 1972. *Person and God in a Spanish valley*.
New York and London: Seminar Press.

Cimetière, J. 1913. "Notice sur Bou Djad." *Revue du Monde Musulman* 24:277–289.

Cohen, Percy S. 1969. "Theories of myth." *Man* 4:337–353.

Crapanzano, Vincent. 1973. *The Hamadsha: A study in Moroccan
ethnopsychiatry*. Berkeley, Los Angeles, and London: University of California Press.

Damis, John. 1973. "Early Moroccan reactions to the French protectorate: The cultural dimension." *Humaniora Islamica* 1:
15–31.

Da'ud, Muhammed. 1959–. *History of Tetouan*. (In Arabic.) Tetouan: Mahdiya Press.

Depont, Xavier, and Octave Coppolani. 1897. *Les confréries religieuses
musulmanes*. Algiers: A. Jourdan.

Devons, E., and Max Gluckman. 1964. "Conclusion: Modes and consequences of limiting a field of study." In *Closed systems
and open minds: The limits of naivety in social anthropology*, edited by Max Gluckman, pp. 158–261. Edinburgh
and London: Oliver and Boyd.

Douglas, Mary. 1966. *Purity and danger*. New York: Praeger.

Doutté, Edmond. 1903. "Les Marocains et la société marocaine."
    Revue Générale des Sciences 14:190–208, 258–274, 314–
    327, 372–387.
Drague, Georges [Georges Spillman]. 1951. *Esquisse d'histoire reli-
    gieuse du Maroc.* Foreword by Robert Montagne. Paris:
    J. Peyronnet.
Dunn, Ross. 1971. "The trade of Tafilalet: Commercial change in
    southeast Morocco on the eve of the protectorate." *African
    Historical Studies* 6:271–304.
———. 1973. "Berber imperialism: The Ait Atta expansion in south-
    east Morocco." In *Arabs and Berbers*, edited by Ernest
    Gellner and Charles Micaud, pp. 85–107. London: Duck-
    worth.
E. SEE Ecorcheville, Claude.
Ecorcheville, Claude. Ca. 1810–ca. 1930. Proclamations. (I have uti-
    lized the French translations of a number of royal procla-
    mations made under Ecorcheville's direction by his inter-
    preter. I have seen the Arabic originals of several of these
    in Boujad and have found their translations to be highly
    accurate; the translations often include the Arabic orig-
    inals for technical terms.) (Abbreviated in text as *E.*)
———. 1938. "Etude sur les Cherkaoua." Typescript. 119 pp. Copies
    in possession of Ecorcheville and the author.
Eickelman, Dale F. 1972–1973. "Quelques aspects de l'organisation
    politique et économique d'une zawya marocaine au XIXe
    siècle." *Bulletin de la Société d'Histoire du Maroc* 4–5:
    37–54.
———, and Bouzekri Draioui. 1973. "Islamic myths from western
    Morocco: Three texts." *Hespéris-Tamuda* 14.
Evans-Pritchard, E. E. 1940. *The Nuer.* Oxford: Clarendon Press.
———. 1949. *The Sanusi of Cyrenaica.* London: Oxford University
    Press.
Fallers, Lloyd A. 1959. "Despotism, status culture and social mobility
    in an African kingdom." *Comparative Studies in Society
    and History* 2:11–32.
Flamand, Pierre. 1952. *Un mellah en pays Berbère: Demnate.* Insti-
    tut des Hautes-Etudes Marocaines, Notes et Documents, 10.
    Paris: Librairie Générale de Droit et de Jurisprudence.
Fogg, W. 1938. "A tribal market in the Spanish zone of Morocco."
    Africa 11:428–457.

Foucauld, Charles de. 1888. *Reconnaissance au Maroc*. Paris: Imprimerie Nationale.

———. 1939. *Reconnaissance au Maroc*. 2d ed. Paris: Société d'Editions Géographiques, Maritimes et Coloniales.

Fustel de Coulanges, Numa Denis. n.d. *The ancient city*. Garden City: Doubleday Anchor Books. (Originally pubished in 1864 in French.)

Gadille, J. 1958. *Exploitations rurales européennes*. Atlas du Maroc, Notices Explicatives. Rabat: Comité de Géographie du Maroc.

Gaussen, H., J. Debrach. and F. Joly. 1958. *Précipitations annuelles*. Atlas du Maroc. Notices Explicatives. Rabat: Comité de Géographie du Maroc.

Geertz, Clifford. 1966. "Religion as a cultural system." In *Anthropological approaches to the study of religion*, edited by Michael Banton, pp. 1–46. Association of Social Anthropologists, Monograph No. 3. London: Tavistock Publications.

———. 1968. *Islam observed*. New Haven and London: Yale University Press.

———. 1971. "In search of North Africa." *New York Review of Books*, April 22. pp. 20–24.

———. 1973. *The interpretation of culture*. New York: Basic Books.

Geertz, Hildred. 1974. "Familial Relationship in Sefrou, Morocco." Mimeographed.

Gellner, Ernest. 1969. *Saints of the Atlas*. London: Weidenfeld and Nicolson.

———, and Charles Micaud, eds. 1973. *Arabs and Berbers*. London: Duckworth.

Gibb, H. A. R., and J. H. Kramers, eds. 1961. *Shorter encyclopaedia of Islam*. Leiden: E. J. Brill.

Gorrée, Georges. 1939. *Au service du Maroc: Charles de Foucauld*. Paris: Grasset.

Gouvion. Marthe, and Edmond Gouvion. 1939. *Kitab aayane al-Maghrib 'l-aksa: Livre des grands du Maroc*. Paris: Paul Geuthner.

Ḥajji, Muhammed. 1964. *The zawya of Dilā': Its religious, cultural and political roles*. (In Arabic.) Rabat: Imprimerie Nationale.

Halstead, John P. 1967. *Rebirth of a nation: The origins and rise of Moroccan nationalism, 1912–1944*. Harvard Middle Eastern Monographs, 18. Cambridge: Harvard University Press.

Hardy, Georges. 1926. *L'âme marocaine d'après la littérature française*. Paris: Larose.

Harrell, Richard S., ed. 1966. *A dictionary of Moroccan Arabic: Arabic-English*. Washington: Georgetown University Press.

Harris, Nigel. 1971. *Beliefs in society: The problems of ideology*. Harmondsworth: Penguin.

Hart, David M. 1973. "The tribe in modern Morocco: Two case studies." In *Arabs and Berbers*, edited by Ernest Gellner and Charles Micaud, pp. 25–58. London: Duckworth.

Hodgson, Marshall G. S. 1975. *The venture of Islam*. 3 vols. Chicago: University of Chicago Press.

Ibn Khaldun. 1967. *The muqaddimah*. Translated by Franz Rosenthal. Princeton: Princeton University Press.

Ifrani, Muhammed es-Sghir al-. 1888. *Nozhet-elhadi*. Paris: Ernest Leroux.

Izutsu, Toshihiko. 1964. *God and man in the Koran*. Tokyo: Keio Institute of Cultural and Linguistic Studies.

Journal Politique des Troupes d'Occupation du Maroc Occidental. 1908–1912. Archives. Ministère de la Guerre, Maroc. Series D. Service historique de l'armée, Vincennes. (Abbreviated in text as *JP*.)

JP. SEE Journal Politique des Troupes d'Occupation du Maroc Occidental.

Julien, Charles-André. 1972. *L'Afrique du nord en marche*. 3d ed. Paris: Julliard.

Kingdom of Morocco. 1961. *Population légale du Maroc*. Rabat: Service Centrale des Statistiques.

————, Ministry of Finances. Circle of Wad Zem. 1951–1968. Rural Tax Records.

Lacoste, Yves. 1974. "General characteristics and fundamental structures of medieval North African society." *Economy and Society* 3:1–17.

Lacouture, Jean, and Simone Lacouture. 1958. *La Maroc à l'épreuve*. Paris: Editions du Seuil.

Lakhdar, Mohammed. 1971. *La vie littéraire au Maroc sous la dynastie 'Alawide (1075–1311 = 1664–1894)*. Rabat: E.T.N.A.

Lanly, A. 1970. *Le Français d'Afrique du Nord*. Paris: Bordas.

Laroui, Abdallah. 1967. *L'idéologie arabe contemporaine*. Paris: Maspéro.
———. 1970. *L'Histoire du Maghreb*. Paris: Maspéro.
———. 1974. *La crise des intellectuels arabes*. Paris: Maspéro.
Leach, Edmund. 1966. *Rethinking anthropology*. New York: Humanities Press.
Le Coeur, Charles. 1969. *Le rite et l'outil*. Paris: Presses Universitaires de France.
Lenski, Gerhard. 1963. *The religious factor: A sociologist's inquiry*. Garden City: Doubleday Anchor Books.
Lévi-Provençal, E. 1922. *Les historiens des Chorfa*. Paris: Librairie Orientaliste Paul Geuthner.
Lévi-Strauss, Claude. 1964. *Le cru et le cuit*. Paris: Plon.
———. 1969. *The raw and the cooked*. Translated by John and Doreen Weightman. New York and Evanston: Harper and Row.
Lyautey, H. 1953. *Lyautey l'Africain*. Vol. 1. Edited by Pierre Lyautey. Paris: Plon.
Mannheim, Karl. 1952. *Essays on the sociology of knowledge*. London: Routledge and Kegan Paul.
Martin, A. G. P. 1923. *Quatre siècles d'histoire marocaine*. Paris: Librairie Félix Alcan.
Martin, J., H. Jover, J. Le Coz, G. Murer, and D. Noin. 1967. *Géographie du Maroc*. Casablanca: Librairie Nationale.
Marty, Paul. 1929. "Les zaouias marocaines et le Makhzen." *Revue des Etudes Islamiques* 4:474–600.
Massignon, Louis. 1924. "Enquête sur les corporations d'artisans et de commerçants au Maroc (1923–1924)." *Revue du Monde Musulman* 58:1–250.
Merad, Ali. 1967. *Le réformisme musulman en Algérie de 1925 à 1940*. Recherches Méditerranéennes, Etudes, 7. Paris and The Hague: Mouton.
Michaux-Bellaire, Edouard. 1913. *Le Gharb. Archives Marocaines 20*.
———. 1927. "Les confréries religieuses au Maroc." *Archives Marocaines* 27:1–86.
Mission Scientifique du Maroc. 1915. *Casablanca et sa région*. 2 vols. Villes et tribus du Maroc, vols. 1–2. Paris: Librairie Orientaliste Paul Geuthner.
Montagne, Robert. 1941. "Un essai de régionalisme au Maroc." Manu-

script. Archives du Centre des Hautes Etudes de l'Administration Musulmane, Paris, 451.

————. 1953. *Révolution au Maroc*. Paris: Editions France-Empire.

Morocco, Kingdom of. See Kingdom of Morocco.

Morsy, Magali. 1972. *Les Ahansala: Examen du rôle historique d'une
famille maraboutique de l'Atlas marocain au XVIIIᵉ siècle*.
Recherches Méditerranéennes, Documents, 5. Paris and
The Hague: Mouton.

Nadel, S. F. 1957. *The theory of social structure*. London: Cohen
and West.

Naṣiri, Muhammed. 1969. "Conditions climatiques, recoltes céréa-
lières et situation des campagnes traditionnelles marocaines." *Revue de Géographie du Maroc* 16: 35–70.

Naṣiri es-Slawi, Ahmed ben Khaled al-. 1906–1907. *Kitāb elistiqṣā li
akhbāri doual el Māghrib el aqṣa*. Translated by Eugène
Fumey. 2 vols. *Archives Marocaines* 9–10.

Niegel, ————. 1913. "La médersa et les bibliothèques de Bou Djad."
Revue du Monde Musulman 24: 290–297.

Noin, Daniel. 1970. *La population rurale du Maroc*. 2 vols. Paris:
Presses Universitaires de France.

Parsons, Talcott. 1964. *The social system*. Paperback ed. New York:
Free Press. (First published 1951.)

Peters, Emrys. 1967. "Some structural aspects of the feud among the
camel-herding Bedouin of Cyrenaica." *Africa* 37: 261–282.

Qadiri, Muhammed al-. 1913. *Nachr al-mathani*. Vol. 1. *Archives
Marocaines* 21.

Rahman, Fazlur. 1968. *Islam*. New York: Doubleday Anchor Books.

Raynal, R., and A. André. 1955. *Elevage, marchés du bétail, équipe-
ment vétérinaire*. Atlas du Maroc, Notices Explicatives.
Rabat: Comité de Géographique du Maroc.

Rezette, Robert. 1955. *Les partis politiques marocains*. Paris: Librairie
Armand Colin.

Rinn, Louis. 1884. *Marabouts et khouan: Etude sur l'Islam en Algérie*.
Algiers: Adolphe Jourdan.

Robert, Jacques. 1963. *La monarchie marocaine*. Paris: Librairie Gé-
nérale de Droit et de Jurisprudence.

Rosen, Lawrence. 1972. "Muslim and Jewish relations in a Moroccan city." *International Journal of Middle East Studies* 3:
435–449.

———. 1973. "The social and conceptual framework of Arab-Berber relations in central Morocco." In *Arabs and Berbers*, edited by Ernest Gellner and Charles Micaud, pp. 155–174. London: Duckworth.

Runciman, W. G. 1970. *Sociology in its place*. Cambridge: Cambridge University Press.

Rural Tax [*Tertib*]. SEE Kingdom of Morocco, Ministry of Finances, Circle of Wad Zem.

Ryder, N. B. 1968. "Cohort analysis." In *International encyclopedia of the social sciences*, edited by David Sills, 2:546–550. New York: Macmillan and the Free Press.

S. SEE Sherqawa.

Salim, Shakir Mustafa. 1962. *Marsh dwellers of the Euphrates delta*. New York: Humanities Press.

Schacht, Joseph. 1966. *An introduction to Islamic law*. Oxford: Clarendon Press.

Scheffler, Harold W. 1965. *Choiseul island social structure*. Berkeley and Los Angeles: University of California Press.

Schutz, Alfred. 1967. *The phenomenology of the social world*. Translated by George Walsh and Frederick Lehnert. Evanston: Northwestern University Press.

Seddon, J. David. 1973. "Local politics and state intervention: Northeast Morocco from 1870 to 1970." In *Arabs and Berbers*, edited by Ernest Gellner and Charles Micaud, pp. 109–139. London: Duckworth.

Sherqawa. 1800–1927. Unpublished correspondence of several families of Boujad. (A microfilm of the correspondence to which I was allowed access will be placed in the library of the University Muhammed V in Rabat.) (Abbreviated in text as *S*.)

Siegel, James. 1969. *The rope of God*. Berkeley and Los Angeles: University of California Press.

Smith, Wilfred Cantwell. 1963. *The meaning and end of religion*. New York: Macmillan.

Smith, William Robertson. 1919. *The prophets of Israel and their place in history to the close of the eighth century A.D.* London: A. and C. Black. (Originally published in 1882.)

Sorokin, Pitirim A. 1937. *Social and cultural dynamics*. Vol. 1. New York: American Book Co.

Terrasse, Henri. 1949–1950. *Histoire du Maroc des origines à l'étab-lissement du Protectorat français.* Casablanca: Editions Atlantides.

Tiano, André. 1968. *Le développement économique du Maghreb.* Paris: Presses Universitaires de France.

Toulmin, Stephen. 1971. "Rediscovering history." *Encounter* 36(1): 53–64.

Troeltsch, Ernst. 1960. *The social teaching of the Christian churches.* New York: Harper and Row.

Turner, Victor W. 1969. *The ritual process.* Chicago: Aldine Publishing Co.

———. 1973. "The center out there: Pilgrim's goal." *History of Religions* 12:191–230.

Van Gennep, Arnold. 1914. *En Algérie.* Paris: Mercure de France.

Vinogradov, Amal. 1973. "The socio-political organization of a Berber *Taraf* tribe: Pre-Protectorate Morocco." In *Arabs and Berbers,* edited by Ernest Gellner and Charles Micaud, pp. 67–84. London: Duckworth.

Waterbury, John. 1970. *The commander of the faithful.* New York: Columbia University Press.

———. 1972. *North for the trade: The life and times of a Berber merchant.* Berkeley and Los Angeles: University of California Press.

Weber, Max. 1952. *Ancient Judaism.* Translated and edited by Hans H. Gerth and Don Martindale. Glencoe: Free Press.

———. 1958. *The Protestant ethic and the spirit of capitalism.* Translated by Talcott Parsons. New York: Charles Scribner. (First published in German in 1904–1905.)

———. 1964. *The theory of social and economic organization.* Translated and with an introduction by Talcott Parsons. New York: Free Press.

———. 1968. *Economy and society.* Edited and translated by Guenther Roth and Claus Wittich. New York: Bedminster Press.

Westermarck, Edward. 1926. *Ritual and belief in Morocco.* 2 vols. London: Macmillan and Co.

Index

'Abd l-Qader l-Jilani (Ṣufi), 26
'ahd. SEE bay'a
'Alawi dynasty (1666–), 17, 26;
    and the Sherqawa, 35, 40.
    SEE ALSO sultans
Ali Bey [Domingo Badia y Leb-
    lich]: cited, 41–42, 257
Almohad dynasty (1130–1269),
    19, 25
Almoravid dynasty (1061–1147),
    19, 25
'ar (compulsion), 62, 124, 149–
    153; defined, 149–150; ḫbir,
    54, 149–150, 174, 223
'Arbawi Sherqawa, 169, 181, 187,
    188, 204, 205, 209, 221–223,
    240–254; origins of, 58;
    shrines of, 198–199. SEE ALSO
    Sherqawa
'Arbi ben Sayh (Ṣufi), 61
Aron, Raymond: cited, 211
'uṣabiya, 96
'ashur, 171

Badia y Leblich, Domingo. SEE
    Ali Bey
Banfield, Edward C., 136
baraka, 6, 25, 26, 27, 37, 48, 61, 62,
    67, 158–159, 160, 162–163,
    166, 167, 171, 179, 180, 181,
    236, 252, 272; attribution of,
    185, 196; colonial conceptions
    of, 221, 257, 267; of sultans,
    42
bay'a, 41, 164, 219. SEE ALSO
    Sherqawa, clients of; Sher-
    qawa, covenants with
bekri, 110, 164
Bel, Alfred, 153, 256; on Islam,
    22–29

Bellah, Robert, 161
bent 'amm marriage, 203–205
Berber Proclamation, 228, 256.
    SEE ALSO nationalism, Moroc-
    can
Berger, François, 274
Berger, Peter L., 233, 234
Berque, Jacques, 12; on Alfred Bel,
    22; on social structure, 89,
    255, 256, 260
Bni Baṭṭu, 106–107, 114, 115
Bni Zemmur, 53, 105–121 passim,
    172, 217, 264, 265; in myths,
    165–167. SEE ALSO Boujad
    region
Boujad, 6; as administrative cen-
    ter, 76; caravan routes to, 44;
    colonial urbanization plan
    for, 74–75; compared by
    French to Mecca, 73; derb-s
    of, 91–99; economic activities
    in, 75–80; education in, 87–
    88; Europeans in, 78; French
    rule of, 75, 85–86 (SEE ALSO
    French); Islam and Islamic
    institutions in, 10, 80–85;
    location of, 33–35; Makhzen
    presence in, 53, 85–88; as
    market center, 44–45; 75–77;
    as pilgrimage center, 8–10,
    33–35; population of, 45, 70,
    71; as sanctuary, 40, 42;
    shorfa in, 82; shrines in, 84,
    262, 263; tariqa-s in, 83–84;
    199, 224–227; urban zones
    of, 72–75. SEE ALSO Sherqawa;
    Sherqawi zawya
Boujad region: climate of, 66–67;
    economy of, 65–70, 77;
    French in, 201, 212–214, 217,